The Poetry of Meng Chiao and Han Yü

The Poetry of Meng Chiao and Han Yü

Stephen Owen

New Haven and London, Yale University Press, 1975

Designed by John O.C. McCrillis
and set in Baskerville type.
Printed in the United States of America by
The Murray Printing Co., Forge Village, Mass.

Published in Great Britain, Europe, and Africa by Yale University Press, Ltd., London.
Distributed in Latin America by Kaiman & Polon, Inc., New York City; in Australasia
and Southeast Asia by John Wiley & Sons Australasia Pty. Ltd., Sydney; in India by UBS
Publishers' Distributors Pvt., Ltd., Delhi; in Japan by John Weatherhill, Inc., Tokyo.

For Phyllis

Contents

Acknowledgments

Of the many people who had some hand in the preparation of this book, I should first thank Hans Frankel, who directed the dissertation from which the book was pared. As a teacher and friend, his help, patience, and understanding allowed me to find my own way without getting entirely lost in the process. Also I thank Professor Shimizu Shigeru of Kyōtō University who gave much of his valuable time listening to ideas, correcting errors, and offering invaluable suggestions. My thanks to the support of the Fulbright Fellowship, which gave me the opportunity to do research at Kyōtō University, and of the Yale East Asian Prize Fellowship on my return to New Haven. I should also thank the members of the Prize Fellowship committee, Arthur Wright, Hans Frankel, Kao Yu-kung, Geoffrey Hartman, and Peter Demetz. For their help in the task of revision I thank Hugh Stimson and Jonathan Spence. Special thanks also go to Robert Somers for his careful reading and copious notes and suggestions. I would also like to express my gratitude to Judith Wile for carefully reading the manuscript and extracting some of the worst infelicities, as well as to Anne Lamont who typed up the final manuscript. And particular thanks to my wife Phyllis who aided me through all the stages of the process, from arguing over poems to making the index.

List of Abbreviations

Introduction

By the time of its full flowering in the T'ang Dynasty (618–907), Chinese poetry already possessed a long and rich history. The poets Meng Chiao (751–814) and Han Yü (768–824), who helped shape the character of Mid-T'ang poetry, were themselves shaped by their consciousness of a poetic tradition that extended back more than a millennium. Poetry (*shih*) had come to be the favorite medium of expression for scholar-officials, who learned its technical requirements in order to pass the civil service examination and used it in their private lives to fulfill the requirements of polite society, to articulate their deepest emotions, and at times to express political and moral commentary on contemporary events.

The first century and a half of the T'ang was an age of imperial glory. T'ang armies marched through central Asia, Korea, and Vietnam, while trade flourished on the caravan routes to the West. Ch'ang-an, the "Western Capital," was the greatest city of its day, with a population that at one time reached almost two million and with a foreign community in which the great religions of the West were tolerated. Buddhism, an earlier importation, had already gained a strong hold on nobility and common people alike, permeating all aspects of T'ang life.

In reaction against the cosmopolitan aspects of T'ang civilization, there was a growing commitment on the part of many intellectuals of the period to the "pure" Chinese tradition. Although their writings show pride in T'ang military power and international success, the intellectuals were just as often disturbed by the incursion of foreign elements into popular culture, elements which they felt presented a threat to the purity and continuity of their own tradition. This ambivalent feeling often emerged as an aggressive cultural confidence, expressed in the perennial theme of the golden age of antiquity, an ideal of humane civilization set in the remote past.

The relationship of political history and literary history is not always direct. The period from 755 to about 790 saw the petrification of the High T'ang poetic style and the concurrent political near-

1

disintegration of the empire. In 755 a Sogdian general in Chinese service, named An Lu-shan, began a rebellion that decimated entire provinces and forced the emperor to flee the capital to Szechwan. After this revolt was put down with great difficulty, there was a string of other rebellions and foreign incursions; and during the decades that followed, the central government lost control of many rich, strategic provinces. Power devolved into the hands of virtually autonomous satraps, *chieh-tu-shih*: the government could muster neither the resources nor the will to oppose them. The poetry of Tu Fu (712–70) comments on the political events of the time with passionate concern, but his work is the exception to the rule. Reading the poems of those poets who were in their own lifetimes thought to be the great writers of this troubled period, one can scarcely tell that such political upheavals were occurring.

By the end of the eighth century and beginning of the ninth century there was a brief restoration of central power—a *chung-hsing*, in traditional Chinese terminology. In the context of this restoration, the idea of "return to antiquity," which had been a brooding undercurrent during the preceding two centuries, found its moment and emerged with a new vigor. Here political, intellectual, and literary history happily coincide; the ability of the central government to consolidate its authority was felt by intellectuals to rest on its ability to approximate the ideal Confucian state and apply its moral power throughout the empire. Meng Chiao and Han Yü, in whose works the theme of return to antiquity finds its strongest poetic expression, show a moral seriousness and artistic self-consciousness far greater than that of any of their predecessors, with the exception of Tu Fu. With them begins a trend, measurable in centuries, of intense critical awareness in Chinese poetry.

The T'ang cultural confidence mentioned earlier is bound up with this "return to antiquity," or *fu-ku*. We do not find the ethnocentric lack of curiosity about the external world evident in some later dynasties, but rather a defensive affirmation of tradition and its associated values. The poet Li Po (701–62) writes:

> Our sage dynasty has returned to primal antiquity,
> The emperor, robes hanging to earth, honors the pure.
> Crowds of talented men emerge in the glorious peace,
> And following the times, leap like fish to greatness.

Culture and basic substance in perfect harmony,
A host of stars arrayed in the autumn skies.[1]

"Return" is the most significant of the many Confucian ideas that fill this passage. To be the equal of antiquity meant to be like antiquity, a state that must be attained by a symbolic "return" rather than by progress. Here Li Po, a High T'ang poet, is consciously blocking from his vision the international empire with its foreign religions, foreign music, and foreign styles. The Confucian pose Li Po assumes here is only one among many possible responses, and elsewhere he affirms the richness and variety of the cosmopolitan empire. In most T'ang writers these two opposing tendencies went hand in hand: "return to antiquity" was counterbalanced by deep religious commitment to Buddhism, fascination with military heroism, and love of all things foreign. However, in looking back over the political and economic turmoil of the last half of the eighth century, some Mid-T'ang intellectuals, like Meng and Han, felt less ambivalence and gave their allegiance more exclusively to traditionally Chinese social and moral values.

Probably all Chinese had admired the international empire, but the concurrent "cultural nationalism," if we may call it that, was felt primarily by the scholar-official class, steeped in the classics and responsible for the internal administration of the empire. This class's long-standing distrust of merchants and military men was exacerbated first by T'ang military and economic success and later by its decline. Although they might revel in the wealth of the capital or gloat over the defeat of a central Asian khan, more often than not their admiration was mixed with distrust, as in the following poem by Wang Tsun (fl. 866):

Ch'in built the great wall like an iron prison
That the barbarian might never dare pass Lin-t'ao,
But though it stretches thousands of miles, to the
   clouds' very edge,
It cannot reach the three feet to the throne of Yao.[2]

Yao, the mythical sage-king of antiquity, represents an ideal of moral power, that no physical force can approach. It was precisely this moral power which the scholar-officials felt they possessed.

1. *CTS*, c. 161, p. 1670.   2. *CTS*, c. 602, p. 6961.

Let us now consider briefly the poetic tradition upon which T'ang poets drew. The earliest body of poems was the *Book of Songs*, the *Shih-ching*, a collection of folk, court, and ritual poems compiled in about 600 B.C. but representing the work of several centuries preceding that date. Since the *Book of Songs* was one of the "Confucian Classics," its influence on subsequent poetry was considerable, and most T'ang poets knew it by heart.

The next important corpus in the poetic tradition was the *Ch'u-tz'u*, a collection of ritual songs and elegies from the late fourth to third centuries B.C. The majority of these poems were traditionally attributed to the poet-courtier Ch'ü Yüan. The Ch'ü Yüan legend of the virtuous minister, maliciously slandered and banished from the court, who vents his grief in poetry and ultimately commits suicide, is a recurrent theme in the poetry of Meng Chiao and Han Yü as well as in the works of other T'ang poets.

Poetry in lines of five or seven syllables, the dominant meter during the T'ang, developed out of the folk poetry of the Western Han (206 B.C. to A.D. 8), maturing during the latter part of the Eastern Han (A.D. 25–220) and Wei (220–64). T'ang poets generally felt that these works of the third century had an appealing simplicity and directness of emotion, a "manly" roughness in contrast to the "effeminate" style of court poetry of the fifth and sixth centuries.

The latter half of the fourth and early fifth centuries saw the development of eremitic and landscape poetry, but this soon gave way to a delicate, sensitive occasional poetry written by aristocratic members of the southern courts. A subgenre of court poetry known as "palace poetry," an ornate and mildly erotic description of the charms of palace ladies, aroused particular ire among T'ang literary theorists, who longed for the simplicity and "serious" themes of ancient poetry. The style of court poetry tended to be paratactic and imagistic, and despite opposition to it, that style formed the basis of T'ang poetic diction.

T'ang poetry is usually divided into four periods: Early, High, Mid-, and Late. This quadrupartite division is basically sound, though the dates assigned to these periods in this study differ somewhat from those assigned by Chinese literary historians. The term "Early T'ang" is a misnomer; it is not really a period style in itself, but rather a continuation of the elaborate court poetry of the Southern Dynasties. This style lasted until a transition period between about 690 and 720 when, due to a change in fashion and the opposition of literary theorists, court poetry ceased to occupy the central position in the world of poetry.

The High T'ang style, which emerged in the first decades of the eighth century, covers a broad spectrum of poets and is difficult to characterize succinctly. Though this style is generally more colloquial and personal than the court poetry which preceded it, from a broader point of view it is a style of clarity and balance, avoiding extreme concision as well as extreme colloquial diction. As in English Romanticism of the latter part of the eighteenth century, spontaneity and naturalness became positive values, set in opposition to the elegant periphrasis of the preceding century.

Tu Fu, generally considered by the Chinese to be their greatest poet, belongs to the second generation of High T'ang poets, but his work is of such scope that it is impossible to confine him to the High T'ang period style. Tu Fu was one of the few admirers of court poetry after its demise, and elements of the seventh-century style appear in his work. Other aspects of his poetry look forward to the Mid- and Late T'ang styles. Apart from Tu Fu, whose work was little understood or appreciated in his own time, the period from 760 to 790 saw the High T'ang style itself descend into hollow convention and stylization. The time was ripe for the poetic reform that will be described in the following chapters.

The three principal genres of T'ang poetry were *yüeh-fu* or imitation folk poetry, "old style" poetry (*ku-shih*), and "new style" poetry (*chin-t'i-shih*) or "regulated verse" (*lü-shih*). The line lengths were predominantly five or seven syllables, with rhyme usually falling on the last syllable of a couplet. There was also a regular caesura before the antepenultimate syllable of a line. Apart from these requirements of line length, rhyme, and caesura, "old style" poetry was free of restrictions. In regulated verse, however, there was a set pattern of tones to be followed, mandatory parallelism in certain couplets, and a fixed number of lines in the two principal subgenres. Due to these limitations, regulated verse developed its own stylistic conventions, as well as a concision and balance which clearly distinguish it from "old style" poetry.

When poets sought to write poetry in the ancient manner, they naturally turned to "old style" verse. The irresistible appeal of the word *ku*, "old" or "ancient," made them associate the genre and the stylistic goal. Furthermore, most High T'ang poets were content to find the ancient manner simply by imitating the poetry of the Late Han and Wei, which was exclusively "old style" verse. Finally, in the case of Meng Chiao, Han Yü, and other Mid-T'ang poets, "old style" verse offered freedom for experimentation, through which they sought their own personal versions of the ancient style.

The search for the ancient style brings us to one of the primary concerns of this study; how Chinese poetry changes and, given the traditional Chinese concern for continuity and normative values, how change is justified. As in the history of Western literature, there has always been in China a creative tension between literary conservatives and progressives, between those who believe in constant values and those who believe in the need for change. However, there is seldom a direct correlation between theory and practice; often literary theory serves the useful function of compensation: a conservative theory may justify a highly innovative poetry and vice versa. Court poets, for example, often spoke of novelty—some clever, original twist of a convention—but the court poetic style dominated two and a half centuries of Chinese literary history with very little change. The eighth and ninth centuries, on the other hand, were periods of great diversity and change in poetry. Their literary theory was China's most reactionary and most influential—*fu-ku*, "return to antiquity." However, in its flexibility and subtle variations, fu-ku offered a compromise between continuity and change which Chinese poets and intellectuals found peculiarly compelling. The fu-ku poetry of Meng Chiao and Han Yü occupies an important place in the history of Chinese poetry not only in its own right, but also because of the fact that Meng and Han set the model for similar fu-ku groups in later dynasties.

The two men are in many ways artistic opposites, and as we trace their development we can see how various their own versions of an "ancient poetry" were and how, considered as a pair, they illuminate each other's work in high relief. The interpretive method I shall use here to describe their development will be extensive analysis and comparison of a selection of poems, arranged in chronological order. This method seemed desirable to me for two reasons: first, to provide specimen studies in the application of various western interpretive techniques to Chinese poetry; second, to show that Chinese poetry is not monolithic, nor that it changes abruptly every half-century, as many Chinese literary histories would seem to suggest, but rather that there is a continuous process of change which can be measured in years and months, even in a body of poetry written over a millennium ago. It is precisely this sense of continuous process which I hope to capture through these analyses.

1

Fu-ku and T'ang Poetry

Meng Chiao and Han Yü were close friends who shared the same convictions about the nature and goals of literature. Yet their experiences, personalities, and art differed radically, and they consequently worked in different directions toward the same goal. They created something new and personal in search of the very old, but ultimately their search led them back to the mainstream of the poetic tradition from which they had originally revolted.

Han Yü's name, as well as Meng Chiao's to a lesser extent, is usually linked with the so-called *ku-wen* ("ancient prose") movement, a literary trend developing through the T'ang toward the straightforward, unrhymed style of pre-Ch'in and Han prose. Earlier in the T'ang and in the period of disunion that had preceded it, prose essays had been for the most part written in a rhymed, antithetical, and highly abstruse style known as "parallel prose" (*p'ien-t'i-wen*). Han Yü's prose is considered the culmination of this stylistic trend toward ku-wen, and he is remembered today even more as a prose stylist and rhetorician than as a poet.

The ku-wen movement was only one manifestation of the larger intellectual trend inspired by the phrase *fu-ku*. Fu-ku was both a slogan and a deeply felt sentiment; it suggests literary reform and ethical regeneration by asserting the vague ideals of antiquity against a corrupt present. However, what constituted these ideals of "antiquity" and how one attained the "ancient" style were largely matters of personal interpretation. As mentioned above, in the realm of prose the Confucian classics and historical writings were adequate models on which to revitalize T'ang essay-writing; but in poetry the situation was more complex. The classically proper model would have been the *Book of Songs*, but poetry in the T'ang, had evolved too far to surrender its own rich and flexible medium to the stiff, archaic

meter and style of the *Book of Songs*. As the dominant literary principle of the period, fu-ku's influence could not be ignored, though it
necessarily had to function more obliquely in poetry than in prose.
To openly contradict the desirability of "return to antiquity," with
its freight of positive ethical implications, was unheard of.

For most poets allegiance to the principle was sufficient in itself.
Though they may have spoken boldly in affirmation of fu-ku, they
ignored it in practice. This in no way impugns the sincerity of their
beliefs; rather, as suggested earlier, a set of fixed, immutable, and
vague ideals could provide a poet with a sense of stability, legitimacy,
and continuity during a period when poetry was undergoing rapid
and profound change. Most T'ang men of letters lacked a highly
developed sense of contradiction.

There were some poets, however, who did try to actualize the ethical and stylistic ideals of fu-ku, and in their hands fu-ku became an
instrument of literary change and, more significantly, of literary self-
consciousness. The very idea of "return to antiquity" implies literary
reform, a conscious rejection of contemporary poetry, to re-create an
antiquity that was at least partly imaginary. Legitimized by the
general acceptance of fu-ku as a literary ideal, such poetry could dare
to be original despite the considerable demands of conformity to conventional poetic taste. Thus we have a peculiarly Chinese phenomenon, a "reactionary reform," the new born of an attempt to recapture the very old.

Although the idea of "return to antiquity" was vague enough not
to limit the kind of poetry written under its aegis, it did move poetry
in certain directions. Such poetry generally tried to express a moral
or philosophical message, setting itself against the objectivity of Bud-
dhist-inspired landscape poetry and the obligatory politeness of vers
de société. In style the poetry tended to be hypotactic rather than
paratactic. While the mainstream of T'ang poetry became increasingly condensed and evocative, fu-ku poetry tended toward bluntness and clarity of statement. Moreover, such popular topics as
women were anathema.

Growing out of an opposition to the court poetry of the Southern
Dynasties, fu-ku never entirely lost its polemical aspect, its sense of
opposition. By creating an "us" and a "them," it became the basis
for the development of a literary group with cohesive and conscious
principles. It was during the T'ang that this self-consciousness came

into being, though it did not develop fully until later in the Sung Dynasty. Although the ideas associated with fu-ku literary theory did not change substantially throughout the T'ang, being virtually the same whether written by the most effete court poet or the most serious "Confucian" poet, we can see in the progression of such fu-ku poets as Ch'en Tzu-ang (661–702), Yüan Chieh (719–72), and Han Yü, increasingly serious attempts to actualize a universally accepted but generally unpracticed poetics. It is through this process that the artist came to have full control over his medium.

Although the idea of fu-ku is as old as the antiquity to which it seeks to return, the tradition we find in the T'ang began during the Southern Dynasties (420–588), when an increasingly effete court poetry produced a violent reaction. In the abstruse parallel prose of Liu Hsieh's *Wen-hsin Tiao-lung*, we read: "When one develops an interest in a career of literature and rhetoric, he seldom realizes that he too should take the Classics as his starting point. The poetry of Ch'u has an alluring charm and the poetic prose of Han is extravagant; but both are deviant forks which never return to the main stream. Would it not be a good idea to curb this tendency to deviate by returning to the source?"[1] Obviously Liu Hsieh felt no contradiction between his fu-ku principles and his own prose style, a development out of the "extravagant poetic prose" of the Han and unlike anything in the classics.

During the Sui and the beginning of the T'ang, fu-ku poetics had become generally accepted. The most important Early T'ang exponent of fu-ku poetry, Ch'en Tzu-ang (661–702), announced:

> The way of poetry has been corrupt for five-hundred years. The Chin and Sung Dynasties did not carry on the style of the Han and Wei, and there are many literary pieces which can attest to this. In leisure hours I have taken a look at poems written during the Ch'i and Liang Dynasties [the Eastern Chin, Sung, Ch'i, and Liang Dynasties are all "Southern Dynasties"], works of flashy beauty that strove for ornateness, but which were utterly lacking in deeper significance. Always then I would sigh, brooding on the ancients, in constant fear lest they become lost in their distance from us and perish. The "Airs" and "Odes"

---

1. Vincent Shih, *The Literary Mind and the Carving of Dragons* (1957; bilingual reprint, Taipei: Chung-hua, 1970), pp. 25–26.

[sections of the *Book of Songs*] are not written today, and thereby I am disquieted.[2]

When Ch'en Tzu-ang wrote this, attacks on the poetry of the Southern Dynasties were already a critical convention. In actual practice, however, Ch'en Tzu-ang was an innovator. Not only was he a pioneer in the lucid, restrained style of High T'ang regulated verse, he also wrote a number of poems in the rugged, simple style of Late Han and Wei poetry, which are taken to be actualizations of his fu-ku sentiment. Among these is a series entitled "Feelings at My Experiences," *Kan-yü*, which are modeled on the Wei poet Juan Chi's "Singing My Feelings," *Yung-huai*. The following is the second poem of Ch'en's series:

> Orchid and turmeric grow in spring and summer,
> Luxuriant and so green.
> Hidden, alone in the beauty of the empty forest,
> Vermilion flowers droop, encroaching on purple stems.
> Gradually the bright sun sinks to evening,
> The trees tremble as the autumn wind rises.
> All the year's flowering flutters and falls—
> What finally becomes of their lovely intentions?[3]

These flowers are traditional symbols of a man of fine character who lives "hidden and alone" and dies without having found anyone to appreciate his goodness. In the course of its development during the preceding centuries, Chinese poetry had left such obvious symbolism far behind, aiming for a richer and more personal symbolic world. Ch'en Tzu-ang, in reviving traditional symbolism, was being consciously primitive, much in the same way that a modern western poet might use allegory. His style is direct but not rough. A different manner may be seen in the following example of Ch'en Tzu-ang's regulated verse.

ANSWERING A POEM GIVEN ME BY THE MONK HUI "ON AN
  AUTUMN NIGHT IN HIS MOUNTAIN PAVILION"

> Gleaming pure, the white woods turn autumn,
> Faintly the azure mountains grow still.
> Fixed in meditation, feeling how things change,

2. *CTS*, c. 83, pp. 895–96.   3. *CTS*, c. 83, p. 890.

Sitting alone, having opened the door to the porch.
Night sounds of wind and streams are mixed,
The sky's gleam of moon and dew is cold.
I am quite grateful to this man with no worldly ambitions,
But cannot put aright my own worldly concerns.[4]

The parallelism we discern in the second poem but not in the first
is a generic difference, but there is also a syntactic complexity and
paratactic style in the second poem that contrast with the syntactic
simplicity and hypotaxis of the first poem. T'ang poetry was tending
toward parataxis and away from hypotaxis, parataxis being more
difficult to understand because of the implied relations between
syntactic units. Both poems do represent a move toward simplifica-
tion and away from the obscurity of the Early T'ang style, but the
first poem does so by syntactic clarity.

The genuine attempt to recapture a lost simplicity and classic
purity quickly turned into a convention itself. In the next generation
we find Chang Chiu-ling (678–740), well known for his ornate regulated verse, producing another series of "Feelings at My Experiences."[5] Ch'en Tzu-ang's personal creation of an ancient-styled
poetry using the poetry of the Late Han and Wei as a model became
a ready mode for poetry written in response to fu-ku sentiment.

Through the example of Ch'en Tzu-ang, fu-ku principles became
associated with the Late Han and Wei poetic style during the High
T'ang. Li Po (701–62) affirmed these conventional fu-ku principles,
writing a number of poems in the Late Han and Wei style that were
collected into a series under the title "Old Manner," *Ku-feng*. The
first poem of this series is a famous statement of fu-ku.

Long have the Great Odes not been written,
Being in my decline, who now will offer up poems that teach?
The Royal Airs have been cast into wild grasses,
In the Warring States thorn bushes grew many.
Dragon and tiger rent and bit one another,   5
Weapons lasted until mad Ch'in.
How faint the proper sounds had become,
When bitter lament rose from the poet of the *Li Sao*.
Ssu-ma Hsiang-ju and Yang Hsiung stirred the falling wave,

4. *CTS*, c. 83, p. 899.   5. *CTS*, c. 47, pp. 571–72.

Until it flowed into the open, vast and limitless.   10
Though rise and fall have occurred thousands of times,
The authoritative models have been engulfed and lost.
Ever since the Chien-an
The lush "prettiness" is not worth valuing.
But our sage dynasty returns to primal antiquity, . . .[6]   15

The "Great Odes," *Ta-ya*, and "Royal Airs," *Wang-feng*, are both
sections of the *Book of Songs*, the ideal of poetic orthodoxy. As the
Chou Dynasty declined during the Warring States Period, the orthodox manner of poetry also declined, and was already considerably
weakened when Ch'ü Yüan wrote his *Li Sao* (ca. 313 B.C.). The two
major writers of *fu*, or prose poems, during the Han Dynasty, Ssu-
ma Hsiang-ju (179–117 B.C.) and Yang Hsiung, opposed the growing
decline, and the Chien-an Period (A.D. 196–219) was the last bright
moment before the "Way" of poetry became utterly lost. Poetry
began like a stream on the right course, gradually losing momentum
until it became lost in the great sea, whose undifferentiated expanse
gave no indication of the "proper channel." But the T'ang, Li Po
asserts later in the poem, has returned to the "authoritative models
of antiquity." This is a succinct history of Chinese poetry from the
fu-ku point of view.

Perhaps the most significant feature of Li Po's reactionary, orthodox poetics is that the same poet was famous for writing verses of the
kind which follows:

White dew appears on the jade staircase,
Night lasts long, it gets in her silken hose.
Back she goes, pulls down the crystal curtain,
And through the latticework views the bright moon.[7]

This is one of the loveliest examples of that "lush prettiness, *ch'i-li*,
characteristic of poetry written during the Southern Dynasties,
which was "not worth valuing." The first poem we quoted was a
statement of Li Po's literary principles; the latter poem is an example
of the style of a sizeable part of his practice. Although Li Po might
have felt that his fu-ku poetry was a more enduring achievement, it is
evident that the problem of the contradiction between his theory and
his practice never arose.

6. *CTS*, c. 161, p. 1670.   7. *CTS*, c. 164. p. 1701.

Avoiding the moribund meter of the *Book of Songs*, most T'ang poets wisely chose the oldest examples of the then dominant pentasyllabic and heptasyllabic line when writing poetry that purported to "return to antiquity." These were, as we have seen, the style of the Late Han and Wei. Besides simplicity and directness, there was also an attempt at ethical significance rather than the delineation of the poet's emotions, as well as a conscious primitivism in the choice of poetic devices. Although such poems did not live up to the high goals of the theoretical "return to antiquity," the poets who wrote them seem to have felt that theirs was a satisfying compromise.

One High T'ang poet, Yüan Chieh (719–72), refused to make the popular compromise and tried to put fu-ku principles into practice in a purer form. His archaized poetry represents a further step in delimiting what constituted fu-ku poetry. Fu-ku had specifically Confucian associations, yet many of Ch'en Tzu-ang's, Chang Chiu-ling's, and Li Po's fu-ku poems were overtly Taoist in inspiration. For them the poetic interpretation of fu-ku meant a poetry of ideas set against a poetry of mere sentiment. To Yüan Chieh the ideas had to be Confucian ideas, the morality, Confucian morality. Furthermore, many of Yüan Chieh's poems are consciously and idiosyncratically archaized, unlike those of Ch'en Tzu-ang and the others who simply used the stylistic model of Late Han and Wei poetry. In this case we have the first example of a style created to match a theory.

Yüan Chieh's critical writings follow the familiar pattern of lament for the idealized past and condemnation of the corrupt present. In the preface to his anthology, the *Ch'ieh-chung Collection* (760), he says:

> The writers of recent times imitate one another still more, being constrained by tonal regulations and delighting in description. Furthermore, they make their diction according to shifts in fashion, not realizing that this does harm to what is right and proper.[8]

Yüan Chieh condemns regulated verse ("being constrained by tonal regulations") outright, as well as imitation. In other words, Yüan takes an extreme and explicit position that was only implicit in Ch'en Tzu-ang and Li Po.

In the first of Yüan Chieh's three chapters of poetry in his col-

8. *CTW*, c. 381, p. 4898.

lected works, he uses the archaic four-character line and Ch'u Tz'u meters. Most High T'ang poets did try their hand at these forms, but Yüan Chieh's experiments with them are distinguished by their quantity, their quality, and by the fact that Yüan took them quite seriously. This can be seen in the prefaces he wrote for the poems. In the "Discussion of My 'Two Kinds of Airs'" (747) Yüan states a specific plan for that series of poems:

> Someone asked Master Yüan, "Why did you compose your 'Two Kinds of Airs'?"
> I answered, "I wished to examine cases of the Ways of Order and Disorder of the kings and emperors, and to continue the mainstream of pattern-setting and satire of the ancients."[9]

Yüan then proceeds to divide the ten poems of the "Two Kinds of Airs" into one group of five tracing various aspects of order in five good rulers, and another group of five tracing aspects of disorder in five bad rulers. Before each poem Yüan writes a few sentences telling what ruler the poem concerns and his particular merit or fault. The significance of these poems lies in their being an explicit attempt to put fu-ku ideals into practice. The didactic ethics permit none of the ambiguity and subtlety which is valued in other High T'ang poetry.

In Yüan Chieh's "Filling in the Lyrics of the Ancient Songs," the poet supplies his own words to the titles of songs that survived without words or music from mythical antiquity. He "sought out their titles and meaning to supply words for them," with the result that "by deep pondering and mysterious reverie [he] had the tones of pure antiquity."[10] These poems do have a certain archaic dignity and simplicity. I quote the third of the series:

> "Cloudy Gates" is the song of the Yellow Emperor. Its general meaning was that just as the clouds go out to enrich and increase all things, there is likewise nothing which the ruler's virtue does not affect.

> Black clouds flood out,
> Sending down rain in steady streams.
> Like unto a sage ruler enriching mankind,
> Endlessly moistening the roots.

9. *CTW*, c. 382, p. 4905.   10. *CTS*, c. 240, p. 2693.

> Black clouds blanket the sky,
> The light within them grows ever brighter,
> Like unto my sagely virtue,
> All-embracing, everywhere.[11]

Like the traditional symbolism of Ch'en Tzu-ang's poem, the similes here have clear meanings. The didactic clarity of the message and the simple one-to-one correlation between the tenor and vehicle of the metaphors are characteristic of fu-ku poetry. The short preface states the message, which is then put into archaic verse.

Yüan Chieh's poetry in the five-character line foreshadows the work of Han Yü and Meng Chiao. Yüan's poetry is often rugged; it frequently uses particles and prose forms, and has a strong ethical orientation. However, he was never able to move far enough away from the High T'ang style to transcend it. His poetry lacks the dynamism and intensity, the world of extremes, which dominate the poetry of Han Yü and Meng Chiao. There is a sense of High T'ang balance and restraint coming through Yüan's roughest diction, a clinging to conventional good taste which he cannot wholly abandon.

Sometimes Yüan Chieh's poetry sounds very much like early Han Yü:

> I didn't know that being among the caps of office,
> Did not go with being without entanglements.
> Yet I struggled hard for what I had not reached,
> Which is somewhat different than other men.
>
>   [from "For Tang, Inquiry Judge"][12]

While most High T'ang poetry tended to be descriptive and nominal, each line a self-contained syntactic unit, the vigorous, hypotactic self-analysis of this passage is something new. At other times Yüan does turn to the casual tranquillity of High T'ang nature poetry:

> No one knows of East Stream,
> Lying east of the mountain to my left.
> To draw from it I come beside the mountain
> Where it flows down, falling into my garden.
> Through the overnight fog it catches dawn's light,
> Its gleam covered like a fading rainbow.
> At times it scatters into rain,

11. *CTS*, c. 240, p. 2694.   12. *CTS*, c. 241, p. 2706.

> Blowing and sprinkling in the clear wind.
>> [from "Written on Drawing from East Stream"][13]

Thematically, Yüan Chieh shows early the eremitism that characterizes much poetry of the last phase of the High T'ang from about
760–90. Faced with an ethical or political dilemma, Yüan Chieh
responds with eremite escapism rather than with the moral outrage
we shall see in Han Yü or the affirmation of ethical values in Meng
Chiao. Thus, in his famous "To the Tax Collectors, After the Bandits'
Withdrawal" (764), in which he soundly berates the tax officials
for being more rapacious than the bandits, Yüan Chieh closes:

> I long to throw away my badges of office,
> Take my fishing pole and punt my own boat,
> With my family go where there's fish and wheat,
> An old man retiring to the banks of rivers and lakes.[14]

Although in many ways his poetry looks forward to that of the
Mid-T'ang (790–815), Yüan Chieh never succeeded in completely
escaping the High T'ang manner. His problem was essentially the
same as that of the earlier fu-ku poets: his archaized verse, like
their primitivism, could not compete aesthetically with the subtler
High T'ang styles. Thus Li Po is remembered more as the poet of
the second poem quoted than as the author of his versified literary
history. Only the complete impoverishment of the High T'ang
manner during the last decades before the Mid-T'ang enabled
fu-ku poetry to oppose it successfully.

With the poetry of Han Yü and Meng Chiao, we have a fully
conscious and original actualization of fu-ku principles. The content
of Han Yü's theoretical pronouncements does not differ substantially
from those of his predecessors, yet we can see in many ways that he
and Meng Chiao felt a close relation between theory and actual
practice. While fu-ku poetry had only been a small part of the poetic
corpus of earlier fu-ku poets, Han Yü's poetry never yields entirely
to the High T'ang style. The prosaisms and archaisms of Han Yü's
early poetry give it a sense of "ancientness," the elusive quality so
many poets had sought. The ethical focus of both Han Yü's and
Meng Chiao's poetry conformed to the high moral standards that
were supposed to accompany fu-ku.

13. *CTS*, c. 241, p. 2713.   14. *CTS*, c. 241, pp. 2704–05.

Finally, the ruggedness of Meng Chiao's poetry in particular seems to have approximated what the poems of the *Book of Songs* must have sounded like to the T'ang poet, in contrast to the smoothness, balance, and parallelism of High T'ang regulated verse. Presumably because Meng Chiao carried this ruggedness to an extreme, his poetry was felt to be more "ancient" than others'. As the *ku-wen* stylist Li Kuan put it: "In the best of his pentasyllabic poetry there is nothing superior in antiquity; in ordinary places he is above Hsieh T'iao and Hsieh Ling-yün."[15] (Hsieh Ling-yün and Hsieh T'iao were two of the best poets of the Southern Dynasties period.) In his "Preface on Seeing Off Meng Chiao," Han Yü says: "At his best he transcends the Wei and Chin style—the others wallow in the style of the Han poets."[16]

In addition to the fu-ku poetry of Han Yü, Meng Chiao, and their followers, a second group of Mid-T'ang poets led by Po Chü-yi (772–846) and Yüan Chen (779–831) built a separate fu-ku style on simplicity, straightforwardness, and the balladry of social protest. Both groups were motivated by the fu-ku sentiment, Han Yü trying to capture the intangible "manner" of antiquity and Po Chü-yi seeking to restore poetry's Confucian function as a means to rectify society. Yet both groups can be equally well understood as separate reactions to the High T'ang period style.

In terms of Western literary criticism it may be difficult to see how one style based on archaism and ruggedness and another based on directness and social criticism are both characteristic of a single period style. Indeed, Han Yü's and Meng Chiao's poetry eventually developed into hermetic symbolism, to be understood only by a moral and artistic Confucian elite, while Po Chü-yi's poetry developed into a simple poetry recording the incidents of everyday life. However, both groups are subsumed under the Chinese idea of *p'ien,* "inclined to one side"—or as we may better describe it, a "poetry of extremes." In contrast, the poetry of the High T'ang is generally one of balance. In entities as elusive as period styles it is often easier to get a "feel" for the differences than it is to define them. With that purpose in mind, compare the following two pairs of poems, the first by Meng Hao-jan and Meng Chiao, the second by the great High T'ang poet Wang Wei (701–761) and Han Yü:

15. *CTW,* c. 534, p. 6875.
16. *HCLW,* p. 137.

NORTH OF NAN-YANG, HINDERED BY SNOW
                                          Meng Hao-jan (689–740)

On my journey I'm hindered at Wan and Hsü,
Day and evening I gaze toward the capitals.
The broad plain stretches into the emptiness,
Where are the mountains of my home?
A single line of smoke rises at the edge of a village,   5
Homeward geese go off beyond the horizon.
Snowdrifts cover the level hills,
Hungry hawks pounce on cold rabbits.
As a youth I played at writing,
Put my mind to composition—   10
After ten vain letters to my lord, I'm ashamed to go home,
Yet pacing about I hold to the homeward road.[17]

SICK ON THE ROAD
                                          Meng Chiao

A sick wanderer with no host,
So hard—always lying down!
Flying sunbeams redden the road,
While an inner fire broils my heart.
Want to drink, but wells and streams, dried up,   5
Want doctoring, but my purse is used up.
How long can a young face last?—
Bold resolution suddenly ruined.
A son doesn't speak of his suffering,
Sending letters home I speak only of calm.   10
But rings of sorrow are in my guts,
Twisting round and round, without any end.[18]

In both of these poems the poet's state of mind is highly complex.
In the first, Meng Hao-jan is torn between a longing to return home
and feeling too ashamed to return home; between a longing to go
back to the capital from which he came and frustration at being unable to go anywhere because he is blocked by the snow. In Meng
Chiao's poem the poet feels longing for companionship, frustration
at being kept in bed, the contradictions between his real state and
the letters he must write home, and suffering both mental and

17. *CTS*, c. 159, p. 1628.   18. *MTYSC*, p. 26.

physical. His longing for someone to care for him, a "host," could
be found at home but, perversely, he can't tell his family of his
need. Meng Chiao's emotions are stated with far greater intensity
than Meng Hao-jan's; and this intensity is an extreme that contrasts
with the restrained brooding and anguish of the first, High T'ang
poem.

In Meng Hao-jan's poem the emotions are balanced by the objective scene, which mirrors the poet's mind yet retains its own
identity: the village suggests communality, geese traditionally mean
return homeward, while the vast spaces heighten his sense of total
isolation. The individual is placed in the greater context of nature,
and aspects of nature have a special meaning for him. In Meng
Chiao's poem the objective scene is subordinated to the poet's
emotions and becomes part of them; nature has existence and meaning only through the poet's state of mind. Red sunbeams burn
the road of his travels like the fever burning within him: this intensifies the relation between the mental anguish of his journey and the
physical pain of his sickness. Nature conspires against him, drying
up the "wells and streams," keeping him from quenching his fever.
Meng Hao-jan saw special aspects of the real world; in Meng Chiao's
poem the external world is bizarre and deformed by the suffering
mind.

Meng Hao-jan's High T'ang poem is also balanced in structure:
first the poet states his circumstances, then gives an objective description of the scene with emotional associations, and closes with a
statement of his emotions. This structure is characteristically High
T'ang—the objective world with its personal associations makes
emotions intelligible, so that finally the poet is able to express them.
Meng Chiao's Mid-T'ang poem jumps from topic to topic, each
one adding another level of suffering. Instead of making emotion
intelligible and therefore controllable, this structure intensifies the
emotion, building up to the final image of mental and physical suffering. The emotion is still in the poet's guts—it never comes out.

WATCHING A HUNT

Wang Wei (701–61)

The wind strong, the horn-bow sings,
The general is hunting by Wei's walls.
The grasses dry, the falcon's eye keen,

Where snow ends, the horses' hooves move light.
Swiftly they pass Hsin-feng Market,
Back they return to Thinwillow Camp.
Looking back to where he shot the hawk—
Evening clouds flat across a thousand miles.[19]

THE PHEASANT STRUCK BY AN ARROW

Han Yü

On the plain fires burn with silent determination,
Field pheasants, fearing the hawk,
   Come out and sink back down again.
The general wishes to humble the others by his skill,
Turns his horse round, bends his bow,
   But holds back and does not shoot.
The area gradually gets narrower, onlookers increase,   5
The pheasant starts up, the bow stretched full,
   A strong arrow in the notch.
It soars abruptly upward, against the people,
   More than a hundred feet,
Red pinions and the silvery barb follow
   Toward one another slanting.
The general looks up and laughs, his officers congratulate him,
As many-colored feathers fall scattering before his horse.[20]   10

There are a number of characteristic differences between the High T'ang and the Mid-T'ang examples. Han Yü dramatizes the situation: the short predicates and nervous action lend a suspense and intensity to the scene which is lacking in Wang Wei's poem. Wang Wei's poem appeals to the senses—the feel of the wind, the sound of the bow, the snow, the dry grass, the expanse of clouds. Of the kill we hear only the sound of the bow and see the scene afterwards, "looking back." Wang Wei builds his scene out of fragments; Han Yü analyzes each movement consecutively. Nature is the focus of the Wang Wei poem: what he sees is the snow, the grass, the falcon, and the evening clouds. Nature is the measure and man is only part of it. To Han Yü the general is the focus: he is placed in a social context, wishing to "humble the others" and being congratulated by his officers. The suspenseful moment when he draws his

19. *CTS*, c. 126, p. 1278.   20. *HCLS*, p. 53.

bow but does not shoot concentrates on human psychology rather than on nature: the human world dominates the natural one. Furthermore, the final line of Han Yü's poem is both lovely and violent, both engaging the reader and repulsing him, in contrast to Wang Wei's poem, where he observes everything dispassionately from a distance.

However, the strongest contrast between these pairs of poems is found in the intensity of Han Yü's poem. The psychological dramatization and the tension between the violence and the beauty of the hunt give his poem an energy that Wang Wei deliberately sought to repress in his poem. Lacking Wang Wei's sense of balance and restraint, Han Yü's poem is *p'ien*, "extreme."

We have taken the long view of T'ang poetry, the trends in literary theory which helped to shape the poetry of the 790s. However, as is often the case in a dynamic period of literary history, it is in the short view of literary development, the style of the preceding two or three decades, that we see the strongest influence exerted over the development of a new style. In departing from the High T'ang style, Meng Chiao and Han Yü were reacting specifically against that style in its declining phase during the decades preceding 790.

Although the poets of this period are often included in the Mid-T'ang, the grounds for their inclusion are historical rather than stylistic. The poets who flourished between 760 and 790, with the exception of Yüan Chieh and Tu Fu, belong spiritually and stylistically to the High T'ang. This poetry is traditionally called the Ta-li style, after one of the reign titles (766–80) of the period. The prevailing poetic vogue was the eremitic quietism and landscape poetry derived from the earlier High T'ang poets Meng Hao-jan and Wang Wei.

Two groups of poets dominated the period; the first, the so-called Ten Talents of the Ta-li, distinguished themselves by stylistic refinement and an easy sentimentality. The second group was from the lower Yangtze region and revolved around the poet-monk Chiao-jan (730–99), whose critical writings set the tone of the group. It was among poets of this circle that the young Meng Chiao first made literary acquaintances.

The best poet of the period was Wei Ying-wu (737–90?), a friend of Chiao-jan. As a landscape poet Wei's name is often linked with those of Wang Wei and Meng Hao-jan, and although he did not move in the direction of a Mid-T'ang style, he might well be called the last of the great High T'ang poets.

Wei Ying-wu's eremitic poetry has an enigmatic beauty and gentleness which also appears now and then in Meng Chiao's early poetry. The following may be taken as an example of Wei's best work:

AUTUMN NIGHT: TO CH'IU TAN

On this autumn night, thinking of you,
I stroll and sing to the cool sky.
The mountains are deserted, a pine cone falls,
I guess my hermit friend hasn't gone to sleep yet either.[21]

Both Wei Ying-wu and Chiao-jan shared a fascination with Hsieh Ling-yün (385–433), the first great landscape poet of China and an ancestor of Chiao-jan. Hsieh's verse, dense and complicated, exerted a strong influence on Chiao-jan's poetry and, through him, on the early poetry of Meng Chiao. In Chiao-jan's essentially High T'ang poetry this influence takes the form of elegant periphrases; but as we shall see in the following chapter, when filtered through the Mid-T'ang sensibility of Meng Chiao, it becomes outlandish hyperbole.

21. *CTS*, c. 188, p. 1924.

2

The Early Poetry of Meng Chiao

Meng Chiao, unlike the younger Han Yü, underwent a poetic apprenticeship in the Ta-li style. But Meng showed little aptitude for the grace and balance which characterized that style at its best. His strong poetic personality seemed awkward in the conventional poems of his early years, but in his mature poetry that awkwardness was transformed into a positive value.

Traditional critics have often called Meng Chiao a disciple of Han Yü, primarily because of the pre-eminent stature of the latter as a prose writer and champion of Confucianism. But Meng Chiao was well on his way to evolving a personal style long before he met Han Yü, fourteen years younger than himself, in Ch'ang-an in 791. Furthermore, it is possible to detect a few traits of Meng Chiao's style in Han Yü's early poetry.

Even so, Meng Chiao's early poetry is decidedly mediocre, though in it the following elements of a growing personal style should be noted:

1. The use of unusual words and images to startle the reader
2. A tendency toward hyperbole showing both cleverness of conceit and awkwardness
3. Absolutes, the natural limit of hyperbole, a tendency to speak in terms of "all" or "none." In Meng Chiao's later poetry this becomes involved with the necessary absolutes of ethical judgment.
4. A personal ethical position. The poet tends to evaluate all phenomena in terms of good and evil.
5. Moral and evaluative metaphor. This is a consistent trait of Meng Chiao's early poetry and the first stage of his mature poetry. Metaphor is used to heighten moral qualities or evaluative distinctions.

All of the above are *intensifying* devices; they all serve to startle, to draw distinctions sharply, and to treat everything as extreme. In Meng's early poetry such "antisubtlety" is usually awkward; in his mature work it becomes a source of strength.

The following poem of 780 is the earliest datable poem in Meng Chiao's works, written even before he became acquainted with Chiao-jan and his circle.

SPENDING THE NIGHT AT HSIA-LING ON MY WAY TO HO-YANG:
TO LI P'ENG

An evening sky, a cold wind—sad, restless,
Crows caw circling the trees, streams choked up.
On the road I take off my saddle, put up at a stone mound,
In the dark sky beyond the mountains I see the faint moon,
An owl screeches, a dog barks, frosty mist at dusk,   5
Open my bag, spread my napkin, face a dish of supper.
Failure and success in human life are owed to understanding
   friends,
So tomorrow I'll send you half a word to express myself.[1]

The structure of this poem is simple: it consists of a description of the scene and the poet's situation, setting the mood, followed by an oblique request for patronage. The description of the wind as "restless" and the streams as "choked up" is unusual, giving the lines an interest otherwise lacking. The original diction of the first couplet can hardly save the poem from falling into the gentle, conventual melancholy which characterizes Ta-li poetry, however. A line like "In the dark sky beyond the mountains I see the faint moon," is unredeemably conventional. The function of imagery in this poem is to create a mood, rather than being symbolic as it often is in the later work. The "cawing crows" and "screeching owls," for example, are melancholy decorations of the scene. As yet Meng Chiao's personal inclinations toward the harsh and bizarre are exerting little pressure on the Ta-li style.

Li P'eng seems to have accepted Meng Chiao as a client, for the

---

1. *MTYSC*, p. 93. *Analects*, XII, 12: Confucius said of his disciple Tzu-lu, "He is one who can settle disputes, though hearing only half a word." Meng Chiao is complimenting Li P'eng, who like Tzu-lu can understand what the poet wants to say, even though he is expressing himself inadequately.

following panegyric of about 781 praises Li with a certain hyperbolic gusto.

To Lord Li P'eng of Ho-yang

Our grand general maintains divine strategies,
His expert troops lack any cruelty.
Though the Triple Army is in a severe winter,
One soothing gesture surpasses thick robes.
His frosty sword outdoes the host of lights,   5
Makes night's stars lose their eternal glimmer.
When this blue falcon stands alone,
Evil birds dare not fly.
Wu-lao locks the Gates to Heaven,[2]
The River Bridge is a narrow stronghold.   10
But how could this great army be at ease?—
Few would vaunt they could hold this place.
This poor scholar is of downcast mien,
At your noble gates are mainly light robes and fat horses.[3]
If one climbs to the height of a great peak,   15
One sees the tininess of trees and bushes,
But since the great peak's compassion is far-reaching,
The hearts of all trees and bushes turn to it.[4]

The maintenance of discipline in the Chinese army was felt to be a function of the commander's moral force. The hyperbole of the second couplet is of a peculiarly Chinese variety; the love and concern General Li shows his troops can conquer the physical hardships the soldiers suffer. When Chinese poets in general, and Meng Chiao and Han Yü in particular, praise military men, they do so in ethical rather than military terms.

All panegyrics tend naturally toward hyperbole, but Meng Chiao shows a particularly extravagant talent in this direction. "One soothing gesture" from the general is better than heavy clothes to keep the soldiers warm in the winter; the general's sword is so bright

2. Wu-lao was on the road to the capital, therefore it is the "Gates to Heaven."
3. "Light robes and fat horses" is a cliché derived from *Analects* VI, 3, ii, meaning the rich and noble.
4. *MTYSC*, p. 98. There is a pun here on *hsin*, meaning "hearts" as well as "stems" or "trunks." Meng Chiao is cleverly suggesting that the reason the trees and bushes grow upward is because they are "turning toward" the superior virtue of the high mountain.

that it makes the stars fade; he is a mountain compared to which Meng Chiao is only an ordinary plant. Certain key words of the "outdoing" trope are present: "surpass" (1.4), "outdo" (1.5), and "losing [some quality by comparison]" (1.6). All qualities are intensified to extremes: "the grand [literally top] general," "expert [literally perfected] troops," "severe winter," "*few* would vaunt," "*all* trees and bushes."

Characteristic of Meng Chiao's poetry as a whole are the moral metaphors, which first make their appearance in this poem. General Li is a mountain, suggesting moral grandeur, to whom all lesser things, "trees and bushes," will turn. "Turn to," *kuei,* has certain ethical associations in addition to the clever pun mentioned in the notes: Confucianism has a traditional idea that when a sage arises all people will naturally "turn to" (*kuei,*) him, influenced by his moral superiority.

Meng Chiao's compliments to Li P'eng were not without foundation; in 781–82 central China was beset by a series of rebellions which nearly brought down the dynasty. Li P'eng, remaining loyal, raised troops to oppose the rebels. The following poem is the finest of Meng Chiao's early works; it goes well beyond the High T'ang style in its vision of order and concluding moral affirmation.

THE MOOD OF KILLING IS NOT ON THE FRONTIERS

The mood of killing is not on the frontiers,
It's an icy chill, this autumn in the heartland.
Roads' dangers are not in the mountains—
There are smashed carriage shafts on the plains.
Even Ho-nan raises troops,   5
Streams pure and foul are jointly locked.
Not simply private troubles for the wanderer,
Boats on official journeys too are delayed.
Worse still, cut off from my duties as a son,
So far from home I'm completely blocked off now.   10
Suddenly my locks turn snowy white
From just one day of sorrow.
Lying alone, it seems night will never turn morning,
Rise, gaze on the stars floating in the galaxy.
A chilly wind sweeps heaven and earth,   15
Day and night its voice moans.

All things lack youth's bright beauty,
A million people grow old and full of cares.
A grown man feels truly ashamed.   20
That magic sound!—What would it do?—
It's a singing sword that longs to butcher the enemy.[5]

The first two couplets give different versions of the topos of the
world upside down. The mood of killing and the broken carriages
belong on the frontiers and in the mountains, but they are precisely
where they do not belong, on the central plains. In these two couplets
the phrase "not on/in," *pu-tsai*, is particularly forceful; the usual way
of expressing location in poetry is by the periphrasis "as for location
x, there is/isn't any *y*" (*x* is *yu*, *wu y*), which occurs in line four. The
world is out of joint. In contrast to the forceful negative location in
the first line, the second line avoids being specific, literally "Chilly—
autumn in the heartland." But it is understood that the chill is from
the *ch'i*, the "mood" or "air" of killing. The moral metaphor of line
six sums up the inversion of the natural order: the pure, General
Li's troops, and the foul, the rebels, are locked in battle; it also
presages the poet's being unable to escape the region by boat.

The following couplet balances Meng Chiao's personal troubles
against public difficulties. The need to perform his filial duties
intensifies his misery at being blocked by the rebellion. As the poem
gradually builds in intensity, the particles of intensification are in
evidence: "even," *yu* (l. 5, meaning "to the extent that") and
"[worse] still," *k'uang* (1.9). The cumulative effect of these national,
official, and personal troubles is that the poet's hair turns white,
hyperbolically, from "just one day of sorrow."

Unable to sleep because of his worries, the poet feels that the
night will never end; this is both the subjective reaction to his rest-
lessness and suggestive of a "dawn" of peace after this endless
"night" of rebellion. As he rises to gaze on the night scene, public
and private troubles become cosmic and universal. The "mood
(*ch'i*, also air) of killing" has been specified as a "chilly wind." A
particular disorder has become a universal vision of disorder: Meng
speaks for "heaven and earth," all time ("day and night," suggesting continuity), "all things," and all people.

In the face of such universal disorder the poet must take a moral

5. *MTYSC*, p. 10.

position; he must rectify the world by carrying out "far-reaching plans" in the service of the empire. The desire to serve becomes a singing sword to oppose the rebellion. The extremity of disorder provokes an opposite extreme in the harsh usage, to "butcher the enemy."

In the mid-780s Meng Chiao fell under the influence of the Chiao-jan circle, and in a number of poems written to its poets, made an uneasy attempt to write with their stylistic grace. However, Meng Chiao's talents lay in the direction of conflict rather than of harmony, and his early experiences with the examination system provided him a source of internal conflict that he was to exploit fully. Until 790 Meng paid little attention to getting a position in the bureaucracy, but with the departure of his uncle Meng Chien to Ch'ang-an in 790 to take the examination, we first see the civil ideal set against the private life.

In the Mountains Seeing Off My Uncle Meng Chien on His Way to Take the Examination

Stone as its roots, a hundred foot fir,
An eye of the mountain, this single spring.
Leaning on one, a Taoist mood prevails,
Drinking from the other, fresh ideas for poems.
But in this field where the mind roams free,   5
Suddenly the strings of parting are played.
But you laugh at this hermit dressed in vines,
Who doesn't share your year for singing and prancing.[6]

Two antithetical points of view contend in this poem: on the one hand, there are the eremitic pleasures of Meng Chiao, and on the other, the joy of Meng Chien at going to Ch'ang-an to take the examination. Through the first four lines the poet builds an ideal scene of Taoist tranquillity; in the sixth line he shatters that tranquillity with "suddenly," introducing the theme of parting and the sorrow that goes with it. The human emotion of sorrow at parting is itself in conflict with eremitic detachment from worldly emotions, but the poet goes even further, completely reversing his point of view in the last couplet. He introduces the seventh line with "contrarily," *ch'üeh* (translated as "but"), to emphasize this shift in viewpoint as

6. *MTYSC*, p. 128.

Meng Chien *laughs* at the idyllic scene of the first five lines and at the
hermit Meng Chiao, who will not have the opportunity to take the
examination and achieve public success.

This technique of building a world in a poem only to destroy it, is
a favorite of Meng Chiao, appearing frequently in his later poetry.
It is another intensifying device, heightening the implicit dichotomy
between two worlds. Its purpose is to shock the reader, particularly
the T'ang reader, to whom a poem usually presented a single point
of view. The reader accepts the world a poem creates on faith; when
that world is destroyed or attacked in the same poem, it challenges
the reader's identification with that world. The T'ang reader, in-
hospitable to contradictions, could accept willingly a poem on either
the joys of a hermit's life or the desire to serve in the government;
here the contradictions are pointed out to him. It is probably in
reference to such devices that the Sung critic Yen Yü said in his
"Ts'ang-lang Poetry Notes": "He [Meng Chiao] gives one an
unpleasant sensation."[7]

In this poem we also see the beginnings of true stylistic control.
The first two lines are nominal sentences, presenting an objective
scene with symbolic overtones. The lone fir tree is a conventional
symbol for the morally pure hermit; the tree and the stone in which
it is rooted are the milieu of the hermit, his "roots." They suggest
firmness, austerity, and integrity. The mountain spring is treated as
an "eye" of the mountain, both in its appearance and in its reflecting
abilities, looking out to apprehend the world around it. The second
couplet relates the hermit, Meng Chiao, physically and spiritually
to this static, symbolic scene. He physically "leans on" the fir, the
symbol of the hermit, and absorbs its qualities—"a Taoist mood
prevails." "Prevails" is literally "high," describing the hundred foot
fir as well as the hermit's mood. He physically drinks from the spring,
the symbolic eye that apprehends the world, absorbing the spring/
eye's view of the landscape as new material and inspiration for his
poetry. The first couplet is verbless, static, and objective; the second
couplet is active (four verbal predicates), as the hermit interacts
with the static landscape. A beautiful, idyllic world has been succinctly created, only to be mocked by Meng Chien, who laughs at
its folly.

7. Yen Yü, *Ts'ang-lang Shih-hua*, reprinted in Ho Wen-huan, ed., *Li-tai Shih-hua* (1770;
reprint, Taipei: Yi-wen, 1959), p. 452.

Soon Meng Chiao found himself going northward to Ch'ang-an
to take the examination. The contradictions between the two ways of
life, a hermit's and an official's, are intensified and internalized. In
the following poem some of the tensions that will tear apart the
superficial balance and restraint of the High T'ang style first appear.

> DESCRIBING MY FEELINGS ON BEING CHOSEN IN HU-CHOU TO
>   TAKE THE EXAMINATION
> In vain the Cha's waters are deep and clear,
> They reflect the form but not the heart.
> A white crane which hasn't risen to the heavens,
> Ordinary birds that compete in floating and diving.
> From here on I'll set my sail and go off,   5
> Then—I'll make a song of return to the mountains.[8]

Meng Chiao himself is going off to take the examination, but he
still longs for the life of a hermit. The Cha River mirrors only external reality, the form of the man who is going north to Ch'ang-an,
but it doesn't reveal the poet's "heart," which longs to return to the
mountains. In this conflict between necessity and desire, the river
is a subtle and complex image. It not only reflects the external truth,
the fact that he *is* going to Ch'ang-an, it also is the instrument of
that reality, for it will carry him there. Extended even further, it is a
symbol of the public life where "ordinary birds," traditional symbols of "lesser men," *hsiao-jen*, contend for personal gain. The inner
world is equally consistent; since the desire to return to the mountain
is internal, it expresses itself by internal means—through poetry—
rather than crossing the boundaries into the physical world and causing him to return physically to the mountains. The crane is an immortal bird, and the phrase "rise to the heavens," *ch'ing-chü*, is a
technical Taoist term meaning to become an immortal; but here, in
connection with the bird image, it means actually to fly upward as
well.

The following poem was written on Meng's journey to Ch'ang-
an to take the examination. The internal tensions are growing even
sharper, but Meng still maintains a High T'ang delicacy.

> HAPPILY COMING UPON UNCLE CHIEN, PASSING IN ANOTHER
>   BOAT
>   I send this to him after parting. At the time my uncle had

8. *MTYSC*, p. 50.

just passed the examination and was returning south. I could
not follow him.

Of one mind, two puffs of cloud,
Gradually joining, then coming apart and away.
Since the southward cloud is borne home on good fortune,
With whom will the northward cloud flock?
I send my voice in a thousand miles of wind—
Did you hear it calling to you?[9]

Like the preceding poem, this poem begins with an image of
contradiction, two separate entities with a single desire, one (Meng
Chien) going in the direction both wish to go, the other (Meng Chiao)
going against his will to a lonely life in the North. The clouds are
images of the sails of the two boats as they come together and pass on
the river. Moreover, clouds are traditional images of wandering
scholars. "Of one mind" refers both to their friendship, that they
feel the same way toward one another, and to their common desire
to return southward.

The technique of the opening couplet is similar to that used in the
beginning of "In the Mountains Seeing Off my Uncle Meng Chien."
The first line is nominal and static; in the second line the static
images are set in motion, "gradually joining, then coming apart
and away." The second couplet explains the internal contradiction.
In the final couplet Meng Chiao seeks to communicate with his
uncle, to cross the gap that separates the two forms that are "of one
mind," but because the physical and spiritual distance between them
is so great, he cannot know whether or not he has succeeded.

The smoothness of the style, the delicacy and sensitivity of the
emotions expressed, and the geometric pattern of the structure (the
two men are apart, then together, then apart, and a final gesture is
made to bring them together again) make this poem much richer
than the average parting poem; but these elements, typically High
T'ang, run at cross-purposes to the strong tensions within the poem.
The unity of the two mens' desires and their physical unity when
they meet on the river is set against the separateness of the directions
in which they are going and their physical parting: these contradictions parallel the split between body and desire in the preceding
poem. Just as the poet built a positive scene only to destroy it in the

9. *MTYSC*, p. 115.

earlier parting poem with Meng Chien, here Meng Chiao holds out hopes for unity, for resolution of the separation and internal contradictions, and then takes the hopes away. First we read "one mind," a unity, but this is followed by a separation, "two puffs of cloud." Then we see the hope of physical unity as the two boats come together on the river, but this hope passes quickly as the boats move apart once again. In the final couplet Meng Chiao makes a last attempt to restore unity by calling to his uncle. Since the great distance between them was implied in the "thousand miles of wind," we guess that the uncle could not hear, but characteristically Meng Chiao ends on a note of uncertainty and doubt—"Did you hear it calling to you?"

None of these poems go beyond the High T'ang style, but within the traditional forms intense emotions and conflicts are driving the poetry in new directions. Just as he feared in the last two poems of this chapter, Ch'ang-an did not bring Meng Chiao success and happiness; it did, however, bring him into contact with Han Yü, Li Kuan, and a new, exciting intellectual world.

3

Han Yü's Early Life and Poetry

Han Yü was born in 768 at Ho-yang in the province of Honan, the youngest son of Han Chung-ch'ing, a county magistrate (*ling*). Members of his family were minor or intermediate officials, lacking the powerful connections necessary to gain important posts in the central government. When his father died in 770, Han Yü was cared for by his brother, Han Hui, and his sister-in-law, née Cheng. Han Hui achieved a minor reputation as one of the "Four Kuei," a group of young Confucian scholars concerned with the political and economic revitalization of the empire, still shaken by the aftermath of the An Lu-shan rebellion (755–62).

Han Hui reached the position of Diarist (*ch'i-chü-she-jen*, sixth grade, third class), probably through his connections with the corrupt minister, Yüan Tsai. When Yüan Tsai fell from power in 777, Han Hui was banished to the post of Prefect of Shao-chou in modern Kwangtung Province. Han Yü accompanied his brother in this southern exile, gaining his first but certainly not his last experience of the shame and hardships of banishment to the South.

In 781 Han Hui died in Shao-chou, probably a victim of the pestilential climate which northern Chinese held in justifiable horror. The young Han Yü accompanied his brother's body north again to Ho-yang for burial, but soon found that conditions there were as dangerous as in the South. In 780 Te-tsung had taken the throne with the clear intention of restoring to the central government the power and prestige it had lost to the provincial governors. The result was a rebellion which very nearly brought the dynasty down, culminating in the flight of Te-tsung from the capital in 783. During this time Han Yü took refuge with his sister-in-law south of the Yangtze River.

After conditions stabilized and the immediate threat to the throne had been removed, Han Yü did what all educated young men who hoped to enter the government did: he went to the capital to take the civil service examination. There he fell under the influence of Liang Su and Tu-ku Chi, leading Confucian intellectuals of the day. When we call someone like Liang Su a Confucian, it does not mean that he was in any way opposed to Buddhism or Taoism—Liang, in fact, dabbled in both. Rather we mean that, just as High T'ang poets affirmed fu-ku principles without rejecting other kinds of poetry, a man like Liang Su could be an upright Confucian and a Buddhist at the same time. Whether it was the influence of his brother or the influence of men such as Liang Su and Tu-ku Chi we cannot tell, but it is evident from his earliest writings that Han Yü's orientation was Confucian; what is unusual is that from this earliest time his principles are *exclusively* Confucian: "I, Han Yü, wear the dress of a Confucian scholar—I would not dare use any other arts to seek official advancement."[1] This was in 790. What the "other arts" might be is unclear, but the emphasis on exclusiveness and the almost belligerent tone are elements that persist throughout his later prose writing.

In 792 Han Yü passed the *chin-shih* examination, presided over by the famous statesman Lu Chih, with Liang Su as an assistant examiner. Han Yü passed fourteenth in a class of twenty-three, a class which came to be known as the "Tiger and Dragon List." From it came such illustrious Mid-T'ang intellectuals and statesmen as Li Kuan, P'ei Tu, Ou-yang Chan, Wang Ya, and Ts'ui Chün. Meng Chiao was the examination's most eminent failure.

For someone with good connections, the *chin-shih* examination was sufficient to start one on an official career. Han Yü, lacking such connections, decided to take an advanced examination, the *po-hsüeh hung-tz'u*, held by the Civil Office (Li-pu). This he failed three times in succession between 793 and 795. He also wrote three petitions to the Minister recommending himself for a position, but his petitions remained unanswered. By 795, at the age of twenty-seven, Han Yü's future did not look bright.

The earliest of Han Yü's poems that can be dated with any certainty are from 791–92 when he met Li Kuan and Meng Chiao in Ch'ang-an. These poems, products of an energetic but untrained talent, can hardly be said to represent Han Yü's best work, but in

1. *HCLW*, p. 383.

their peculiar awkwardness they indicate the course Han Yü's poetry was to take in later years.

During the first phase of Han Yü's poetic development, ethical and intellectual concerns dominate personalities and events. While in his later poetry an intellectual framework served to make experience meaningful, in the early poems experience is deformed to illustrate ideas. Taking the self-conscious role of Confucian moralist and intellectual, Han Yü sought to create a poetry to fulfill the same didactic impulse which inspired his classical prose. The most common critical cliché about Han Yü's poetry, that he "makes poetry out of prose," is accurate only in this early period, when it seems that Han Yü felt there was no fundamental distinction between prose and poetry except for rhyme and line length.

None of Han Yü's prose writings of the period articulate a poetic reform; in literary theory he certainly accepted the prevalent fu-ku principles of the age. Against the decadent High T'ang style of the Ta-li, the stylistic associations of fu-ku took on new meaning and force. Han Yü's early poetry represents such a radical departure from what had generally been considered "poetic," that there can be little doubt it constituted an attack on poetic decorum. From the poems we shall discuss later in this chapter we can abstract three elements to form the nucleus of a poetics. These are: (1) a rejection of emotional responses in reaction to the sentimentality of Ta-li poetry; (2) an affirmation of the didactic responsibilities of poetry, the most important idea associated with fu-ku poetry; and (3) a stylistic and thematic fascination with bareness and harshness, coupled with a distaste for rich, descriptive language.

As we have seen in some earlier fu-ku poetry, a conscious archaizing of poetic style goes along with the idea of "return to antiquity." Rejection of the smooth, balanced, and subtle style of the High T'ang necessarily accompanied the rejection of the moral unconcern in that poetry. The eremitic escapism which characterized much of the poetry of the last decades of the High T'ang was intolerable. The "moral man" was to live in harsh, impoverished surroundings, neither becoming one of the corrupt rich nor escaping his duty to society by flight into the world of nature. These surroundings were to beget a bare, harsh style. Ethical judgment had to be courageous and absolute; subtlety and indirect allusion were despised. Furthermore, prosaisms in the poetry carried the moral authority of the Confucian classics.

Lyric poetry was rejected in favor of the narrative and didactic modes; metaphor and other poetic devices had a secondary role in the poems if they had any role at all. The didactic message was carried in stories, myths, exempla, and other techniques that were associated primarily with prose essays. Han Yü avoided a High T'ang treatment of a theme even when the occasion seemed to call for one.

Although the ethical focus of these poems unites them, the poems themselves are quite diverse. Han Yü's poetry is in an experimental stage; he is trying to invent a new style appropriate for his ethical concerns. As experiments, many of these early poems are total failures, while all show stylistic immaturity. The poetry of these early years constitutes an embryonic poetic reform. In the following poems we shall see a conscious attempt to actualize fu-ku principles, not using the late Han and Wei style of earlier fu-ku poetry, but *creating* a new style for them. These poems possess the same belligerent affirmation of principles we found in other fu-ku writing, but unlike earlier poets Han Yü allows himself no alternatives—he never falls back into a more aesthetically pleasing style. Furthermore, unlike Yüan Chieh who slipped back into the High T'ang style as he grew older, Han Yü developed a new kind of poetry out of this early reform poetry. The difference between the early poetry and Han Yü's later poetry is subtle: in the aggressive assertiveness of his pose of Confucian rectitude, we see the reformer, the man trying to fit poetry to principles; later his poetry develops to suit his personal needs, and the fu-ku principles become excuses for originality.

The following poem, perhaps Han Yü's earliest, was written in 791–92 when he met the prose stylist Li Kuan in the capital.

THE FAR NORTH: A POEM TO LI KUAN

There were vagabond wings in the far north,
There were sunken scales in the Southern Sea.[2]
Stream and plain stretched vast dividing them,

2. *Chuang-tzu*, I: "In the Northern Seas there is a fish called the K'un which is countless thousands of miles long. It changes into a bird called the P'eng which is also countless thousands of miles long. When it stirs and flies, its wings are as clouds stretching over both horizons. If it wants to move in the ocean, it goes off to the Southern Sea."

Neither had a way to know the other, his voice or form.
Then in wind and cloud they met one morning,   5
Transformed, became one body.
Who could object that their ways were far?
Heart's harmony came swift as the spirit.
I am now twenty-five years old,
Seeking friends, ignorant of such as you.   10
Sadly I sang in the market of the capital,
Then I became close to you.
If their aspirations rush in the same direction,
Could even sage and fool fail to be friends?
Now our friendship is as metal and stone—   15
A thousand ages without thinning or darkening.[3]
Nor do we have that babyish attitude
Which, broken-hearted, grieves over poverty.[4]

The allegorical fable was a staple of Chinese essay-writing and is found in Chinese poetry only occasionally. Although later in his work this device will develop into mythopoeia, in this poem the use is relatively simple. Han Yü tells a little story about the "original" fusion of the K'un and the P'eng, Chuang-tzu's dual-natured leviathan, as a metaphor for his meeting with Li Kuan. To alert the reader that he is elaborating the story rather than simply alluding to it, Han Yü purposefully reverses the locations, placing the P'eng in the North and K'un in the South. The original purpose of the fable by Chuang-tzu, to emphasize limitless immensity, is retained as a metaphor for the two men's talents.

The style of this piece is consciously that of the poetry of the late Han and Wei, the basis of the High T'ang "old style," *ku-feng*: it is rugged in texture and "manly," *hsiung,* in contrast to the delicate, lyrical style of Southern Dynasties poetry, felt to be effeminate. The style is verbal, particles abound, and allusions are made to the classics and philosophers rather than to other poetry.

Despite certain devices which show Han Yü was trying to imitate the late Han and Wei style, the resulting poem is much further from its model than Ch'en Tzu-ang's or Li Po's fu-ku poetry. The use of

3. *Analects*, XVII, 7: "Is it not Strong which can be ground and thins not; is it not Pure White which can be dyed and darkens not?"
4. *HCLS*, p. 4.

fable in such poetry is uncommon, and it is never created ad hoc as here. Furthermore, late Han and Wei poetry is rarely as intellectual and abstract as the above poem; for example, there are lines such as:

Seeking friends, ignorant of such as you.

or:

If their aspirations rush in the same direction,
Could even sage and fool fail to be friends?

Han and Wei poetry, like most of the poetry that followed it, was openly emotional; in contrast, here every emotion is treated in moral or intellectual terms. Because of their talents they are *suited* for friendship; their meeting involves knowledge and judgment: Han Yü was "ignorant" (*mei*, an intellectual term, meaning literally "to be in the dark about") of "such as you" (*ch'i-jen*, implying certain moral qualities, "what kind of person"). Friendships are not founded on emotion, but have intellectual and political motivation—their (political) aspirations are the same. In a similar vein, the last couplet is an explicit rejection of emotion in favor of resolute endurance of hardship.

The diction of this poem is unusually bare of ornament. There is not one purely descriptive adjective in the entire poem, nor are there many concrete nouns to be described. Han Yü has gone out of his way to replace concise poetic constructions with longer prose ones. The trend over the course of six centuries toward the creation of a dense, ambiguous poetic diction has met its first setback. The aim is a special archaic tone rather than the symmetrical and tight structure of High T'ang poetry. It is this very looseness of diction and rambling structure which, along with the ethical focus, immediately sets Mid-T'ang poetry off from the preceding and following period styles.

In the following poem by Meng Chiao, written before he took the civil service examination in 792, there is a focus on ethical concerns similar to Han Yü's, but in the treatment of the theme there are important differences between the two poets.

ANCIENT ATTITUDE: TO LIANG SU

A twisted tree hates its shadow in the sun,

As a slanderer fears the wise man's brilliant perception.
Things are self-evident before such shining candles,
And will allow no disparagement by the evil and corrupt.
Without a hundred smeltings in the fire,
How could one tell the essence of the heart's speck of gold?
Gold, lead, are verified in the same forge,
Wishing to separate essence and dross.[5]

Here we can see tendencies of Meng Chiao's earlier poetry growing more extreme: the world is dichotomized into good and evil, the valuable and the worthless, while judgment between the two is the most important activity. As in earlier fu-ku poetry, the metaphors are direct and obvious, here suited to the "self-evident" nature of such judgments. The pose of ethical rectitude is reinforced by the title, "Ancient Attitude," implying that it was thus that the ancient sages viewed the world.

Meng Chiao's stylistic control is evident in the last couplet. Asyndeton, the most common way of joining two nouns in Chinese poetry, is used in line seven, but in this case it is used to emphasize that the "gold [and] lead" are together in the forge. When they are separated into "essence and dross," a connective "and," *yü*, is used to emphasize the division.

Comparing this poem to the preceding one by Han Yü, we find a similarity in the rugged diction, the moral imagery, and the disdain of ornament. However, Meng Chiao's poem is more tightly constructed; it has only one message and repeats it with power and precision. Han Yü's poem is looser: it makes a metaphor, develops it, and comments on it. The devices of Meng Chiao's poem, the parallel construction of metaphors and the asyndeton, serve structural purposes. Han Yü, on the other hand, seeks a special archaic tone rather than symmetrical tightness of structure.

One reason for these differences is that Meng Chiao matured in the more tightly knit style of the High T'ang. The beginnings of Han Yü's poetry were more independent, more characteristically Mid-T'ang. Meng Chiao also came to use this loose diction, but he never escaped entirely from the elliptical density and antithetical symmetry of the preceding period.

The following poem by Han Yü is also from the early 790s.

5. *MTYSC*, p. 107.

Those Who Make Friends in Ch'ang-an: A Poem to Meng Chiao

Of those who make friends in Ch'ang-an,
Whether rich or poor, each has his followers.
When friends or relatives visit one another,
Each also has something by which to please the other:
In the humble house there is literature and history, 5
In the noble mansion there is music of fife and pipes.
How then can we tell the grand from the distressed?
Rather I would distinguish sage and fool.[6]

This is the first of a number of experiments by which Han Yü hoped to develop a style appropriate to didactic poetry. The prosaisms of this poem are even more salient than those of "The Far North." The nominal phrase of the first line and the subordinate clause of the third line both require enjambement in each of the first two couplets. Syntactically required enjambement is comparatively uncommon in Chinese poetry, and when it is found, it is usually in the last couplet.[7] The fourth line is decidedly antipoetic, and in the entire poem only the third couplet is faintly recognizable as poetic diction.

The consciously unpoetic style of this poem diverges sharply from the poetic tradition. It is associated with the moral man, the "sage" of the last line who lives in a "humble house" with his books. The blunt ugliness of the style is meant to match the sage's harsh surroundings, but from both the plain truth is supposed to emerge. The enemy are the rich, the "fools" who live in the "noble mansions," to whom belongs the delicate, effete style of courtly poetry. Although no poetic reform has been articulated, the style of this poem is a slap in the face of what was conventionally considered to be "good taste" in the poetry of the early 790s.

In addition to the unpoetic style, the poem cleverly manipulates the reader in a game of wit through which Han seeks to trap him into accepting his values. To bring this out, let us paraphrase the argument of the poem: "Each has something to please a visitor: the poor man his books, the rich man his music. Since everyone is pleased, how

---

6. *HCLS*, p. 5.

7. An exception occurs in *yüeh-fu*, real or imitation folk poetry, written in irregular lines that use many prose forms.

can we distinguish the happy-successful from the sad-unsuccessful? This is a distinction we *cannot* make, but we *can* make a distinction between the wise man who loves learning and the fool who loves only music and sensual pleasure." This is craftily done: Han Yü's satirical malice is reserved for the last line, and the satire is never made explicit. Han has used his rhetorical talents to build a logical trap. Beginning innocently with the joys of life in Ch'ang-an, Han Yü creates a positive situation in which everyone is happy. The reader accepts such positive statements because they offend no one—everyone is satisfied with his station. Having lured the reader into accepting his premises in one set of criteria, those of happiness, Han then changes the criterion of judgment in the last line, to virtue. The reader finds that he has accepted the premise that the rich care only for sensual pleasure while the poor scholar loves learning, and now under different criteria he finds he must censure the rich. Han skillfully leaves the extrapolation from the new criteria to the reader, simply stating the new criteria themselves in the last line.

Parallel to Han Yü's affirmation of the sage's resolute endurance of hardship is a fascination with antiquity. In a long narrative poem of 792 Han Yü describes his friend Meng Chiao:

Master Meng is a scholar from the rivers and seas,
An ancient appearance, also a heart of antiquity.
He has read the books of the ancients,
That one might say in him antiquity is like the present. . . . [8]

The magic word "ancient," *ku*, means nothing definite here: it is an imaginary world in which Han Yü's ethical, stylistic, and political ideals are realized. Although we must keep in mind that Han Yü's conception of "antiquity" is fundamentally not historical, it is equally true that he sincerely took it to be real and fervently believed in the values it embodied.

The above lines are from "A Poem for Master Meng Chiao," Han Yü's first experiment in narrative verse, a form in which he was later to excel. In this first attempt, however, the idiosyncratic grammar, the prosaisms, the verbal lines, and the rambling structure conspired against him. Searching for originality, Han Yü found only awkwardness: for example, instead of saying, "He came to see me occasionally," Han Yü says, "From time to time my humble eaves were ap-

8. *HCLS*, p. 6.

proached." Perhaps aware of how grotesque this poem had turned out, in his next narrative poem Han Yü depended on an honest simplicity of statement to create a moral, "ancient-styled" poetry.

POEM OF HSIEH TZU-JAN

In Kuo-chou, in the county of Nan-ch'ung,
Was a poor girl named Hsieh Tzu-jan.
Young and foolish, ignorant of everything,
All she had heard was the existence of the gods.
With no care for her life she studied their lore,   5
It was on Goldspring Mountain.
From worldly splendor and her budding desires cut off,
The love and concern of mother and father renounced.
Concentrating her heart she stirred demons and spirits,
The blur of a trance is hard to tell completely.   10
One morning she sat in her empty house,
Clouds and fog rose therein.
It was as though you could hear the music of ocarinas
Coming from the dark, dark sky.
Bright sunlight changed to gloomy darkness,   15
The scene was cold and desolate.
Lights flickered around beams and eaves,
Multicolored rays clung to them.
Onlookers were startled, but in vain,
Mulling about, how could they dare come forward?   20
Suddenly she rose into the air,
Wafting upward like smoke in the wind.
Immense is the vastness of the universe,
Nothing more of her was seen or heard.
The village elders made a report of the matter,   25
To the prefect, who was astonished and sighed.
Speeding his carriage he led his subordinates there,
And peasants vied to be the first to arrive.
Entering the gate there was nothing to be seen,
But her cap and slippers like shed locust shells.   30
All said this was a matter of gods and immortals,
So clear that it can be told and handed down with certainty.
I have heard that under the rule of the Hsia Dynasty
One knew which were holy creatures and which evil demons.

People could enter the forests and mountains   35
And never meet an ogre.
Times twisted, it will never happen again,
Deception and fraud are rampant in later ages.
The worlds of darkness and light got scrambled together,
Men and demons did even more harm to one another.   40
Though the Ch'in emperor doted on them,
It was the emperor Wu of Han who enlarged their source.[9]
Ever since those two rulers
This kind of calamity has been continuous.
Trees and stones undergo miraculous transformations,   45
Foxes bewitch and bring disaster as they please.
No one can finish even his natural span,
Much less get to prolong his life.
Human life is set amid thousands of different kinds,
It is knowledge most of all that is virtuous.   50
How can they not trust in themselves
But instead wish to stray seeking strange beings?
She who is gone cannot repent,
Her lonely soul harbors a deep wrong.
Coming generations can still take warning,   55
How could what I say be vapid, elegant verse?
There are constant principles in human life,
For male and female there are fixed relations.
Clothes for the cold, food for hunger
Are to be found in weaving and tilling.   60
Downwards such principles preserve children and grandchildren,
Upwards they are to preserve parents and ruler.
If one deviates from this Way,
It will always result in the loss of the body.
Alas—that poor girl   65
If forever given up to the hordes of weird beings.
Feeling the sorrow of this I compose a poem—
The ignorant should write it on their sashes.[10]

9. I.e. Emperor Wu, by his delvings into the occult, opened up the way for demons to get into the human world.

10. *HCLS*, p. 14. *Analects*, X, 15. After Confucius explained to his disciple Tzu-chang the proper modes of behavior, Tzu-chang wrote the master's words on his sash.

In his *Discussion of the Heart of Han's Poetry*, the critic Ch'eng Hsüeh-hsün says of this poem: "It's nothing but rhymed prose—you can put it aside and not bother to read it."[11] Disregarding the evaluation, there is some truth in Ch'eng's comment. The poem is like a T'ang tale, *ch'uan-ch'i*, with a didactic essay appended to it. Caesura violations (e.g. l. 60) and prose constructions (e.g. l. 63) add to the prose flavor. However, in this poem for the first time we are given a hint of the purposes of such a style:

> How could what I say be vapid, elegant verse?

Wen, which I have freely translated as "elegant verse," means both literature and pattern, the manner of a piece in contrast to its substance, its *chih*. *Wen* and *chih*, manner and substance, formed a traditional dichotomy in literary theory. Ideally *wen* and *chih* should be balanced, but it is clear that here Han Yü is consciously emphasizing the "substantial," cognitive aspect of literature. Han is reacting, perhaps too extremely, against "vapidity," *k'ung*, and overemphasis on the artistic aspect of literature in the preceding age. The result is straightforward didacticism. We are given a "true story" from which a moral lesson is to be drawn.

The almost Augustan humanism of the homily has its own beauty; behind the style and message of:

> How can they not trust in themselves,
> But instead wish to stray seeking strange beings?

we can hear:

> Know then thyself, presume not God to scan,
> The proper study of mankind is man.

In trying to create his own kind of didactic poetry, Han Yü strips away "decoration," poetic devices that are superfluous to the story and moral. We may presume that Han feels such devices have been devalued by their use in "vapid, elegant verse." Simile is used rather than metaphor, and that only twice. Simile is more appropriate to didactic poetry than metaphor because, by maintaining a barrier between tenor and vehicle, it allows nothing to stand for anything else—the simple truth must always be stated.

11. Quoted in *HCLS*, p. 17.

Among these early poems no two pieces are alike. In the following poem we find still another experiment in integrating Han's lively intellect with poetry. The actual situation here is uncertain, but it is clear that the coincidence of Li Kuan's sickness and the natural phenomenon of thick clouds blotting out the sun has been interpreted by Han Yü to be Li Kuan's grief to the point of sickness at cosmic disorder.

THICK CLOUDS: A POEM TO LI KUAN WHO IS SICK

Heaven's motions have lost their measure,
The Yin Spirit comes to oppose the Yang.
Thick clouds block off the bright sun,
Blazing heat becomes chill and cold.
The lesser man just sighs in resentment,   5
But the good man can only be stricken by sorrow.
You have been cutting down on food and drink,
So how can your body keep calm and well?
Your intention to do so is quite honorable,
But I fear you're not fulfilling an obligation.   10
When vegetable soup still must be eaten,
How can others taste meat dishes?
At the end of winter when all plants are dead,
The hidden cassia is then most fragrant.
But above all between Heaven and Earth   15
The Great Cycle has its own constants.
I urge you to look favorably on food and drink,
For phoenixes by nature fly high.[12]

Since the complex reasoning of this poem will not be immediately apparent to the Western reader, let us here outline the argument:

1. Lines 1–4: We can see that the natural order is out of balance because clouds have caused darkness and chill in a season of light and warmth. (This may be either a passing phenomenon of the weather or a real and serious cold spell which damages crops, cf. ll. 11–12.)

2. Lines 5–10: You, a "good man," *chün-tzu*, are moved in sympathetic resonance with natural disorder, and are consequently eating less. Since this is bad for your health, your intentions, though good, are misdirected.

12. *HCLS*, p. 13.

3. Lines 11–14: Although, on the one hand, it is improper to over-indulge in the presence of need and hunger (ll. 13–14), it is equally in the nature of a "good man," whose purity is symbolized by the cassia, to flourish under the worst conditions. (This line of reasoning is more comprehensible if we assume that there is a real famine; how-ever, we need not so assume, because it is possible Han is caught up in his own fiction.)

4. Lines 15–16: Nature has a fixed pattern, so we can be certain that order will be restored.

5. Therefore, you must strive to maintain your health, because a "good man" must stay healthy (ll. 13–14, 18) and because the natural order will be restored of itself without your intervention (ll. 15–16).

It is important to remember that underneath the complicated "logic" of the argument, this is simply a poem encouraging a sick friend to take care of himself. This is a common theme in occasional poetry, but Han sees fit to give it deep moral and cosmic significance and rejects the ample store of conventions associated with the theme. "Looking favorably on food and drink" is a variation on the conven-tion "eat more," meaning "take care of yourself"; however, the train of thought that brings him to say this is anything but expected or conventional, as we can see in the conclusion (sec. 5) of the argument above.

This is an early example of an important thematic mode in Han Yü's poetry, the imposition of cosmic and moral meaning on natural phenomena and the human condition. Everything is interpreted in terms of a holistic, organic cosmic order, a world divided into ma-crocosms and microcosms dominated by a constant pattern, a fixed order of relationships and changes. Han Yü views phenomena as manifestations of this higher pattern and order which simultaneously informs everything.

Complementing the logical play and cosmic mode of the poem, Han Yü's language is intellectual and abstract. The terminology of Chinese cosmology is present in abundance: "Heaven's motions," the Yin and Yang, the "Great Cycle," "constants." There are em-blematic images such as "thick clouds," "sun," "cassia," and "phoenix," all of which have a fixed, traditional set of meanings and associations. Although Han does use "vegetable soup" and "meat dishes" (even they have ethical implications in this context), he prefers generic nouns such as "all plants," *pai-ts'ao,* and "the body," *shen-t'i,* to specific ones. It is an expected part of Han Yü's world of order that the language of order, abstractions, and generalizations, be used. The pseudological argument of the poem, the attempt to give the occasion universal meaning, and the abstractions, all run counter to the mainstream of the Chinese poetic tradition in general and to High T'ang poetry in particular, in which there are tendencies toward juxtaposition rather than logical argument, toward the occasional, and toward the specific.

At this stage of his life, however, Han Yü had little energy to devote to the composition of poetry. In 796, after fruitless years of office-seeking, Han Yü finally got a position on the staff of General Tung Chin, a former chief minister. He was the general's aide (*kuan-ch'a t'ui-kuan*), an office barely within the official hierarchy. To Tung Chin had been entrusted the troublesome Hsüan-wu satrapy in present-day eastern Honan and northwestern Anhui provinces. This was hardly a desirable post, but it was still better than staying in the capital, begging fruitlessly.

With Tung Chin in the strategic city of Pien-chou, Han Yü was given charge of the local qualifying examinations to choose candidates to take the *chin-shih* examination in Ch'ang-an. One of his discoveries was Chang Chi, who was to become one of his lifelong friends and turned out to be an important poet in his own right. Another discovery was a young philosopher, Li Ao, who was to become the most important Confucian theorist of the T'ang and a forerunner of Sung neo-Confucianism. In 797 Meng Chiao, who had finally passed the chin-shih examination in 796 and had not gotten a post either, followed Han Yü to Pien-chou, where he was a guest of Lu Ch'ang-yüan, Tung Chin's subordinate. These four men, Han Yü, Meng Chiao, Chang Chi, and Li Ao, formed the nucleus of a group of scholars and poets who dominated the intellectual literary world for the next three decades.

In 799 Meng Chiao, unhappy with political conditions in Pien-chou, left in a huff for the South, followed by Li Ao. In the same year Tung Chin died and as Han Yü was following the funeral cortège to the capital, the Pien-chou army revolted against the overzealous Lu Ch'ang-yüan, killing and eating him.

The poetry written by Han Yü during his stay in Pien-chou shows a growing mastery of style. He is still experimenting, but there is none of the awkwardness which characterizes much of his poetry of the early 790s. In Han's narrative technique are a new conciseness and dramatization, indicating a growth of his artistic self-consciousness and control. Most important, the belligerent assertiveness of his reform style disappears, without a return to the gentle High T'ang manner. There is a shift also from didacticism to persuasive rhetoric: as a didactic poet Han Yü was primarily concerned with the affirmation of principles, but as a rhetorician he was more concerned with results. Thus the blunt forthrightness of a piece such as "Poem of Hsieh Tzu-jan" changes into a conscious effort to persuade without giving offense. The brash young man never disappeared entirely from Han Yü's poetry, but he learned to temper his brashness.

The growth of Han Yü's stylistic control is evident in the following parting poem. The formal dignity with which Han seeks to infuse it is, perhaps, to counteract the banality of the compliment Han is paying Yang Ning. Poetry occupied an important position in T'ang official society: meetings, partings, invitations, thanks, congratulations—all demanded a certain kind of poetic response. Believing in the didactic and rhetorical powers of poetry, Han Yü, before the last years of his life, showed a certain embarrassment at the poetic requirements of social intercourse, and sought to give such occasions a broader meaning. Yang Ning has been sent by Tung Chin to convey the customary New Year's greeting to the emperor from a provincial governor, but Han Yü dramatizes the situation far beyond its real significance.

HEAVEN'S STARS: SEEING OFF YANG NING AS HE TAKES NEW
    YEAR'S GREETINGS TO COURT

Heaven's stars grow sparse, the cock crows,
A servant prepares breakfast, carriage smeared with grease.
It's right at the end of winter, the cold not yet gone,
May I ask you, sir, whither you go—
"Meeting at court on New Year's, all must come.   5
I've orders from the commander, must be there on time."
Among the attendants of the throne, positions are empty.
Now, sir, you leave here, but return—when will that be?[13]

The first line of this poem is a *hsing*, a line of description of nature

13. *HCLS*, p. 34.

at the beginning of a poem whose relation to what follows is enigmatic or indirect. It is also possible to interpret the line allegorically, stars being traditional metaphors for court officials; thus their sparseness would suggest the empty positions mentioned later in the poem. Primarily, however, this *hsing* sets the scene as morning. Han then focuses on the servant preparing breakfast and the carriage made ready, hinting at an early morning trip. The very indirectness the poet uses here to tell us that someone is making an early morning journey is indicative of a change in Han's poetry from blunt statement to suggestion.

The narrative, if one may call it that, is suspensefully dramatized. The hints of a journey and the query of the speaker arouse the reader's curiosity as to what is occurring. As suggested earlier, it makes the situation seem more important and interesting than it actually is. The convention of worry that the one who departs will not return is transformed into a moral compliment: Yang will be detained at court because the court will recognize his value and give him a position.

The style is simple, restrained, and somewhat archaized. Every line but the seventh has a multiple predicate, and topic-comment constructions are favored over more direct syntactic constructions. For example, "whither you go," *hsing an chin*, is literally: "As for [your] going, whither arrives it." "Return—when will that be?" is used rather than the more direct "When will you return?" What I have translated as "you leave here," is likewise inverted in the original to "hence you leave," *tz'u-ch'ü*. These unnecessary topic-comment constructions, along with the multiple, unsubordinated predicates, create heavy caesuras within the line and "slow" the poem down. This likewise lends gravity to the treatment.

The same kind of dramatization can be seen in the following poems, which protest the imperial policy of leniency toward the mutinous army of Pien-chou.

REVOLT AT PIEN-CHOU

I

The city gates at Pien-chou didn't open that morning,
Heaven's Dog Star fell to earth, its voice like thunder.
Soldiers competed in boasting they'd killed the governor,
Linked roofs and joined beams were burned to ashes.

The other princes nearby couldn't save him,   5
So why should this lone scholar lament by himself?

II

Mother following, child running—who are they?—
The lord's wife, the governor's son.
Yesterday she mounted a carriage and he rode a huge horse,
People sitting hurried to stand, riders got down.
The Imperial House is unwilling to use shield and spear,   5
Alas, then, what can be done about mother and child?[14]

Regrettably, Han Yü soon abandoned this concise dramatic technique for more discursive narratives, but the lessons he learned in such poems as these made his later narrative technique much more vivid and energetic. The opening line of the first poem is ominous: one morning, routine is violated and the city gates don't open. The fall of the Dog Star, an omen of rebellion, is a more specific hint that a rebellion is taking place; the sound of thunder is probably the sound of fighting in the city. Next we see the aftermath, burnt houses and soldiers boasting of the murder of Lu Ch'ang-yüan. As in a Greek play, all the violence takes place offstage. Since the other governors couldn't save Lu, Han asks, why should he lament? The second poem explains the reason.

Han Yü answers the question raised in the first poem with another question, to double the reader's curiosity about the pathetic scene. He asks the identity of the mother and child whom he imagines to be fleeing the rebels, then answers, saying they are the wife and son of Lu Ch'ang-yüan. To heighten the pathos of their situation he contrasts their proud state the day before, when everyone rose to their feet in respect while they rode by, to their having to flee on foot on the day of the rebellion. By evoking this scene of Lu's wife and son, Han criticizes the government's policy of not putting the rebellion down by force.

The vitality of this poem derives from the persuasive art of the rhetorician. No longer simply stating principles, Han Yü is seeking to stir the reader's emotions in the service of principles. Just as the omens in the opening poem are to create suspense and stir the reader's curiosity, Han Yü prejudices the reader against the rebels by saying

14. *HCLS*, p. 35.

that they are "boasting" of Lu's murder. The term Han Yü uses for soldiers means literally "strong lads," *chien-erh*, suggesting the physical strength that was repugnant to the scholar class. The obviously pathetic scene of the mother and child in flight is used to condemn both the rebels and the government's lenient policy toward them.

Also from Han Yü's stay in Pien-chou we have the following poem, in which the humanism and sense of humor that are to characterize his subsequent poetry first appear.

WHILE SICK: TO CHANG CHI

My innards were emptied, I suffered a serious decline,
To avoid the cold I lay by the north window.
I didn't pace with the morning drums to audience,
But slept peacefully, listening to their banging.
As for Chang Chi—he then lived in a village,   5
Full of capability not yet bestowed on the state.
He amuses himself with essays and poems,
Which always ring solidly as of metal and stone.
His brush so strong it can tote by itself
A hundred gallon caldron, patterned with dragons.[15]   10
My chattering tongue hadn't wagged a long time,
Who else but you could be my match?
Leaning on the table, I led you to speak,
And at first the melody was strong and sonorous.
Halfway through, you cheerfully bored open a channel,   15
Then splitting into tributaries you lost the great river.[16]
Hoping to bring your spirit to the fullest,
I didn't let you see my battle-flags.
Since only sheep and cattle filled field and plain,
You took down your standards and bundled the bare poles.[17]   20

15. This metaphor compliments both the power and antiquity of Chang Chi's style. Han is playing on the term *pi-li*, "force of brush," which usually refers to the vigor of style. Here the "force of brush" becomes the physical strength of the writing brush which, placed over Chang's shoulder like a carrying pole, supports a heavy caldron. Figuratively, carrying the caldron means that Chang's style is powerful enough to handle "weighty," ancient themes.

16. This means that Chang got off the track of his discourse.

17. Han Yü is comparing his dialogue with Chang Chi to a battle. In this couplet he is referring to a stratagem mentioned in the "Essay on the Hsiung-nu" in the *Han History*: the Chinese told the Khan that they were giving him one of the border cities, and when the Khan approached the place with his warriors he saw only livestock grazing unat-

When you downed a cup, I poured you more,
Until jugs and winepots were heaped all around the room.
Coal-black curtains kept us from wind and snow,
And shining on the stove was spiked a bright lantern.
At night's end you went wild with exordia and epilogues,   25
You opened your mouth wide, knit your white-flecked brows.
While I looked just like the old man of Kao-yang
Right when he was plotting T'ien Heng's downfall,[18]
For a few days he can cherish what he has,
His body suddenly swelling tumorous with pride.   30
As you were ready to go I addressed you slowly:
"Isn't there a bit of gibberish in what you've been saying?"
I brought back my army, locked horns, pursued you,
Cutting down a tree I got my poor P'ang.[19]
With a soft voice I spat forth the essentials,   35
A wine jug followed by a sheep's breast.[20]
"You," he said, "are a water course from off Mount K'un-lun,
I'm just a brooklet from the Ling Range.
I'm comparable to a tiny anthill—
How could I rise above a towering peak?"   40
Now at last I send you this with my good wishes,
I've cut out the stumps and pulled up the stakes.[21]
From now on you'll know the direction to go,
Like the roaring rush of eastward flowing waters.[22]

---

tended in the fields. The Chinese army in the meantime was waiting in ambush at the city. Fortunately for the Khan, he captured a Chinese official who told him of the plan, so he took his troops back. Han Yü is suggesting that, in his discourse, Chang Chi is walking into just such a trap.

18. In the struggle for power after the fall of the Ch'in Dynasty, T'ien Heng had made himself minister of the state of Ch'i and his brother, the king. The founder of the Han Dynasty sent Li Yi-chi of Kao-yang to bring about his downfall. Li got T'ien Heng to disband one of his armies while a Han army was attacking Ch'i. Han Yü is comparing his own stratagems with Chang Chi to the plan of Li Yi-chi.

19. Sun Pin set a trap to kill P'ang Chüan by felling a tree across the road and leaving a letter that said, "P'ang Chüan will die by this tree." Then Sun hid his archers all around the place. When P'ang came riding past, he read the letter and dismounted to burn it, at which point he was killed by the archers.

20. This image seems to mean that Chang Chi's drunken rhetoric of the "wine pot," hard on the outside but hollow within, is followed by Han Yü's soft but firm rebuttal, like a "sheep's breast."

21. Han Yü has cleared out all the obstacles to Chang's intellectual progress as one clears a field for plowing.

22. *HCLS*, p. 31.

The tone of the narrative in this poem shows significant change from that of "Poem of Hsieh Tzu-jan." This is not simply a narrative experiment but represents a fundamental change of attitude. The focus is on the two men as individuals rather than as moral types: the foibles as well as the virtues of Han Yü and Chang Chi clearly emerge. The ethical problem is subordinated to the intellectual encounter between two men. From this point on in Han Yü's poetry morality is involved in true human experience, and if there is an ethical lesson, it is learned from experience. Although there are exceptions, it is generally true that Han Yü no longer deforms experience to illustrate an ethical idea, as he did in his early poetry. Even in "Revolt at Pien-chou" a strong sense of humanism is present, although in that case it is subordinated to the ethical judgment demanded by the persuasive structure of the poems.

There are still a number of archaic and prosaic elements present in the style of this poem, but in comparison with Han's early poetry they are unobtrusive. The style is neither as limpid as that of "Poem of Hsieh Tzu-jan" nor as self-consciously awkward as that of "Poem for Master Meng Chiao." Furthermore, we find in this poem for the first time phrases and images used for their shock value; for example, there is Chang Chi toting the ceremonial cauldron over his shoulder with a writing brush, his body swelling with pride like a tumor, his speech "gibberish," and the images of the wine jug and sheep's breast.

The humor of the poem is another new feature in Han's poetry, here serving as a necessary counterbalance to the seriousness of the encounter. Chang Chi is evidently very anxious to impress Han Yü, and his efforts are met with a devastating rebuke. The gentle humor of the poem, in which Han laughs at himself and at Chang, defuses the potential bad blood that could have arisen between them. It is true that there is a great deal of vanity on Han Yü's part about the way in which he tripped Chang Chi up, but he does not treat the episode in piously didactic terms. He freely admits the stratagems of the interpersonal relation and the gamelike nature of his behavior. In this sense, the poem is no less suasive than "Revolt at Pien-chou." Han excuses his own bad behavior by laughing at it (though not without pride in it also), praises Chang Chi, and thereby tacitly begs Chang's forgiveness by asking him to treat the episode as lightly as he does.

4

Meng Chiao's Poetry on His Failure and After

Meng Chiao's poetry of 792 and 793 is dominated by one theme, his failure to pass the *chin-shih* examination, the gateway to an official career. Out of this failure emerge Meng Chiao's first great poems. The confident morality of "Ancient Attitude" (p. 39) caught the poet in a destructive contradiction: the examiner Liang Su and his colleagues applied the discriminating judgment called for in the earlier poem; however, although the examiners accepted Han Yü and Li Kuan, Meng Chiao was rejected.

Even though he felt the fu-ku sentiment as strongly as did Han Yü, it is in his intensely personal poetry that Meng Chiao finds his true voice. In his poetry inner experience dominates and shapes the phenomenal world, in contrast to the intellectually structured world of Han Yü's poetry. While Han imposes cosmic order on emotions, Meng Chiao's emotions define both the cosmic order and the world.

In didactic pieces such as "Ancient Attitude" we can clearly see the ethical focus fundamental to fu-ku. However, Meng Chiao is quick to transfer the harshness and bluntness of didactic poetry to lyric poetry. His failure in the examination is treated in ethical terms—as the failure of the examiners in rejecting his virtue, as aspersions on the quality of those accepted, and as a moral failure within himself. The stylistic directions and intellectual basis of fu-ku combine with Meng's own lyric talents to broaden fu-ku into a new kind of lyric poetry. The emotional intensity of these poems is no less a reaction against the Ta-li style than are Han Yü's didactic and intellectual poems. Indeed, the harshness is often self-conscious ugliness, carrying the Confucian principle of uncompromising bluntness to an extreme. Such poems are intense, straightforward outbursts of the poet's indignation and bitterness.

Sharp dichotomies dominate Meng Chiao's poetry. The world of the capital is set against the eremite landscape, the poet's heart against his body, his will against his actions. In "To Li Kuan" (p. 60) his own failure is contrasted with his friend's success; in "Expressing My Feelings" (p. 59) Meng's alienation and emotional solitude is set against the unity of his friends and that of all men under nature. The vigor of Meng Chiao's early poetry usually lies in the violent conflict between the two halves of the dichotomized world, nor is there ever any resolution to that conflict.

The first two couplets of the following poem are among the most quoted portions of Meng Chiao's works. The pompous moralizing, technical brilliance, and firm control of "Ancient Attitude" is here transformed into something entirely different by the force of Meng Chiao's bitterness.

DRIVING OUT MY FEELINGS ONE NIGHT

Studying one night, by dawn haven't stopped,
Reading bitter poems aloud, gods and demons grieve.
How come I'm not at peace with myself?—
Heart and body are enemies!
The shame of death is an instant's pain,   5
The shame of living is long years of humiliation.
On the pure cassia, no straight branches,[1]
So I long for my former travels over emerald rivers.[2]

The structure of this poem is what we shall call a "release structure": the poem gradually builds in intensity until the last line gives some form of release, here the "former travels over emerald rivers." The poet studies through the night, into the morning with no end in sight, while the grief in his poetry grows so intense that it crosses over into the spirit world. The mention of "demon," *kuei*, a melancholy and dangerous ghost, hints at the relation between such intense grief and death. The cause of this grief is the dichotomized self, in which the "heart and body are enemies." We saw this same division of self in "Describing my Feelings on Being Chosen in Hu-chou to

1. "Plucking the cassia" is a literary cliché for passing the examination. Cassia itself is also a symbol of the pure, honest man. Here we can interpret it in one of two ways: the cassia (places of success in the examination) had no straight (morally upright, suited to his nature) branches to pluck; or the poet is as pure as a cassia, but withered by defeat in the examination.

2. *MTYSC*, p. 51.

Take the Examination"; however, the violence of opposition in the failure poem goes far beyond a melancholy division of self such as we find in the earlier example. The violation of the regular caesura in the fourth line heightens the shock value of the line, and the connective *yü*, "and," is again used to indicate separation.

In this context, the "shame of death" implies suicide, a major sin against filial piety. The "shame of death," an "instant's pain," relates to the body; "long years of humiliation" relates to the heart, which will suffer as long as the poet remains alive. On the surface it appears that these two alternatives are at war; however, the juxtaposition of an "instant" with "long years" clearly suggests that death is the preferable alternative. Thus Meng Chiao retains the *illusion* of conflict, while implying that his sorrow is so great he wishes to die. The ambiguity of the cassia metaphor sums up both the cause and the effect of his grief. Finally Meng obtains release from his intense misery by longing for the happy past, "travels over emerald rivers." This release structure is important in Meng Chiao's poetry, both as an artistic device and as an emotional device to counterbalance the intensity that often builds up in his poems.

The following poem balances the world of ambition and failure against a pastoral landscape to which the poet longs to return. Remembering how these two worlds were juxtaposed in Meng's earlier poems, the ugliness and bitterness in this poem makes us feel something akin to a lost innocence in the poet. Unlike his earlier poems and very much unlike the poetry of T'ao Ch'ien (365–427), who is the poet of the pastoral world Meng Chiao invokes, here the ugly world of his failure and rancor dominates the pastoral elements. The pastoral scene is stiff, emblematic, and conventional; the ugly world of Ch'ang-an is personal and original.

BALLAD OF A WANDERER IN CH'ANG-AN

Ten days—fixed my hair just once,
Each time I combed it, dust of travel flew.
Three weeks—nine times drank too much,
Each time I eat, it's only the usual poor fare.
For all things the time has come,   5
I alone am unaware of spring.
Who will visit me now that my good name's lost?
Successful, they're busy making friends with each other.

> In straight trees are found contented wings,
> By tranquil streams are no bothersome scales.   10
> Now I know that this land of raucous contention
> Is no place for a good man's body.
> For a staff on the plains, bamboo and rattan are light,
> For mountain vegetables, fern and bracken are fresh.
> T'ao Ch'ien sang "Let's go home,"   15
> Beyond the world's troubles, the landscape is pure.[3]

The first two couplets, deceptively simple, show Meng Chiao in full control of his style even at his most impassioned, bitter moments. In what he *should* do—comb his hair—he does too little: one in ten; in what he *should not* do—drink—he does too much: nine in three. What I have translated as "three weeks" is really "three decades," thirty days. Even though he has drunk too much only nine times in thirty days, the juxtaposition of three and nine gives the illusion of "exceeding," *kuo* (rendered in the translation as "too much"). More important, the play on numbers indicates the poet's disequilibrium; he is out of harmony, not "one to one," but "one to ten," or "nine to three." The poet's numbers and real numbers are not in balance. Thus when the "time comes" for everything else, springtime, Meng Chiao alone is not in harmony with the season. Such spiritual isolation is quickly translated into physical isolation: no one will visit him.

In Meng Chiao's poetry the worlds of emotion and imagination merge with the real world. The inner world transforms the external world into a mirror of itself. Spiritual isolation becomes physical isolation; disequilibrium between the numbers of events becomes spiritual uncoordination between the poet and the season. A second kind of transformation also takes place: emotion becomes moral principle. Ironically, Ch'ang-an becomes a "land of raucous contention" where "good man" does not belong. By making this transformation from emotional judgment to ethical judgment, Meng Chiao can reject Ch'ang-an and his failure there in favor of the pastoral landscape, likewise morally judged as "pure."

The hermit's isolation in the landscape is preferable to isolation in the capital, the mountain vegetables are preferable to the "poor fare" he had in Ch'ang-an. The spring that Meng could not feel in Ch'ang-

---

3. *MTYSC*, p. 2.

an is present in the countryside. The objective conditions of life he describes are remarkably the same in both places; however, the values and emotional coloring he projects on them make the two worlds antithetical.

EXPRESSING MY FEELINGS

Pull up the stems, grass doesn't die,[4]
Take out the roots, the willow still flourishes.
Only the man who's a failure
As in a trance walks, strengthless.
Before he was a branch entwined with others,   5
Now is the sound of a breaking lutestring.
As a twined branch—then he was honored,
Now as a broken string he is made light of.
I will go forward in my lonely boat
To the great Gorges where the water isn't smooth,   10
I will ride my carriage and horse
Over the T'ai-hang Mountains where the roads are rocky.
A single spirit lies at the root of all things—
How can they then destroy one another?[5]

In the first two couplets the durability of nature is put into contrast with the fragility of man because of his emotions. Unlike the heart of the poet, the roots and stems of plants can survive being torn up. Again the poet finds himself out of harmony with nature. A further plant image, the "branch entwined with others," shows that earlier Meng had been in a state of harmony. Now that he has fallen out of harmony with nature, the poet resolves to go to the Gorges and the T'ai-hang Mountains, where the violent state of nature mirrors his own heart, which "isn't smooth/peaceful," *pu-p'ing,* like the waters of the Gorges. By such action harmony with nature will be restored. The yearning to restore unity with the natural world is stated abstractly in the last couplet: "A single spirit lies at the root of all things," using the root image of the first couplet, here in a figurative sense.

The image of the lutestring in lines six and eight shows the complexity and associative resonance of Meng Chiao's metaphors. On a visual level, though not explicitly part of the plant imagery, the

---

4. "Stem," *hsin,* also means "heart," as previously noted.   5. *MTTSC,* p. 33.

broken lutestring is a concrete image of separation from the twined branches. A single strand/branch is like a broken string, once supported by unity with others, once playing in harmony, now limp and alone. As the branch depended on the others for support, so the string depended on other strings for music and harmony. But the poem mentions the *sound* of a breaking/broken lutestring; with this in mind, the present participle goes better. The "sound of a breaking lutestring" to represent the poet's disillusionment and grief is an image both appropriate and inexplicable. Thus the image of the lutestring can be understood on both an intellectual and on an immediate, emotional level.

Li Kuan, like Han Yü, was successful in the 792 examination, thus becoming the barely disguised object of Meng Chiao's jealousy.

To Li Kuan

Who says form and shadow are kin?
The lamp goes out, shadow leaves body.
Who says fish and water are lovers?
Water dries up, scales dry and rot.
Before we were wanderers with the same grief—   5
Now you are one who laughs alone.
You cast me behind in a muddy rut,
As your floating steps ascend the ford of clouds.
A fallen tree goes easily to grubs,
A cast-off flower will not turn spring again.   10
How can I say I face a lovely spring scene?—
I gaze in sorrow to the end of this gloomy morning.
Of the buried sword who knows the spirit?
The boxed lute grows daily more dusty.
I wish you would speak to the high wind   15
To question for me the blue, the high skies.[6]

As in most of the poems on his failure, here there is a thematic dichotomy to match the emotional and stylistic extremes: the ruined "me" is set against the successful "you." Han Yü cleverly manipulates his audience; Meng Chiao shouts at it. The rhetorical questions of the first two couplets are bitter and ironic, almost sarcastic. In these couplets the technique employed is that of "In the Mountains

6. *MTYSC*, p. 102.

Seeing Off My Uncle Meng Chien"; the first line of each of these couplets postulates a harmonious unity, while the second line destroys that unity in a particularly cruel way. That a shadow leaves the body when the light goes out is usually no tragedy, but in this case the shadow is the body's "kin," and by its loss a kinship is broken. The accusatory tone is heightened by lines like:

> Now you are one who laughs alone.
> You cast me behind. . . .

Instead of this the poet might have said, "We are now apart," something more neutral to emphasize Meng's sense of spiritual isolation, rather than treating Li Kuan's success like a personal offense.

Comparison between the fifth and seventh couplets, both containing images of the fallen poet, show the change in direction from self-pity to a request for aid. The fallen tree and the cast-off flower emphasize *permanent* ruin; the buried sword and boxed lute describe hidden talents awaiting discovery. The plant imagery of the fifth couplet fits with the familiar theme that the poet is not in harmony with springtime: while other plants are flourishing in the "lovely spring scene," Meng is a fallen tree and a cast-off flower. In the last couplet Meng's request for aid is explicit, the skies being a traditional metaphor for the court.

The accusatory tone, the bitter irony, the morbid ugliness of the imagery, and the violence of emotion all violate T'ang poetic decorum. If the T'ang poet attacks, he almost always does so by indirection, never through the invective we find here. From the ethical bluntness and honesty valued in didactic poetry we have moved to emotional bluntness and honesty; and given the emotion that Meng Chiao felt, the result was a shock to conventional poetry. Breaking down much of the distance between the poet and the reader by direct address and rhetorical questions, Meng simultaneously draws the reader in and attacks him.

The following poem is probably a result of Meng Chiao's second examination failure in 793.

FAILING

> For a dawn moon, hard to hold its light,
> For a sorrowful man, a heart troubled.
> Who says that all things flower in spring?—

Can't they see the frost on the leaves?
An eagle, losing its powers, sick,   5
Wrens that soar on false wings.
Cast off once, cast off again,
My feelings are like a knifeblade's wound.[7]

Once again we find the poet rejecting springtime; he sees only the frost on the leaves, either remaining from winter or, more likely, a vision of future autumns in the poet's mind. The strong emphasis on the cyclical aspects of nature in the Chinese tradition permits the viewer to see any moment in the cycle of the seasons as presaging another. A positive view sees spring in winter; a negative one may see autumn in spring. In "Failing" Meng Chiao sees spring only as a movement toward autumn and death. The magnificent bird image juxtaposes his own innate greatness failing, with lesser talents succeeding, not under their own power but on "false wings." The last couplet is an emotional outburst of the pain he feels at his failure.

In the preceding poems we can see ideas and images beginning to be repeated again and again. If Meng Chiao does not find new directions for his poetry, such straightforward statement of intense emotion will ultimately be a deadend. The following poem points out those new directions.

To Ts'ui Ch'un-liang

Eating greens my belly too is bitter,
Force a song, no joy in the sound.
I go out the door and there's a stumbling block—
Who claims Heaven and Earth are broad?
There is a stumbling block—not far away,   5
Beside the great highway in Ch'ang-an.
The lesser man wisely considers it dangerous,
And level land becomes the T'ai-hang Mountains.
A mirror, broken, doesn't change its light,
An orchid, dead, doesn't change sweet smell.   10
Now I understand the good man's heart—
His friendship endures, his way fully clear.
Your heart and my feelings
At parting both confused, bewildered.

7. *MTYSC*, p. 50.

Compare it to a stream that soaks the shoots,   15
Flowed on, the withered bitterness will grow in coming days.[8]
Enduring these tears my eyes age quickly,
Enduring this grief my form is quickly harmed.
Not that Hsiang Yü was not strong,[9]
Not that Chia Yi was not good,[10]   20
But at the time of their failures,
Each soaked his robes with rolling tears.
The ancients urged one to eat more,
This meal I find hard to force down.
In one meal I pray nine times I won't choke,   25
With one sigh my heart breaks ten times.
Even stronger this childish resentment,
Whose spirit rises to the blue heavens.
Long ago the heavens were aware of such,
And in broad daylight sent down clear frost.[11]   30
This morning for the first time I sigh startled
At the empty expanse of the azure sky.[12]

The powerful first four lines of this poem are the most quoted and,
sad to say, often the only quoted portion of Meng Chiao's work.
Separated from the whole, however, these lines do a disservice to the
complexity of the poem. One need only compare line four to the last
line to realize that the poem is far more complicated than the emotional outburst of the first four lines.

We may read these four lines as a rejection of conventional responses. "Eating greens" should be one of the simple pleasures of the
hermit; greens do represent poverty, but a poverty that is noble and,
if we are to believe poems such as "Ballad of a Wanderer in Ch'ang-
an," desirable. Reality intrudes upon the convention, and the greens
give the poet a stomach-ache. Singing is the traditional response to

8. *K'u*, "bitterness," the word used here, is occasionally employed as a variant for *k'u*,
"withered tree." So a pun is involved, that like a "withered trunk," their "bitterness"
will grow.

9. Hsiang Yü was the unsuccessful contender with Liu Pang, the future Han emperor,
for the empire after the fall of the Ch'in Dynasty. Hsing won the battles; Liu, the war.

10. Chia Yi was an important writer and intellectual figure of the early Han who lost
favor in the court and was given an undesirable position in the south.

11. When King Hui of Yen unjustly imprisoned Tsou Yen, Heaven was disturbed,
making frost appear in broad daylight as a reproof to the king.

12. *MTYSC*, p. 101.

overwhelming sorrow; hence this response offers the poet no consolation: he has to "force" the song. "Going out the gate" is a traditional
opening of a poem in which the poet "goes out" to brood on transitoriness and death. Here reality intrudes on the poet and he trips.
Finally, an awareness of the "vastness of Heaven and Earth" is a
summation trope in which the poet places his experience in relation
to the immensity of the universe; Meng Chiao rejects this response—
the universe that blocks his going out the door seems too narrow to
him. In all of these examples the conventional poetic response fails to
satisfy the poet. Like the metaphors at the beginning of "To Li
Kuan," each of these traditional responses offers some hope of escape
from his overwhelming grief, and Meng destroys each hope in turn.
In terms of fu-ku this means something else—that the conventional
poetic responses no longer work, they are not consonant with reality.

Meng proceeds to consider his failure as a "stumbling block" on
the road in Ch'ang-an. Then he ironically shifts to the point of
view of the "lesser man," *hsiao-jen,* who "wisely" knows the danger of
the search for position. Meng himself lacked that wisdom and failed.
Again Meng shifts the viewpoint to that of the "good man," *chün-tzu,*
whose virtue is enduring and does not alter with failure, using the
moral metaphors of the broken mirror and the dead orchid.

Next we move to the parting scene with Ts'ui Ch'un-liang. Their
sorrow at parting is compared to "shoots from a withered stump."
Out of the pun discussed in the notes comes the metaphor that as a
withered stump washed by water will sprout, their *bitterness* washed by
tears will also grow. As in Elizabethan and Metaphysical poetry, the
pun here is exploratory. The accident of language which brings
together a "flowed-upon witheredness" and a "flowed-upon bitterness" leads the poet to explore the similarities.

The poet follows this with the effects of his sorrow on his body,
then a comparison between himself and Hsiang Yü and Chia Yi, each
of whom wept at his failure. Next the theme of harm done to the body
by sorrow is resumed by the therapeutic suggestion to eat more, a
convention equivalent to the English "Take care of yourself." Once
again the conventional response is negated by the fact that the poet's
grief is so intense he can't swallow. "Praying" that he won't choke
anticipates the hope that Heaven will sympathize with him.

From grief Meng Chiao turns to resentment at the wrong done
him by those who failed him in the examination. The poet imagines

that Heaven might sympathize with this injustice as it once did to the wrong done Tsou Yen, and show its displeasure by sending down frost in the daytime. Seeing that Heaven will not do the same for him, Meng Chiao sighs in disappointment and recognizes a new aspect of the heavens—they have become an "empty expanse." This not only means a negative answer to the hope that Heaven will show its displeasure on his account, it is also an ironic counterstatement to the poet's earlier denial of the "vastness of Heaven and Earth"—the heavens *are* vast, but they are empty, caring nothing for him.

That critics seized upon the first four lines while ignoring the rest of the poem gives us some clue about Meng Chiao's neglect by later ages. The first four lines are striking, but they are part of a highly complex whole. The entire poem twists and turns with counterstatements: for example, the heavens are narrow, the heavens are vast; the "lesser man" is wise, the "good man" is superior. These could be compared to John Donne's logical arabesques, but in Meng Chiao's poetry such convolutions find expression in imagery and changes in attitude rather than in logic. Furthermore, the resumptions ("my form is quickly harmed . . . eat more . . . pray I won't choke"), the pun, and the moral affirmations (the way of a good man is clear and his friendships endure), which go against the cynical irony of most of the poem—all these tend to complicate the clarity of the poem's argument.

When we discussed "In the Mountains Seeing Off My Uncle Meng Chien," we spoke of the unpleasant, unsettling effect of shifting viewpoints and of destroying a scene that the reader has already accepted. The complex turns of this poem are a stylistic advance over the earlier poem and an *internalizing* of the shifting viewpoint. The poem has become a *process of discovering* meaning rather than a simple record of thought. The poem becomes an "act" rather than a "thing"; it makes mistakes, corrects them, discovers partial truth, and rejects it. Sometimes it even fails to discover the meaning for which it is searching. Meng Chiao has shown himself quite capable of writing a poem with perfect structure and geometrical unity, but this poem-as-process is a new kind of structure. In "To Ts'ui Ch'un-liang" the poet has at last reached a tentative understanding of his problem, but it leaves us unsatisfied, facing two partial and contradictory truths—a world that cramps and blocks him by its narrowness, and one that is vast but hollow.

"To Ts'ui Ch'un-liang" stands out from the other poems on Meng's failure because of the uncertainty, the process of discovery, we have just described. In evaluating the other poems on his failure, we must simultaneously concede their greatness and their limitations. The greatness lies in their straightforwardness, the power of their images, and the intensity of the emotions. But the straightforward expression of intense emotion is a self-limiting mode. To fulfill his promise as a major poet Meng Chiao had to develop further; his poetry had to gain more depth, sacrificing in the process some of the immediacy of these poems on his failure. However, before he attained this new style, Meng Chiao underwent a long period of relative infertility.

Meng Chiao's experiences between 793 and 805 were varied. After his second examination failure of 793 he journeyed south, returning to Ch'ang-an in 795 to take the examination for the third time. This time, in the spring of 796, he passed it, but like Han Yü he found no ready employment awaiting him. As mentioned in the preceding chapter, he joined Han Yü in Pien-chou in 797 and left in the early spring of 799, just before the rebellion. In 800 he received the post of office chief (*wei*) of Li-yang County in Kiangsu Province. In 801 someone else was given charge of his duties, and his salary was reduced accordingly, reputedly because he devoted more time to writing poetry than he did to his official duties. Meng remained at Li-yang on half-salary for some years before returning to Ch'ang-an in 806, where he again met Han Yü, who had just returned from exile in Kwangtung.

During these thirteen years, years in which Han Yü was developing his poetic personality, Meng Chiao was writing elaborate poems for patrons, increasingly hollow recapitulations of the poems on his failure, and landscape poems. Meng's best poems of the period are from his short residence in Pien-chou and just afterward. These poems show at least two of the four major developments in his poetry which occurred during these years.

First Meng Chiao turned away from the simple, blunt, and intense metaphor of fu-ku primitivism to a more complex and personal symbolism. Second, the bizarre aspect of Meng Chiao's imagination came more and more to the fore. Meng Chiao's fascination with the bizarre and grotesque, much rarer in Chinese poetry than in western literature, is an important factor in the self-consciously "strange"

poetry that developed after 806. Third, Meng Chiao turned away
from the occasional to the universal, from poetry of immediate emotion toward a poetry of vision. Instead of transforming the external
world by his emotions, he created his own worlds in his imagination.
After 806 Meng lived in a private, hermetic world all his own. A
fourth innovation toward the end of this period was his first tentative
experiment in the poem sequence.

In the following poem from his stay at Pien-chou, Meng Chiao
seeks to give universal significance to the occasion of a friend's
departure; Meng's bizarre vision of eternity may well be contrasted
to Han Yü's classical restraint in "Heaven's Stars" (p. 49).

AT TA-LIANG: SENDING OFF LIU CH'UN GOING INTO THE
    PASSES TO CH'ANG-AN

Their wheels have ground the green mountains into dust,
Under the bright sun is no man at ease.
Since ancient times they've hurried high carriages,
Competing for gain, westward into Ch'in,
Where gates of princes and gates of lords   5
Receive the rich, don't receive the poor.
In vain with one bundle of books in your hand,
You go farther and farther away—who shall be your friend?[13]

Meng Chiao's use of hyperbole, which in his early years was so
contrived, develops real power. The carriages of men going to
Ch'ang-an to seek their fortunes have raised so much dust over the
centuries that the mountains have been worn away. It seems to the
poet that no one has been free of this mad struggle for position and
gain. The second line suggests that the mountains, which have
traditionally been the abode of hermits, now can afford no one any
refuge; the green, shade-giving trees are gone into clouds of dust,
and the recluse is left "under the bright sun."

This is the poetry of vision; it has all the intensity of the failure
poems, but it is the power of imagination rather than of direct
emotion. Parallel to the development of Meng Chiao's poetry from the
metaphorical to the symbolic, there is a development from the statement of immediate emotion toward the imagination. While the
western idea of eternity is endless time stretching forward from the

13. *MTYSC*, p. 129.

present, the most common Chinese idea of eternity is of remote antiquity stretching forward to the present. Thus, in this visual image of a constant stream of carriages grinding away the mountains, the poet's imagination compresses eternity into a single scene.

Moral metaphors still play a large role in Meng Chiao's poetry during this period, but the boundaries that separate the real world from the metaphorical world are breaking down. The following poem occupies an important position in Meng's works, for in it we first see the metaphorical world assuming primacy, as though it were teaching the poet how to evaluate the real world. Here the meaning of the metaphorical world is clear; but in later poems we will find the poet confronting a hermetic, symbolic world, and by understanding the meaning of that symbolic world, becoming able to evaluate and understand the real one.

AT PIEN-CHOU: PARTING FROM HAN YÜ

I won't drink from waves of muddy water,
So it's in vain that I linger here by the Yellow River.
To no purpose do I see the ice that rings the shore
All become waves returning to the sea.
Through four seasons not at home,   5
Wretched clothes full of broken threads.
A distant wanderer, alone and haggard,
As spring flowers fall from dying trees.
The River here at Pien has many twistings in its flow,
No straight boughs on the wild mulberry here.   10
Only for *your* good heart
Do I sigh—and for nothing else at all![14]

Nature, names, and moral qualities converge strangely in this poem. In the ascendance of the metaphorical world there is a great deal of word magic; Meng won't drink the muddy water because physical muddiness means moral turpitude—he "thinks its name evil," *wu ch'i ming*, as in the following story about Confucius:

> Confucius came to Conquering-mother [place-name] in the evening, but he would not spend the night; he passed by Robber's Stream, but he wouldn't drink—this was because he thought their names evil.[15]

14. *MTYSC*, p. 153.
15. This story occurs in various places. In the *Huai-nan-tzu*, Confucius's disciple Tseng-

Just as the muddy water represents moral turpitude, the twisting of the Yellow River and the crooked mulberry branches suggest "warped" moral qualities. Following the traditional assumption that the state of nature and that of government are related, Meng concludes that the muddy water and the twisted branches reveal human evil.

Nature is sending other messages to the poet. The melting of the ice and its return to the sea indicates the arrival of a new year and that the poet likewise should "return" homeward. He has seen this hint of nature, but "to no purpose," for he still lingers at Pien-chou. Meng continues by lamenting his aging, his long absence from home, his poverty, and his loneliness. The powerful simplicity of lines like, "Through four seasons not at home," are still in the style of his poems on failure. Instead of grief at parting, Meng Chiao delivers a harsh attack on the place he is leaving; however, his statement that his only regret is parting with Han lends both dignity and credence to Meng's feeling for Han Yü.

Meng Chiao wrote the following poem in response to the rebellion at Pien-chou and the assasination of his former patron Lu Ch'ang-yüan.

Parted by Rebellion

There is no righteous sword in all the world,
The central plains are full of gashes.
Alas, alas!—my lord Lu,
Perversely the gods have cheated your honesty.
Tzu-lu has become but blood,[16]   5
Hsi K'ang is still mocking the world.[17]
Each time I feel a pang for you,
It's as though the sword were in my own limbs.
Your broken wings will never more fly,
Water passing by will never more return.   10

---

tzu supposedly wouldn't drink the water of Robber's Well. However, in the *Later Han History* the story is twice associated with Confucius. The version used here is quoted by Li Shan in his *Wen Hsüan* commentary on Lu Chi's "Ballad of the Fierce Tiger" from a now lost portion of the *Shih-tzu*.

16. Tzu-lu, one of Confucius's favorite disciples, here stands for Lu Ch'ang-yüan.

17. Hsi K'ang (232–62) was a famous recluse and lutanist who scorned the world. When condemned to death on false charges, he went calmly to his execution playing his lute. This may refer either to Lu or to Meng himself.

The high bough of the upright pine is ruined,
What now will this weak vine rely on?
This morning I had the joy of a spring day,
But this evening I have an autumn day's sorrow.
Tears fall, not just a little,   15
But in a downpour, the strands of Heaven's rain.
The bitterness grows becoming sickness,
Sorrow grows becoming madness,
No edge to the grasses of bitterness,
No shores to the waters of sorrow.   20
Sorrow and bitterness drive my heart,
Through vast reaches, whither do I go each day?[18]

In contrast to Han Yü's rebellion poems, in which the focus is on
the social and political context and human tragedy serves a persuasive purpose, Meng Chiao is primarily concerned with the personal
tragedy of Lu Ch'ang-yüan and with his own emotional reaction to
the rebellion. Meng Chiao may speak of righteousness and injustice,
but he does not call for judgment or political action. Han Yü's
"emotional" exclamation is pointed:

The Imperial House is unwilling to use shield and spear,
Alas, then, what can be done about mother and child?

In contrast to Han Yü's implied call to political action, Meng Chiao's
emotional exclamation is bewilderment at cosmic injustice:

Alas, alas!—my lord Lu,
Perversely the gods have cheated your honesty.

This is reminiscent of Meng's reaction to his failure in "Expressing
my Feelings"

A single spirit lies at the root of all things
How can they then destroy one another?

Many of the metaphors have the blunt directness of those in the
poems on his failure. On the other hand, while an image such as
that of the sword in the limbs (l. 8) is reminiscent of "My feelings are
like a knifeblade's wound," in "Failing," the image here is much
richer within the context of Lu's assasination: the sword that killed

18. *MTYSC*, p. 38.

Lu can be felt in Meng's own body. However, we can also see the bizarre and imaginative metaphors of Meng's new style. Lu Ch'ang-yüan's personal wounds and the figurative wounds inflicted on the empire by the rebellion become "gashes" in the land itself. The closing lines combine hyperbole and pathetic fallacy: either Meng's tears are so copious that they seem like a rainstorm, or the real rain seems like Heaven's tears, or both Meng Chiao and Heaven are weeping for Lu. The end is as frantic as the madness it describes. This madness caused by his grief over Lu's death "drives" Meng's heart across vast stretches of "waters of bitterness" and "grasses of sorrow" to an unknown destination. As in the case of the gashes in the land, a bizarre visual image results from the translation of an idea or an emotion into external terms.

The following poem is a mellower, more elegiac treatment of the subject.

AFTER GRIEVING OVER THE REVOLT AT PIEN-CHOU, REMEMBERING HAN YÜ AND LI AO

Once we met together weeping,
At parting, three broken hearts.
Remaining flowers that don't wait for the wind,
But, when spring ends, each flies off by itself.
Joys are gone—can't gather them back,   5
Grief comes—hard to guard against it.
Lonely gate, night in a cool inn,
Lying alone, bed covered with bright moonlight.
Loyalty, honesty bloody silver blades,
On the road, voices in confusion.   10
Three thousand troops that fed on imperial favor
For one morning became jackals and wolves.
On some ocean isles the troops are all upright,
But at Pien-chou the troops are not good.
Human hearts have not behaved of their kind,   15
So Heaven's way too has reversed its constants.
Killing oneself or letting them do the killing—
I don't know which one is better.[19]

This poem is another fine example of a midway-point between

19. *MTYSC*, p. 118.

Meng's style of the early 790s and his style of his last years in Lo-yang. In comparison to the poems on his failure and, to some extent, to the preceding poem, the emotions here are deeper, the images more complex, and the thought more mature. The poem begins with a moment of togetherness like flowers blossoming, then the scattering of both friends and flowers. The flowers fall because it is their appointed time to do so, and not because of the wind. "Wind and dust" is a cliché for rebellion; thus, in terms of the friends, the wind which their parting precedes is perhaps the wind of revolt.

In Han Yü's poems on the rebellion personal tragedy was a stimulus to action and only an element of cosmic disorder. Here, as "Loyalty, honesty bloody silver blades," morality is inextricably bound up with the living human being—it is literally his blood. As in the preceding poem, there is an element of bewilderment at the presence of evil; there is a simple, almost naive understatement that the rebel troops are "not good."

Heaven responds to the immorality of the troops, the fact that they are "not good": humans did not behave "humanely," therefore Heaven's balance is upset. Given this disruption of human values rather than of the social order, Meng Chiao wonders whether suicide—firmly forbidden by Confucian ethics—or being killed by the rebels is worse. However, Meng Chiao phrases the question, "which one is better": despite the disruption of values, it is still one's obligation to chose the *best* alternative, the most human, the most "of his own kind."

There is, too, an enigmatic relation between this question of suicide and the earlier image of the three friends as falling flowers.

> Remaining flowers that don't wait for the wind,
> But, when spring ends, each flies off by itself.

In each of the three cases—flowers, friends, and the ethical problem of facing the rebels—self-imposed death or scattering contrasts with destruction brought from outside. This is not an exact or explicit comparison; rather it is exploratory comparison, in which the poet feels that there is a similar structure underlying the three situations and seeks to give that structure meaning by juxtaposition, without defining the relation between the situations. Like "To Ts'ui Ch'un-liang," this poem searches for meaning but does not necessarily find it.

5

The Growth of the Narrative: Han Yü

When Han Yü heard of the revolt of the Pien-chou army, he hurried back toward the east, fearing his family had been trapped in the city. It turned out, however, that they had escaped, and Han Yü rejoined them in Hsü-chou, an important city in east China, governed by Chang Chien-feng. Chang Chien-feng had a reputation as a patron of unemployed scholars, and it had been to him that Han Yü recommended Meng Chiao when he failed the *chin-shih* examination in 792. On this occasion Han Yü himself had need of Chang Chien-feng's support, and he took the post of aide again, as he had under Tung Chin in Pien-chou.

In 800 Chang Chien-feng died and, predictably, the Hsü-chou garrison mutinied against his successor. In the ensuing struggle for power between the central government and the rebellious troops supporting Chang Chien-feng's son Chang Yin, Han Yü again found himself without means of support. So he journeyed west to Lo-yang, then on to Ch'ang-an in the winter of 800 in order to try and gain a government appointment.

Chinese poets tend to write more as they grow older, and Han Yü was no exception to this rule. With the increase in the quantity of his poetry, we find a complementary increase in quality. Still managing to avoid the conventions of High T'ang lyric poetry, Han forged a personal style in the following narratives of his experiences. The exemplary "types" of his earlier narrative poems such as "Poem of Hsieh Tzu-jan" disappeared, and there was a new concentration on personality and ethical character responding to concrete circumstances. The narrative poems recounting personal experiences fall into roughly three categories. First, there are humorous, mock-ethical stories, such as "While Sick" in chapter three and "To Hou Hsi" (p. 83); in both cases the humor offsets a serious problem, Chang

Chi's potential anger in the former and Han Yü's sense of personal failure in the latter. Second, there are the persuasive, rhetorical narratives such as "Returning to P'eng-ch'eng" (p. 80), in which Han Yü seeks to justify himself and his actions in political affairs. Third, there are the seriously personal narratives in which Han seeks to give pattern to his own experiences, exemplified in this chapter by "How Sad This Day." Even though these categories overlap—for example, the persuasive is part of "While Sick" along with the humorous—they do form the three-principle directions of his personal narratives in the future. Other poems in this chapter show Han Yü's balance of the serious and comic aspects of a situation in a non-narrative poem and his first attempts at descriptive poetry.

Safe with his family in Hsü-chou, Han Yü reviewed his experience of the revolt at Pien-chou in the following poem.

How Sad This Day: A Poem to Chang Chi

How sad this day!—
This wine I cannot taste.
I put the wine from me and talk to you,
Since together we're fated but a single day's light.[1]
I think on the past before I met you,   5
Master Meng Chiao had come from the south,
Boasting he'd found someone
And saying you were good at writing.
I was then attached to the Minister's bureau,[2]
I wanted to go to you, but couldn't get to travel.   10
I longed for you but couldn't meet you,
For a hundred reasons emotions filled my heart.
At that time the dark of the moon was dying,
At dawn the winter sun was in the Fang Constellation.
I left the frenzy of official business   15
When I heard you had just arrived in the city.
I ordered my carriage to bring you to me,
Then I led you to sit in the middle of the hall.
Opening my heart I listened to what you said,
Everywhere I seconded what you hoped for.   20
Confucius perished in the remote past,

1. I.e. because Chang Chi is leaving, they only have one day left together.
2. The "Minister" here and elsewhere in the poem is Tung Chin.

The path of virtue and kindness has long been overgrown.
In confusion a hundred schools of thought arose,
Ranting and raving weird, fantastic things—
The elders preserved only what they had heard, 25
While those born later practiced such things as constants.
Even the least knowledge is truly hard to obtain,
Since the pure and unadulterated disappeared long ago.
I compare you to that tree planted in the garden,
Which, having roots, will easily grow tall. 30
I detained you and didn't send you away,
But set you a place to stay by the west wall.
The year was not at its end,
When I gazed on the vastness of the lakes and rivers.[3]
Ordinary people pointed at you and laughed, 35
As if to say my knowledge was not illuminating—
Children who fear thunder and lightning,
Fish and turtles dazzled by light in the dark!
From local families they recommended men for the doctorate,
But in choosing an examiner they erred in what was right.[4] 40
Swiftly came the phrases to answer my questions,
The organization of your essays was brilliant.
The Minister stood in his court uniform,
And the musicians played "A Deer Sings" at the banquet.[5]
The rites were over, the music also ended, 45
Paying my respects I sent you off to court.
This man had been gone only an instant
When his rising fame circulated in bright splendor.
I rejoiced then, but also sighed,
For, though knowing well you had accomplished something, 50
How can anything human stay constant?—
In a moment I suffered a great wound.
The day when I heard of your high rank in the examination
Followed right on the Minister's death.
Feelings of lament met words of good fortune, 55
I was greatly confused, for they went not well together.

3. "The vastness of lakes and rivers" is to describe the breadth of Chang Chi's talent.
4. This is a humble way of saying that they chose Han himself as the examiner.
5. *Book of Songs*, 161. It expresses friendship, praise for a man of fine quality, and conviviality—hence its appropriateness at the feast.

I stayed the evening west of Yen-shih County,
Tossing in vain on my bed and turning.
That night I heard Pien-chou had revolted,
And I went pacing around the walls of my room.   60
At the time I had left my wife and children there,
In the confusion I hadn't gotten to take them with me.
I had no hope of seeing them ever again,
And accepted their fall and ruin as what must be.
My favorite daughter had not yet left the breast,   65
I thought of her and could not forget—
Suddenly it was as though she were right there,
And my ears seemed to hear her voice crying.
In mid-journey how could I turn back?
For an entire day I couldn't change my course.   70
Then all at once there was a report from the east
That my family had avoided meeting disaster,
They had gone by boat down the Pien River
Off eastward, hurrying to P'eng-cheng.
That morning I reached Lo-yang with the funeral cortège,   75
Then I rushed back without a chance to stop.
I took a shortcut through Meng Ford,
In and out over streams and hills.
When the sun was in the west, I came to an army camp,
Where my worn-out horse fell and lay stiff.   80
My host wished to detain me a short while,
Inviting me in, he set out winecups.
My position was such that I dared not decline,
Though my heart was agitated to the point of madness,
I couldn't taste what I ate and drank,   85
Pipes and lutes seemed to boom on meaninglessly.
At daybreak I took my leave and left,
As abruptly as a startled duck wings upward.
By dusk I had come to the Ssu's waters,
I wanted to cross but there was no boat.   90
I yelled and shouted a long time, then one came
And by night we crossed the ten miles to Huang.
In midstream we went up over rapids and sandbanks,
You couldn't tell the sand from the water,
Frightening waves massed huge in the darkness,   95

Constellations struggled in the overturning floods.
My carriage horse pawed his hooves, whinnying,
Right and left, the servants sobbed.
On the twentieth of the month we rested at Shih Gate,
Looking down in the stream I spied dragons fighting.[6]　　100
To the southeast I came out into Ch'en and Hsü,
Far and wide, level marshes and embankments,
By the roadside trees and plants were in flower,
Red and purple above and below me.
For a hundred miles I met no one,　　　　　　　　105
Only the calls of the pheasants singing.
On and on I went until the end of the second month,
When I reached the boundary of Hsü-chou.
I got off my horse, walked up the slope of the Dike,
Then onto a boat, where I greeted my elder brother.　　110
Who would imagine that, having gone through such hardship,
None of the hundred in the family had died before his time.
Chang Chien-feng of the Board of State, Duke of Nan-yang,
Quartered me on the north bank of the Sui River.
In my trunk there were plenty of clothes,　　　　　115
On my platter there was plenty of food,
I closed my gate to read the classics and histories,
And a clear breeze made the window cool.
Daily I longed that you come visit me,
But how could you have known what I felt?　　　　120
It hadn't been a long time since our parting,
But our experiences had been mostly misery and suffering.
Facing one another at meals, neither of us ate his fill,
Nor did we tire of talking together.
Continuously for thirty days　　　　　　　　　125
We sat from dawn until four o'clock in the morning.
Of my friends, two or three
Are on official visits to the capital;
Meng Chiao is peeking into Yü's cave,
Li Ao is gazing at the billows on the Yangtze.　　　130
A million miles of empty desolation—

6. The image of fighting dragons refers to a passage in the *Tso Chuan*, Chao, XII, in which it is told that dragons were fighting outside the Shih Gate. Han Yü is just spicing up his narrative with a little local legend.

Where else can I find a meeting?
The Huai's waters go slowly, slowly,
Ch'u's mountains are straight up in clusters.
You also cast me off and go,   135
How can my melancholy ever end?
But a man is not young and strong a second time,
A hundred years pass like a whirlwind.
May you be able to find high position
And not keep to one small region.[7]   140

The narrative of personal experience is an important subgenre of
Chinese poetry, reminiscent of the Latin verse epistle. From the
specific one divines the universal or, as in this case, seeks to give
pattern and perspective to experience. In the exordium Han Yü
rejects the conventional response of losing one's sorrows in wine. Such
a rejection of escape and emotionalism is consistent with the attitudes of Han Yü's early poetry, but in this case escape into wine is
not rejected on ethical grounds but in order to master his own depression by recapitulating his experiences. The theme is a friend
found, lost, then found again, and about to be lost again. Parallel to
the relation of the two friends is Han Yü's good fortune possessed,
lost, regained, and by implication, about to be lost again.

The account Han Yü gives here of his first meeting with Chang Chi
is quite different from the one we saw in "While Sick." In the earlier
poem their discussion of Confucian principles was treated as a game,
while here the same discussion is described as if it were serious. In
"While Sick" Han Yü made fun of Chang Chi's earnestness and
laughed at how he led Chang into a trap; in "How Sad This Day"
Han overflows with sincerity:

Opening my heart, I listened to what you said,
Everywhere I seconded what you hoped for.

It is important for the reader who seeks biographical truth in verse
narratives to remember that events are structured and given meaning for literary rather than historical or biographical purposes. In
this case, Han's friendship with Chang Chi in Pien-chou is so idyllic
in comparison to what followed, that for the sake of the pattern of his
fortunes, Han considers their friendship perfect.

7. *HCLS*, p. 40.

The statement of the Confucian theory of cultural decline in this context prepares the way for the disaster to follow:

> The path of virtue and kindness has long been overgrown,
> In confusion a hundred schools of thought arose,
> Ranting and raving weird, fantastic things.

Such intellectual and ethical disorder translates into political disorder, the rebellion, which proves their point. Although Tung Chin's death preceded the news of Chang Chi's success in the examination, Han Yü rearranges them in the narrative in order to keep the pattern of his fortunes consistent. Chang's success is the peak of good fortune, after which everything goes wrong—Tung Chin's death, the revolt, the fear that his family has been killed.

On hearing that his family has escaped to safety, the wheel of Han's fortunes starts its slow swing upward again, in the journey from Lo-yang to Hsü-chou. Beginning with his unpleasant experiences in the army camp, the landscape becomes increasingly idyllic as he nears Hsü-chou. Han's state of mind changes from the beginning of the trip when

> I couldn't taste what I ate and drank,
> Pipes and lutes seemed to boom on meaninglessly

to the end of his journey when he is moved by the beauty of the landscape:

> By the roadside trees and plants were in flower,
> Red and purple above and below me.
> . . . .
> Only the calls of pheasants singing.

Once in Hsü-chou, Han Yü finds all his wants satisfied except for one thing—he longs for Chang Chi's presence. When Chang appears, the wheel of fortune again reaches its apex. Then, after thirty days of bliss together Chang is about to leave, and Han Yü laments his impending solitude. At the end of the poem, however, Han corrects his attitude, realizing that Chang must fulfill his potential in government service.

The poem begins in depression and ends in resolution; through the narrative Han has exorcized his self-pity about his experiences and his impending loneliness. By giving his experiences pattern, albeit a very simple one, he can control them. The discovery of meaning and pattern in this poem is much subtler than in Han's early poems; however, in the new version of his meeting with Chang Chi, in the rearrangement of the sequence of Tung Chin's death and Chang's success, and in the progression of his mood in the journey to Hsü-chou, we can see Han Yü is still trying to force reality into a coherent order.

In contrast to the hyperbolic and humorous metaphors of "While Sick," here we find metaphors of simple clarity such as the tree well planted, the children who fear thunder and lightning, and the fish dazzled by light in the dark. The narrative style is chatty, using some prosaisms but none in extreme. Action rather than description still dominates the poem, but short descriptive passages are beginning to occur. As in "While Sick," ethics are far less important than human experience. Although it is the similarity of Han's and Chang's ethical viewpoints which brought them together in the first place, the poem is about the two friends, not about morality. Instead of seeing experience in terms only of traditional Confucian ethics, Han is now primarily interested in human experience and the intellectual order he finds in it.

Late in 799 Han Yü left Hsü-chou for a short visit to court, and on his return in the spring of 800 we have the following poem.

RETURNING TO P'ENG-CH'ENG [HSÜ-CHOU]

Again arms are in motion in the world,
When, at last, will there be an age of peace?
What fellows have given their "mikel conseile?"—
Haven't they in some way failed what is proper?
Year before last, drought in the capital region,   5
Most of the villagers died of starvation;
Last year, floods in the eastern provinces,
Live population became floating cadavers.
High Heaven doesn't make such responses for no reason,
Good fortune and misfortune both have a cause.   10
I had wished to offer some insufficient plans,
But had no way to reach the inner sanctum.
I hacked up my heart to make the paper,
Spilled blood to write my words,

In the first part I explained of Yao and Shun,   15
Below I drew examples from Lung and K'uei,[8]
The language was quite stirring,
The diction rarely florid.
First reading it I amazed myself,
But looking it over I had my doubts—   20
Eating celery may please most of us,
But offering it to the emperor would be stupid indeed!
I wrapped it up, sealing it with marrow,
Ill-at-ease, pointlessly thinking it special.
A while ago I arrived in the capital,   25
Rode often with lords in fine carriages,
Perfect in actions, most were exceptional,
Nor was there any flaw in their discussions,
I was treated with special courtesy,
But I couldn't get beneath the pelt.[9]   30
I dared not spit out the words that came to my tongue,
Patiently I waited for a crack.[10]
Then I returned among war horses,
Gazing about shocked, like a lone, wandering bird.
For days on end I wouldn't speak,   35
Whole mornings I would feel as though deceived.
When I got a free moment I would abruptly ride my horse off
Through the vast spaces till I reached an empty slope,
Find wine and get dead drunk—
You know who I am![11]

Topical political poetry, so far removed from a modern western
reader's concern, often made up a sizable portion of a poet's opus.
Han Yü, perhaps desiring above all else the political power to put his
Confucian values into practice, invested a great deal of himself in
poems about state policy and his political experiences. As one might
expect, the persuasive component of such poems is large, and as here,
the personal narrative often turns into a defense of his political

8. Lung and K'uei were two ministers of the legendary emperor Shun. Cf. *Shu-ching*
II, i.
9. Han seems to be saying that they were courteous and proper, but he couldn't get
beneath the surface to find out what they really felt.
10. I.e. to get beneath the armor of their courtesy (?).
11. *HCLS*, p. 57.

actions. Han Yü loads his case against the ministers from the very
beginning: the world is at war, and peace is nowhere in sight; Han
questions with ironic tact if they haven't failed "in some way." The
catastrophes that have befallen the empire are made more horrible
with shock phrases such as "floating cadavers." Having set up his
case, he then offers the proof of the ministers' faults: natural disaster
is a direct consequence of governmental failure.

The use of the term "mikel conseile" from the *Book of Songs* is an
excellent example of Han Yü's rhetorical abilities. The phrase comes
from *Song* #256, a didactic encomium of the ruler's potential to serve
and educate his people. I quote the second stanza (in modern
English, the archaism "mikel conseile," was used only to approximate the force of the phrase in Han Yü's poem).

> Nothing is more powerful than a man,
> He influences the entire state.
> When there is upright and virtuous conduct,
> All the nation obeys him.
> *Grand plans* ("mikel conseile"), fixed orders,
> Far-sighted counsels, timely announcements—
> He whose manner is reverent and reserved
> Is the model of the people.

Against this grandiose vision of the Confucian ideal Han Yü uses the
colloquial phrase *shui-tzu*, "what fellows," to heighten the irony.
The juxtaposition of the archaic, formal phrase with the colloquial
serves Han's persuasive purposes by contrasting what a minister
should be with the banal reality of what Han feels the ministers are.

With polite humility Han Yü suggests "insufficient plans."
Humility serves the purpose of winning the reader's sympathy, but
if overdone, it runs the risk of convincing the reader that the rhetorician actually is unworthy. Han resolves this complication by
simultaneously complimenting his letter and saying it is unworthy of
the emperor. Han's frustration at trying to deal with the court
officials is vividly described, but he is careful not to criticize them
too openly; hence we have the explicit praise of their conduct, while
his criticisms are phrased in the obscure metaphors of the "pelt"
and the "crack." Pointedly, Han speaks of his return "among war
horses" to remind the reader that the situation hasn't improved. In

a final bid for the reader's sympathy Han assumes the traditional role of the worthy official who, spurned by the court, escapes to seclusion, drowning his sorrows in wine.

Poems like this one (and there are a good many) are closest in spirit to Han Yü's prose writing. As a prose writer he is admired for many of the same reasons as Cicero is admired in the West—as a stylist, a rhetorician, and a culture hero. Han Yü is indeed a master rhetorician, not only in his overtly persuasive poems, but also, in more subtle ways, in his other poetry. However, although ethical judgment plays an important role in such poems as this one, circumstances have begun to determine principle rather than principle altering circumstances; in short, as he becomes more involved in public life, his rhetoric serves his personal ends rather than affirming traditional ideals.

The following is one of Han Yü's most delightful poems, possessing a good humor unlike anything in earlier Chinese poetry. Like "Poem of Hsieh Tzu-jan," "To Hou Hsi" offers us a short narrative from which a lesson is drawn, but unlike the earlier poem, which is genuinely didactic, "To Hou Hsi" is mock-didactic. The didactic assumptions and form remain; the message, however, is against Han's traditional ethics—it is to give up and become a hermit.

To Hou Hsi

A Mr. Hou of my circle, Hou Shu-ch'i,[12]
Called to me, "Get your pole and we'll fish in the Wen River."
At daybreak we whipped our horses out the capital gates,
Then on and on all day long among thorns and brambles.
The Wen is a rather hazy affair—it stops, then flows again, 5
As deep as a cart track, wide enough for a carriage pole,
Frogs leap over it, there baby wrens can bathe,
But even if there were fish, they wouldn't be worth the trouble.
For Mr. Hou's sake I could not give up,
So we bent needles for hooks, 10
      broke grains for bait,
           cast them into the slime.
Ramrod stiff we sat from noontime on to yellow dusk,
Hands tired, eyes sore, then finally we got up—

12. Hou Shu-ch'i is Hou Hsi.

It moved a moment!
      then stopped,
            we couldn't hope—
Shrimps moved, leeches crossed over as though all were in doubt,
I raised the pole and pulled in the line—   15
      suddenly I had something!
An inch's worth—just old enough to tell the fins from scales.
At this moment Mr. Hou and myself
Gazed mournfully at one another, sighing a good while.
Everything I do these days turns out just like this,
So this experience may well serve as an example for me: 20
Half of my life spent in a fluster to get chosen for a post,
When I first get that single title, my once young face is old.
Why didn't I see the way things are in this human world?
Bringing pointless suffering on myself, and ultimately for what?
I just ought to take my wife and children by the hand,   25
Go south into Ying and Chi, never to return.
Hou Hsi, your spirit is at its keenest now—
What I say is really important—don't laugh at me!—
If you want to go fishing, you have to go really far,
Do you think a big fish would live in this backwash?[13]   30

    The gentle cynicism and good-humored irony of this poem stands in sharp contrast to the pious idealism of Han Yü's early poetry. The poem is delicately balanced between humor and depression: the fishing episode is clearly comic, but its analogue, Han Yü's futile experience in public life, is decidedly not. The humor dulls the biting edge of Han's sense of failure, while the personal analogy lends a mock dignity to the fishing episode. What is important is that Han Yü never lets the poem sink into gloom. When he gets too serious about his personal failure, he adds: "What I say is really important—don't laugh at me!" Han Yü is going to some lengths in this passage to suggest that his own serious extrapolation from the fishing experience also has its comic aspects. Besides being funny, the fishing episode is futile and frustrating; besides being frustrating and futile, Han Yü's experiences in public life are a ludicrous example of a man struggling frantically for something not worth having—the poem tells us both these things.

13. *HCLS*, p. 68.

In "To Hou Hsi" Han's experiments in vivid dramatization, such as "Revolt at Pien-chou" and "While Sick," bear fruit. The style is nervously active, to parallel the futile efforts to catch a fish in the Wen River. Of the first sixteen lines, six have three verbs each. The tendency toward hyperbole that we saw in "While Sick" is far more prevalent here, being the source of the humor in the description of the river and the fishing experience. As in Meng Chiao's poetry, extreme situations—or, as here, mock-extreme situations—call for hyperbole, the poetic device of extremes.

The following poem from the same period shows a similar balance between the serious and comic aspects of a situation.

LOSING A TOOTH

Last year a molar fell out,
This year an incisor fell.
All of a sudden six or seven more fall,
And this tooth-falling condition is hardly over.
Those left are all shaky,   5
And I suppose this won't stop till they've all fallen.
I remember when the first one fell,
I felt only that the gap was embarrassing.
When two or three had fallen,
I began to worry that this decline meant death.   10
Now every time one's going to fall,
I feel a constant trembling within.
A shaky tooth prevents me from eating,
I'm so upset I fear rinsing my mouth with water.
Finally it will desert me and fall,   15
My mood likens it to an avalanche.
Recently I've grown used to the falling,
When one falls, there is similarity in emptiness,
The remaining ones, twenty-odd,
I know they'll fall in succession and that's it.   20
Now supposing one falls each year,
I've got enough to last me two decades,
On the other hand, if they fall together, emptying me,
It's still the same result as gradually.
People say when the incisors fall,   25
You can't hope for long life,

But I say life has its limits,
Long or short, all die anyway.
People say when you've got a gap in the incisors,
Those around are startled when they look closely,   30
But I say what Chuang-tzu said,
Trees and geese each have something to be happy about.[14]
Silence is certainly better than telling lies,
Chewing doesn't work, but soft things still taste good.
Thus I sang and finished a poem on it,   35
With which I inform my wife and children.[15]

The witty play on numbers, teeth falling, and Han's personal reactions, form a rhetorical game played by the poet to deny and, by humor, to devalue the importance of a very serious problem, his own aging. At the fall of two or three teeth (l. 10) the poet begins to worry about death, and a loose tooth prevents him from eating (1.13), but the gravity of these. situations is counterbalanced by the hyperbolic absurdity of: "I'm so upset I fear rinsing my mouth with water" or "My mood likens it to an avalanche." His resignation that all his teeth will eventually fall out is balanced by the witty similarity of the empty spaces (ll. 17–18). The poet speculates that at the rate of one a year, they'll last twenty more years, but that the result is the same even if they were all to fall out at once. Han counters each serious implication with a playful sophistry. Against the threat of impending death he points out that everyone dies sometime anyway. Against the ugliness of a missing tooth Han uses Chuang-tzu to suggest that there are advantages to ugliness. If the lack of teeth prevents him from talking, well, "Silence is certainly better than telling lies."

14. This refers to the first story in the "Tree on the Mountain" chapter of the *Chuang-tzu*. Chuang-tzu's disciples saw that a tree was spared the woodcutter's axe because it lacked quality; then they observed that in a choice between a goose that could cackle and one that couldn't, the goose that couldn't cackle—the one that lacked quality—was selected to be killed. Perplexed at this contradiction, they asked Chuang-tzu about it. Chuang-tzu replied that he would take a position between quality and lack of it, but that even that position was incorrect because it allowed consideration of the distinction between quality and its lack. Han Yü is saying that such things as whether one has teeth (quality, like the goose that could cackle and survived) or has not teeth (lacks quality, like the tree that survived), do not determine survival because they are meaningless distinctions. The tree was happy to lack quality; the goose that survived was happy to possess it.

15. *HCLS*, p. 81.

Though tame in comparison with the logical wit of the English Metaphysical poets, this poem is an oddity in the Chinese poetic tradition. For example, the use of "fall," *lo*, fifteen times in the poem, without even bothering to use elegant variations, is against all T'ang standards of poetic good taste. The style is unusually prosaic. In contrast to the usual poetic practice of using a number of events or images to develop one idea or emotion, this poem extrapolates a number of emotions and ideas from one thing, his teeth, and one event, their falling out.

In this poem and the preceding one a consistent trait of Han Yü's poetry is revealed: Han is a poet who must maintain a barrier between his emotions and their expression in poetry. Wit and humor are two important devices he employs to achieve such distance, and he seems to use them to convince himself, much as the rhetorician in him tries to convince others. Although his poetry lacks the direct emotion, the "sincerity" (*ch'eng*) so prized by Chinese critics, it makes up for the lack by the complexity of Han's attitude—his real feelings, the logical counterstatements to those feelings, and often a self-mocking humor in his counterstatements, devaluing both his feelings and his evasions.

Until this period, Han Yü has shown very little inclination or aptitude for description. It is not surprising, therefore, that when he does try his hand at descriptive poetry, he falls back on the precedent of the *fu* or "prose poem," in which description and persuasive rhetoric are supposedly joined.

THE PIEN AND THE SSU FLOW TOGETHER: TO CHANG CHIEN-
FENG

Where Pien and Ssu flow together, at the city wall's corner,
There's a rammed-earth field of a thousand paces,
　　　　flat as though shaved.
A short wall on three sides, long and circling,
Where they beat drums booming and plant crimson flags.
The morning cool from recent rain, the sun not yet seen,　　　5
Our Duke Chang has made arrangements for early morning,
　　　　and for what do they come?—
They'll divide into teams to decide a victory,
　　　　a meet set previously.
Hooves of a hundred horses gather, bright and close together,
The ball leaps up, the stick drives it,

as they ride together and apart,
Of red oxhide their straps, of yellow gold their bits.   10
They lean their bodies and bend their arms
    around the horses' bellies,
A thunderclap answers hands' movement, the divine bead races,
Far away it rolls—both teams rest a moment,
Then fleet-galloping hosts struggle to change the outcome.
The shot was hard, making it, skillful—his breath rasping,   15
As strong warriors all around him shout cheering.
This is really practice for battle—it's not just sport.
It would be better indeed to sit at rest, making good plans.
Nowadays loyal subjects are hard to find—
Don't run your horse too hard, sire, you must kill rebels.[16]

Han is describing a game that resembles polo. The peculiarly Chinese notion that a commander should concentrate on strategy rather than training his troops, thereby stirring their more violent emotions, seems to indicate that Han Yü has the Pien-chou rebellion in mind here. Chang should not encourage his troops in such behavior lest their bloodthirstiness get out of hand, and he find himself in the same infelicitous position as Lu Ch'ang-yüan.

The indirect satire of the Western Han fu is a submerged form in this poem. Such fu would describe a thing or activity lavishly, and by descriptive excess, criticize it indirectly. Usually they would close with a direct expostulation, as we find here. The most famous example is Ssu-ma Hsiang-ju's *Fu on Shang-lin Park*, in which the emperor's park and a hunt are described with unparalleled hyperbole, supposedly for the purpose of criticizing the emperor's lavishness, although the emperor doubtlessly felt more flattered than criticized. The evident inconsistency between the purpose and the effect of this structure was already apparent by the end of the Western Han; in the famous words of the repentant fu author Yang Hsiung: "That's satire??!—I'm afraid it doesn't avoid encouraging."[17] This wise observation notwithstanding, Han Yü is using the same technique in the above poem. He elaborately describes the polo field and game, without injecting any note of evaluation. Since we can see at the end that the poem's express purpose is to remonstrate with Chang Chien-

16. *HCLS*, p. 49.
17. Yang Hsiung, *Fa-yen*, (SPPY reprint, Taipei: Chung-hua, 1966), c. 2.1a.

feng, such objectivity is curious, considering Han Yü's earlier tendency to evaluate constantly.

In the descriptive section Han Yü still relies heavily on action verbs, but concrete nouns are plentiful. Consistent with the fu form, but striking in comparison to Han Yü's previous poetry, is the fact that prose constructions and particles are almost completely absent. This denser descriptive technique will develop into Han's principle style in the later part of his exile and after his return north in 806. The two main characteristics of Han Yü's later descriptive style, vivid realism and extravagant hyperbole (strange bedfellows), can be seen in the descriptive part of this poem, from

> Far away it rolls—both teams rest a moment,
> Then fleet-galloping hosts struggle to change the outcome.
> The shot was hard, making it, skillful—his breath rasping,

to "A thunderclap answers hands' movement, the divine bead races" (in other words, the crack of the polo stick against the ball answers the swing of the stick by the hands. The "divine bead" is the polo ball.)

The final expostulation is there to give the poem a sense of moral purpose—albeit an acknowledgedly ineffective one. However, later poems in this style will lose this very facade of moral purpose. It is significant that Han Yü chooses the submerged form of the fu in his extended descriptive poem, for the fu does offer a superficial compromise between enthusiastic description and moral purpose.

6

Han Yü's Exile: 804-806

In 803 Han Yü received a minor position in the censorate (*chien-ch'a yü-shih*), an area of the Chinese civil government requiring both moral courage, of which Han Yü had an ample supply, and tact, in which Han Yü was singularly lacking. During the same year there was a drought in the capital region, and Han Yü, along with his friend Chang Shu, memorialized the throne. Something in the memorials particularly angered the emperor, and as a result, in late January or early February of 804, Han Yü and Chang Shu were exiled to Yang-shan, in Lien-chou in modern Kwangtung. With the ascension of Shun-tsung to the throne in 805, Han Yü received a partial pardon and was transferred north to Chiang-ling on the Yangtze River. Finally in the summer of 806, the emperor Hsien-tsung ascended the throne, and Han Yü was recalled to the capital.

This period of exile is an important transitional period in the development of Han Yü's poetry. Although Han had written many fine poems before this time, none can stand against his best poetry. However tempting it is to say that his exile gave Han full poetic maturity, the directions his mature poetry took have been pointed out in the poems we looked at in the preceding chapter. In this chapter we will consider first the development of Han's descriptive technique and of landscape poetry *within* the narrative and, following that, two other elements found first in this period of exile in Yang-shan: Han Yü's early experiments in regulated verse and purely descriptive poems.

For a poet whose primary concerns had been ethics and personalities, the transition to landscape poetry was neither easy nor expected. "Seeing Off Reverend Hui" (p. 92) is a character-sketch that shows Han Yü's fascination with the personality of an eccentric Buddhist monk. Hui's main love in life is fine landscapes, and in the course of this poem Han describes them. This presents little problem because such landscapes are adjuncts of the monk's personality and events in his life rather than things in themselves. In "Visiting a Temple on Mount Heng," (p. 97), one of Han Yü's greatest poems, Han has a profound experience in viewing a mountain, not uncommon for most Chinese poets, but new to Han Yü. Unable to accept the beauty of the landscape on its own terms, Han Yü uses the mode of understanding in which he feels most comfortable; he writes a character-sketch about his relationship with the "god of the mountain." By anthropomorphizing the landscape he can deal with it in human terms, which he knows best.

Han Yü, however, develops another way of understanding the landscape more satisfying than looking for gods in the mountains he visits. Just as he had tried to give pattern to his personal experience in "How Sad This Day," (p. 74), here Han tries to find a deeper meaning, a cosmic pattern reflected in the landscape, which somehow correlates with his personal experiences. In other words, Han Yü's landscape poems are peculiar in the Chinese poetic tradition; his landscapes are not simply aspects of nature to be appreciated in themselves but actualizations of cosmic patterns. The assumption underlying this view of nature is that of the organic universe in which fixed cyclical structures inform all aspects of the world of phenomena. On the simplest level this can appear in the alternation of Yin/dark and Yang/bright: for example, in "Hindered by Winds at Lake Tung-t'ing" (p. 102) when the Yin essence is ascendant, Han Yü's fortunes are "dark" and the lake is stormy. Both the poet's life and the landscape actualize the cosmic state. In the poems in this chapter such landscapes are still bound up with the personal narrative, but after 806 we have poems we can truly call symbolic landscapes existing independent of the narrative. In such poems the landscape becomes a great hermetic portent through which Han can understand the cosmic structures that govern his life and all other phenomena. Yet throughout this complex poetic development one thing remains constant: from his earliest poetry Han Yü has sought to impose order and meaning on, and to find pattern in, chaotic or meaningless phenomena.

"Seeing Off Reverend Hui," written during his stay in Yang-shan, is the finest of a number of character-sketches Han wrote at this time and includes an important early example of landscape description.

SEEING OFF REVEREND HUI

Reverend Hui, as a Buddhist,
Is not a man for the halter.
At fifteen he loved mountains and rivers,
Transcending earthly ties, left friends and relatives,
Took off his cap and shaved his head,   5
With flying footsteps left tracks in the dust behind.
Then it came to pass that he went on Ssu-ming Mountain,
The void as his ladder, he ascended autumn's skies.
Next he climbed T'ien-t'ai to gaze
On a host of crevasses all fathomlessly deep.   10
That night he spent on the highest summit,
Raising his head he saw stars and planets
Which were sparkling candles shining on him,
North and south vying to form the finest patterns.
This place was cut off from bird and beast alike,   15
Where nature was most severe and mysterious,
A faint wind blew over trees and stones,
In the rush of waters he heard celestial harmony.
At midnight he rose and gazed down
To where ocean waves enclosed the sun's orb.   20
Fish and dragons leaped about frightened,
Their shrieking and howling was the harshest misery.
Then strange vapors, reddish and purple,
Spiraled together knocking and grinding.
The sun, the Golden Raven, had soared aloft,   25
Suddenly the ends of the earth were clear anew.
Having long heard the marvels of Yü's cave,[1]
He went eastward to have a look at Ou and Min,
But Yüeh customs don't favor what's ancient,[2]
And have lost their purity as they were handed down.   30

1. On Kuei-chi Mountain in Che-chiang Province was supposedly located the grave of the legendary emperor Yü, the founder of the Hsia Dynasty. It became common practice for literati visiting the region to go in search of it. Cf. "How Sad This Day," l. 129.

2. Ou and Min are areas in southeast China, while Yüeh is a general term used for the whole region.

Yü's hidden traces were so remote he couldn't find them,
And he sighed that the way to/of the sage was blocked forever.
Turning back, he looked down on the Che's billows,
Which rose steep, high as E and Min Mountains;
In them was a strong spirit that rested not in death,   35
It was a thousand years ago and it seemed but yesterday
    morning.[3]
Finally, not knowing if the tale be true or false,
He rejected it as not being of his principles.
Crossing the Yangtze he reached Lu Mountain,
From whose limitless view he saw all he had transversed,   40
Its towering cliffs lost beyond the clouds,
The lower slopes drenched by the eddies of a lake.
At that time a rain was just clearing,
A cascade formed a ribbon hanging from the sky.
Two years ago he went to mount Lo-fu,   45
And his steps struck the stand of the South Seas.
Here the mighty Yang Essence is at its peak,
Where all flourishes in a spring that lingers forever,
Here the roc mounts, drooping its long pinions,
And the whale sports, leaning his long flippers.   50
Since he came to the temple in Lien-chou
He has never come to the city walls,
Daily he joins fellow wanderers among the blue clouds,
Seeking scenic spots he has run out of cliffs and shores.
The governor invited him, but he wouldn't come,   55
A host of magistrates asked him often, but in vain.
There is not a coin in his purse,
But contrarily he calls rich men poor.
Yesterday he was suddenly nowhere to be found,
So I had someone go inquire of his neighbors.   60

3. This refers to the legend of Wu Tzu-hsü. During the Warring States Period, Wu
Tzu-hsü fled from Ch'u to Wu, where he became a trusted advisor of the king. Although
he had greatly helped the king, he eventually fell out of favor because of his hostile attitude toward the neighboring state of Yüeh. Finally, slandered by a pro-Yüeh minister,
Wu Tzu-hsü was ordered to commit suicide. Before he died, he ordered his retainers to
take his eyes out and put them on the capital gate facing the state of Yüeh, so that he
could view the destruction of the state of Wu. One story goes that the king was enraged
when he heard this and ordered Wu Tzu-hsü's body to be put in a sack and thrown in the
Yangtze River. Popular legend tells that at times he can be seen there, riding a white
horse among the whitecaps.

Then swift as a wave I rushed after him,
And grasping his hand, asked him why he went.
Looking at me he gave a sigh:
"Are you so different from everyone else?—
There are meetings and separations—it's always been so,   65
Is parting really worth cherishing?
I've heard the Chiu-yi Range is nice,
So now I would fulfill an abiding wish.[4]
The mottled bamboo wept on by Shun's wives,[5]
The clear Hsiang that sunk the subject of Ch'u,[6]   70
Heng Mountain and Lake Tung-t'ing—
This indeed is where my road follows,
Visiting Mount Sung, then down into Lo-yang,
Across Mount Hua and next into Ch'in.
Roaming about, never a fixed place,   75
Unexpectedly going, then crossing another ford."
I said, "You must go,
Your way is not to be followed by me—
A river fish can't stay alive in a pond,
A bird from the wilds is hard to tame in a cage.   80
I think the Western Teaching is wrong,[7]
But love your passion and purity.
I loath lazy wanderers,
But love your simplicity and resolution.
Go off then! We each have different inclinations,   85
Why should I weep on my kerchief to no purpose?"[8]

In contrast to Hsieh Tzu-jan, who was an illustration of a character "type," the monk Hui has a real personality, a cavalier aloofness both convincing and amusing. The structure of this poem reflects Hui's life: the poem moves from place to place, lingers a while on a scene, then moves on, "roaming about, never a fixed place." Looking into the future at the end of the poem, we see only constant wandering in Hui's condensed itinerary (ll. 67–74).

4. "Abiding" may here have the implications of "from a former life," but not necessarily.

5. The speckles on a certain variety of bamboo were said to have been originally formed by the tears wept on them by the wives of the legendary emperor Shun, on hearing of his death.

6. This refers to Ch'ü Yüan and his suicide by drowning.

7. The "Western Teaching" is Buddhism.   8. *HCLS*, p. 91.

Han Yü's personal liking of Hui, his principles that oppose Hui's
Buddhism and "lazy wandering," as well as his emotional reaction
to Hui's cold rebuff, all come into conflict at the end of the poem:

> I think the Western Teaching is wrong,
> But love your passion and purity.
> I loathe lazy wanderers,
> But love your simplicity and resolution.

Instead of saying, "The Western Teaching is wrong," *Hsi-fang chiao
fei,* Han qualifies his principle as opinion, "*I* think it is wrong,"
wu fei. Han Yü's sense of principle is no longer rigid enough to bring
him to reject Hui outright; his appreciation of aspects of Hui's
character, his "not being a man for the halter" and his "not having a
coin in his purse/but contrarily calling rich men poor" (Han made a
similar point himself in "Those Who Make Friends in Ch'ang-an"),
puts Han in an ambivalent situation. By mentioning that he
"loathes lazy wanderers" (the category into which Hui definitely
falls according to Han's utilitarian ethics), Han both affirms his principles and repays Hui's aloof rejection of him in kind. But Han cannot ignore the "simplicity and resolution" in Hui, which he admires.

The first couplet might well be prose. Hui is described as possessing the two essential qualities of a hermit or itinerant monk, the love
of freedom and of landscapes. Even though Han Yü offers no judgment on Hui's decision to become a monk, it is clear that the social
implications of the act are foremost in his mind:

> Transcending earthly ties, left friends and relatives,
> Took off his cap and shaved his head.

The "cap" is associated with adulthood as well as with service in the
government, as is the style in which the hair is worn. Taking off the
cap and shaving the head, the symbolical acts of assuming monk-
hood, sever all familial, social, and political ties.

From the world of men Hui moves into the transcendent world of
the landscape. The poem's style likewise leaves the prosaic and
turns strange. In line eight Han uses the noun *t'i,* "ladder," as a
verb when Hui "ladders the void," suggesting both that he climbed
a high mountain and that he became a flying immortal. The descriptive style of Hui's stay on Mount T'ien-t'ai is similar to that of
"Pien and Ssu Flow Together" (p. 87). The vision of the sunrise over

the ocean shows particular imaginative power; even in describing scenery Han Yü's poetry is rarely static. Rather, it possesses a violent energy that sets him apart from most Chinese landscape poets.

> Fish and dragons leaped about frightened,
> Their shrieking and howling was the harshest misery.
> Then strange vapors, reddish and purple,
> Spiraled together, knocking and grinding.

On and on Hui wanders until he comes to the South Seas, the most exotic landscape of all, full of rocs and whales and existing unnaturally in a state of eternal spring. But when we turn again to Hui's relations with men, the style becomes rough and prosaic once more:

> Then swift as a wave I rushed after him,
> And grasping his hand, asked him why he went.
> Looking at me he gave a sigh:
>
> "Are you so different from everyone else?—
> There are meetings and separations—it's always been so,

Han Yü's answer is equally prosaic:

> I said, "You must go,
> Your way is not to be followed by me.

It is hard to say to what extent these two passages are colloquial because we know very little about T'ang colloquial language. Yet there is no "more poetic" way in which Han Yü might have said this; rather, the uniqueness of the passages lies in the fact that he does record conversation in such a natural, matter-of-fact way. Most of the prose usages in these passages can be found in earlier T'ang poetry; however, one usually does not find so many used together. Pronouns, for example, *are* used in T'ang poetry, but sparingly, for special emphasis. Of the ten characters in the couplet quoted above in which Han Yü answers Hui, four characters are pronouns (two *wu*'s, "I," and two *tzu*'s, "you"), three characters are verbs, two are particles, and only one character—*Tao*, the "Way"—is a noun. A similar preference for verbs, particles, and pronouns, and an avoidance of concrete nouns are evident in the passage preceding the couplet. This prosaic style, used primarily to describe events, human relationships, and in speeches, carries over into Han's descriptive style. There we find a similar preference for verbs; for example, "bird and beast" (1. 15) is literally "flying and walking [creatures]," *hsiang-tsou*. Or there is the description of the vapors which "spiraled together knocking and grinding." The result of this influence on his descriptive style is, as suggested earlier, that Han Yü's descriptive poetry has a violent tension unique in Chinese poetry.

The following work, one of the finest of Han's exile poems, was written during his journey north from Yang-shan to his new post at Chiang-ling. Han's narrative technique is getting less diffuse, his descriptive powers richer, his humor sharpened by adversity, and his humanism is still intact.

Visiting a Temple on Mount Heng

Afterwards I spend the night in a Buddhist temple on the peak and write this on the gate tower.

The Five Mountains I've worshiped in their ranking,
    All great lords,
They ring and guard the four directions,
    Mount Sung is the middle.
Toward the fiery pole where the earth is wild,
    One fit for goblins,[9]
Heaven lent it divine power,
    Making its might unique.
Spurting clouds and oozing fog,   5
    Half hide its belly,
Though it does have an uppermost peak,
    Who could ever reach all the way there?
I have just come, meeting with
    The season of autumn rains,
The Yin Spirit made it dark and dismal,
    There was no clear wind.
Deep in my heart I prayed silently,
    And it seemed there was a response—
Of course it is because there is one honest and upright,   10
    That it can feel and comprehend.[10]

9. The Mount Heng referred to here is the southernmost of the Five Mountains. The south is associated with the fire element.

10. I.e. the god of the mountain responded to Han's prayer because of his good character.

In an instant it was swept clear,
  A host of peaks came out,
Looking up I saw them thrusting forward
  To prop up the blue sky.
Purple Cover stretched out to reach
  Heaven's Pillar Peak,
Stone Granary flings itself upward,
  Heaped up against Firegod Peak.[11]
Darkly my spirit was moved,   15
  I got off my horse and bowed,
Pines and cypresses were all along the path,
  As I rushed to the god's palace.[12]
Through its white walls and crimson columns
  Moved colored beams of light,
Paintings of demonic creatures filled it
  With greens and reds.
I mounted the stairs, back bent in reverence,
  To offer meat and wine,
Wishing by such trifles   20
  To make clear my inner feelings.
An old man, the temple guardian,
  Who knew the god's will,
With eyes bulging looked me over
  And was able to bow down.
In his hands he held the oracle stones
  And taught me to cast them,
Saying, "This one's the most lucky,
  The rest can't beat it."
Hiding banished in barbarian wilderness,   25
  Fortunate I'm not dead,
Clothes and food just enough,
  Feeling it sweet to die an old man,
To be duke or prince, general or minister
  Hope long ago gone—
Even if the god wants to bless me,
  It will hardly do any good.
That night I put up in a Buddhist temple,

11. These are peaks of Heng Mountain.
12. I.e. the temple of the mountain god.

> Climbed to the highest room,
> The brilliance of stars and moon   30
>   Hidden faint through the clouds,
> Gibbons cried, the bell toned—
>   I didn't know it was dawn
> Until gradually brightening, a cold winter sun
>   Rises in the east.[13]

Landscape poetry is one of the dominant subgenres of Chinese poetry, one hitherto disdained by Han Yü. The problem, stated earlier in this chapter—of how a poet who is primarily concerned with ethics and personalities understands a landscape—is resolved by Han Yü's postulating an agent who controls the landscape, an anthropomorphic god with whom Han may have a human relationship. So we have an intermediate stage between Han Yü's humanism and his symbolic landscapes; the landscape is personified in the god who responds to the poet and tries to console him.

The Five Mountains (Sung, T'ai, Hua, and the two Mount Hengs) have a ritual, cosmic significance to the Chinese, and it is therefore not surprising to find that the poet begins by considering the relation of these mountains to the cosmic order:

> They ring and guard the four directions,
>   Mount Sung is the middle.

Mount Heng, the mountain of the south, is representative of his exile, his life in the south. Thus his experience with this mountain is a portent of the poet's future.

The theme of concealment and revelation is important in the poem, so it is appropriate that Han comes upon the mountain when it is hidden by clouds and mist, just as his future is still hidden from him. When Han's prayer for clear weather is fulfilled immediately, he is astounded, acknowledging that the mountain must be aware of him. A relation is established: the mountain reveals its majesty to Han Yü in response to Han's "honesty and uprightness."

The second revelation is less sublime. Han proceeds to the temple of the mountain-god to pay his respects, to "offer meat and wine." A formal, almost ritual, gesture-response relation has developed between Han and the mountain. Han prays to the mountain and is

13. *HCLS*, p. 128.

of good character, therefore the mountain-god reveals its majesty to him. Han Yü responds to the god's gesture by going to the temple to pay his respects, and the god in turn responds to this gesture by way of the oracle. But the superstitious gaudiness and grotesqueness of popular religion—the "demonic creatures" and the old guardian with bulging eyes—devalue the purity of the relation between Han Yü and the mountain. Thus when the oracle (not unexpectedly) reveals a prediction of good fortune, Han receives it with cynicism mixed with gentle humor. First he contrasts the prediction with his present state of exile and unhappiness (it might be added here that Han was equally unhappy about his transfer to Chiang-ling, for his post there was a low one). Han Yü grants that the god is sincere in his desire to bring him good fortune, but denies that he is potent enough to do so:

> Even if the god wants to bless me,
> It will hardly do any good.

The majestic mountain we saw in the first scene has been transformed into a well-meaning but overly optimistic godling. Although he could accept the existence of a god of the mountain in the first scene, Han probably did not trust such oracles; awe at divinity has become a humorously cynical fiction.

The third and final example of concealment and revelation occurs as Han spends the night in the Buddhist temple on the summit of the mountain. During the night the light from moon and stars is "hidden faint through the clouds." But at dawn

> . . . gradually brightening, a cold winter sun
>   Rises in the east.

This revelation is the most enigmatic of the three, involving traditional Chinese light and sun symbolism. The warmth of sunlight implies a relation of kindness from those above to those below— nature's kindness to living things, the ruler's grace toward his subjects, a parent's love for his children, etc. If we were to treat this metaphor of the cold sun rising as allegorical, we might say that the emperor who recently ascended the throne (like the sun rising) will show no grace to Han Yü (will shed no warm light on him). Doubtless this is one aspect of the ominous image; however, the implications are probably broader—in general, a bleak future for the poet.

The first revelation in which the god unveiled the mountain was hopeful and majestic; the second, in which the god of the mountain promised him good fortune, was positive but unacceptable. This third revelation is ominous and grim. The god of the mountain did wish to bring Han Yü good fortune, but he is overridden by some mightier power of nature which seems to bear the poet only ill-will.

We can see still another level in the growth of Han Yü's landscape poetry in the following lines from "Accompanying Censor Tu, I Visit Two Temples on the West Bank of the Hsiang River: Staying the night there alone I write a poem on it and present it to Yang P'ing," also written on Han Yü's journey north to Chiang-ling.

> The mountain buildings are black with no moonlight,
> But fishermen's fires sparkle like dots of stars.
> How the wind moans tonight!
> Often fir and juniper wave in wind, rubbing together.
> I imagine that I am among huge waves,
> In my terror, dreams have become nightmares.
> Then calming, I think on Ch'ü Yüan's drowning, . . .[14]

The mountains, covered with trees waving in the wind, begin to seem like immense rolling waves, and Han feels he is lost in their midst. This immediately brings Ch'ü Yüan's drowning to the poet's mind. Three associations bring about Han Yü's comparison of himself to Ch'ü Yüan: first, Han is actually in the region where Ch'ü Yüan was supposed to have drowned himself; second, Han Yü views himself as a Ch'ü Yüan-like figure, wrongly banished from court by the lies of slanderers; and third, there is his fantasy of being lost amid the mountains/waves.

The mountains, the southern landscape of his exile, have been transformed into a metaphor for the dangers of his exile. This is a step beyond his personification of the landscape in the preceding poem; however, the mountain landscape is still not symbolic: by using "I imagine" Han keeps the mountains from actually being waves, nor does he develop the metaphor beyond this one aspect. Han Yü still maintains a barrier between fact and fiction, between narrative "truth" and metaphor.

The two following poems integrate the narrative of events and the symbolic landscape. In them we first see the landscape understood in

14. *HCLS*, p. 141.

terms of the structures of change of the organic universe. This is the
end toward which Han Yü's landscape poetry has been developing,
and once it is attained, the narrative of events begins to drop away,
for experience can be understood through the landscape itself.

HINDERED BY WINDS AT LAKE TUNG-T'ING: TO CHANG SHU

In November the Yin Essence is ascendant,
The north wind never ceases.
On the vast shores of Tung-t'ing
With you I bind our two boats together.
A foggy rain drizzles in the darkness,   5
Huge waves fling themselves at us in rage.
No dogs or chickens can be heard around us,
Provisions gone, with whom can we arrange for more?
Not even a step away from each other,
It's as dangerous as if blocked by mountains.   10
Of pure talk we can have our fill,[15]
But our daydreams have no way to reach their goal.
Our boys and girls howl right and left,
Only the moaning of hungry cries.
If I didn't feel elation at returning north,   15
How could I overcome the sorrow of these travels?
Beyond the clouds there is the bright sun,
Its cold winter light has gotten far, far away.
If I could order it to open and clear but for a moment,
Beyond this I would seek nothing.[16]   20

"Hindered by Winds at Lake Tung-t'ing" begins with a statement
of the cosmic condition: the moment in the cycle of the seasons, in
the weather, and in the pattern of Han Yü's experiences, is when the
Yin, the force of darkness, is on the rise. This cosmic state accounts
for the weather and for the sufferings of the travelers. The poem
focuses downward from the cosmic state (l. 1), through the state of
the weather that actualizes the cosmic state (l. 2), to the general
location (l. 3), and thence to the specific scene (l. 4). This focusing

15. "Pure talk" is *ch'ing-t'an*, a form of philosophical dialogue prevalent in the Chin
Dynasty, combining a Taoist proclivity to paradox with aristocratic elegance and wit.
Han is saying that all talk of going home is only clever speculation, devoid of concrete
reality or hope.
16. *HCLS*, p. 143.

not only gives the humans a sense of smallness and insignificance in relation to the world around them, it isolates them at the same time. Cut off from human society (l. 7), the two men try to find unity by tying their boats together, but the storm seeks to isolate them from each other (ll. 9–10).

In the final two couplets Han Yü binds together the real scene and the metaphorical world of the cosmic structure. The "cold winter sun" we saw in "Visiting a Temple on Mount Heng" appears again. The clouds block its brightness, the kindness it could show to Han, so that he only gets cold light, far in the distance. His longing to clear away the clouds is a desire to change the entire cosmic state. Again the allegorists, who would have the sun equal the ruler's grace and the clouds equal slanderers, catch only one aspect of the organic whole. In face of such real hardships, the dangers of the storm, Han does wish the weather to change for the better as well as the present "stormy" condition of his life. While the first part of the poem treats the narrative of experience as an actualization of the cosmic state, these last lines join the two together in the symbol of the cold winter sun, as Han finds the means to understand his experiences as well as his own kind of symbolism to express that understanding.

AT YÜEH-YANG TOWER: PARTING WITH TOU HSIANG

Within China's nine provinces, Lake Tung-t'ing,
In its largeness, to what would it yield?
To the south converge streams from a crowd of slopes,
In the north they gush out, how swift and free!
It amasses them into seven hundred miles,   5
Swallowing them in, each in a different form.
Since ancient times, never clearing,
Whirling around, mixing, with no place to go.
Parching winds agitate it each day,
Weird things hidden therein are tediously many.   10
High upward huge waves rise,
Even the sky's vault is too narrow and blocks them,
Wavecrests above Sung and Hua Mountains,
They spring upward like strong youths.
How its sounds echo and resound!—   15
The crash and rumble of thousands of chariots.
It seems as though the Yellow Emperor

Has come to these vast and empty spaces to play his music,[17]
Dragons appear as his chime-frames,
White-silken foam blows as his tent tassels.   20
Gods and demons, not of the human world,
Whose rhythms are especially wild and erratic.
When the bright Yang acts we see wondrous beauty,
When the dark Yin covers we feel deep melancholy.[18]
At dawn we passed by Yi-ch'un Harbor,   25
Then directly north, where there's no quay or embankment.
At night we tied up at Pa-ling Island,
Only then could we rest among clumps of waterplants.
The entire River of Stars lay submerged,[19]
So that, looking up and down, I was confused which was
    which.   30
The breakers raged endlessly,
Their din, like plates and jars knocking together.
The next morning I climbed Yüeh-yang Tower,
The dawn sun bright in shimmering brilliance.
Fei-lien, the wind-god, subdued his might,   35
So that, calm and clear, even the tiniest thread was still.
Then I saw a frozen green deep and transparent,
In which the images of things competed in artfulness.
Often porpoises jump out in play,
Then, startled, the waves will suddenly ripple.   40
The time is the first month of winter,
When into the earth's fissures shrink the cold floods.
Stepping forward I look down, pointing to the near shore,
I sit straining, but it's blurred and hard to see.
Purified, cleansed my soul awakes,   45
Brooding emotions are relieved and exhilarated.
You, my host, have been a friend since childhood,
Clasping hands we are happy and sad by turns—
Happy at my return from banishment,
And that we can see each other without ill effect.   50

17. The "T'ien-yün" chapter of the *Chuang-tzu* mentions that the Yellow Emperor held a great concert at Lake Tung-t'ing. In Han Yü's imagination Lake Tung-t'ing becomes that orchestra, its dragons forming the chime-frames; foam, the tent tassels.

18. Mori Kainan in his *Kanshi Kogi* suggests here that Yin and Yang refer to musical modes. They probably also refer to the weather and the cosmic state in general.

19. I.e. the Milky Way is reflected in the lake.

You held a banquet to which many guests came,
Where your sparkling, homemade wine was poured,
The goblets passed from hand to hand without halting,
The high frets of lutes sent off clear singing.
On the middle of platters they brought in oranges and
    chestnuts, 55
Flinging these away, we drank down meat broth.
My joy exhausted, grief rises in my heart,
Unable to forget the sweetness of youth.
I think on when I could first read long ago,
My desires, my ambitions sought to be chief among leaders. 60
I wasted a fortune learning the craft of dragon-butchering,
And in practicing this art I was on a rather high level.[20]
I loved only talent, was not selective about behavior,
So that in everything I handled I got vilified.
As for the cause of my leaving office two years ago— 65
That calamity was most undeserved.
The minister had selected me for my groundless reputation,
I was chosen to know the emperor's own entourage,
The evil were suspicious, fearing my accusations,
They let loose deceit and lies, driving me away. 70
Due to the new emperor's grace my post has been transferred,
I am forced into the company of military commanders.
I sigh that I am so slow and dull-witted,
Fearing only that I will fail in what is right and proper.
I think back on when I crossed the lake southward, 75
When I gladly would have been buried in a fish belly,[21]
A harsh journey which forced the wind-blown sails
As an arrow splitting into the high waves.
We could have overturned and sunk in an instant—
Who then would ever again consider my loyalty and
    forthrightness?[22] 80

20. The "Lieh-yü K'ou" chapter of the *Chuang-tzu* tells how Chu P'ing-man studied how to butcher dragons for three years, using all his family's wealth. In the end he had become quite accomplished in the art, but of course he had a certain difficulty putting it into practice. Probably Han is referring to studies in high statecraft, that he never got a chance to put into practice.

21. "Buried in a fish belly," as Ch'ü Yüan supposedly mused before drowning himself.

22. A pun is involved here. "Loyalty and forthrightness" is the primary meaning of *chung-keng*, but it can also be translated as "loyal fish-bones," absurd in any other case, but here a humorous reference to l. 76.

Truly I can be happy that I have returned alive,
And in the course have become chastened to subdue myself,
So that from this day onward
I have a rough idea of how success and ruin occur.
In most matters I have changed my former likes,   85
And my interests have taken on new directions.[23]
I vow to till a ten-acre field
And not try to get a minister's position.
My wife knows about silkworms and weaving,
My sons can already get provisions for me.   90
Soon I must hang up my cap and retire,
I want you to come visit me then, alive or dead.[24]

"At Yüeh-yang Tower" is perhaps the best narrative of Han Yü's exile. Lake Tung-t'ing is both the physical location of the poem and the central symbol in which the cosmic cycles are actualized. Conveniently absent-minded about the storm he has just experienced, Han Yü considers the calm beauty sailing northward and remembers the storm of his southward crossing, going into exile. Tung-t'ing reflects these cycles of mood and fortune:

When the bright Yang acts we see wondrous beauty,
When the dark Yin covers we feel deep melancholy.

The lake is a celestial orchestra, playing Yang music for moments of joy and Yin music for gloomy periods of the cycle.

The style of the poem is immensely varied. The calculated grandeur of the opening couplet, meant to lend the lake a special significance, is achieved by what may be called the "retentive style." The heavy use of topic-comment constructions creates strong caesurae and slows the lines down. The first couplet is literally:

As for Tung-t'ing, as for its being in the "nine provinces"
As for its size, who to it yields?
[Tung-t'ing Chiu-chou chien / chüeh ta shui yü jang.]

There are, of course, much simpler ways to say "Tung-t'ing is the largest lake in China." Han uses the archaic possessive pronoun *chüeh* to add to the dignity, as well as the periphrasis "as for its size,

23. With no little cynicism Han Yü is saying in this and the preceding lines that he will never again get himself into trouble by being too forthright.
24. *HCLS*, p. 144.

who to it yields?" It is particularly characteristic that in creating a periphrasis for "largest" Han uses this active, verbal construction which implies a tensional, competitive relation.

After a lively description of the lake's waters, showing Han Yü's growing penchant for hyperbole, Han begins his description of his journey north across the lake. The playful hyperbole that the lake reflects the heavens so clearly he can't tell which is up and which is down has a more serious implication: Han is reinforcing the idea of the lake as a reflection and microcosm of the cosmic state. The symbolic lake and the real lake are one. Later on Yüeh-yang Tower, as he faces the calmness and clarity of the lake scene, he himself is purified and calmed; as the lake was previously almost the instrument of his destruction, so it has now become the instrument of his regeneration.

Tou's banquet and the music-making echoes the concert of the Yellow Emperor earlier in the poem, still another way in which the lake reflects human experience. As Han meditates on the storm he met on the southward crossing of the lake, the tortured syntax reflects the harsh state of his emotions at the time:

> Harsh journey//force wind sails
> Split arrow//enter high waves
>
> [ll. 77–78]

In the first line the logical order is turned around: the wind forced the sails and made the journey a harsh one, the journey didn't force the sails which were (by chance) full of wind. In the second line "splitting" is the effect of the arrow (boat) entering the waves, but it is used to modify the subject (the usual way one handles such a construction is to put the two verbs together, the result after the cause, i.e. "enter-split").

Han has organized the poem well: first, he suggests that Tung-t'ing is the microcosm of change; then he recounts his recent positive experiences with the lake (remembering that he has omitted the storm described in the preceding poem); next, he thinks back on the storm he experienced during his trip southward. From these experiences he has learned his lesson:

> So that from this day onward
> I have a rough idea of how success and ruin occur.

Through the cosmic pattern revealed to him in Lake Tung-t'ing, Han has learned the fate of those who become involved in politics. He makes the appropriate traditional response, vowing to withdraw from government service and become a farmer (a response we need not take too seriously in his case). But it is characteristic of Han's utilitarian Confucianism that he vows to become a farmer rather than a hermit.

Han Yü is not known to us primarily for his accomplishments in regulated verse, although in the last years of his life these accomplishments were considerable. During the 790s, when the tendencies toward reform were strongest, Han Yü's poetry was almost exclusively "old-style" verse. He seems then to have associated regulated verse with its common function as occasional poetry demanded by polite society at social gatherings and partings. In the one regulated verse we are certain Han wrote in the 790s, "Seeing Off Chü Wen-chen," he makes the point in the preface to the poem, that he was ordered to write it by Tung Chin.[25]

Han Yü was one of the first admirers of Tu Fu after his death, and Tu Fu's regulated verse is equal, if not superior, to his "old-style" verse. Echoes of Tu Fu are noticeable in Han's narratives of his stay in Hsu-chou and the exile period. Han Yü again turns to the model of Tu Fu when beginning to write personal regulated verse. However, during this period Han Yü's talent is too nervous and violent, too energetic, to stay within the bonds of restraint that regulated verse style imposes. In the following "old-style" verse, written on his journey south to Yang-shan, we see Han Yü trying to assume the manner of Tu Fu.

T'UNG-KUAN GORGE

Mid-March in the Southland,
Things of spring have already gotten fewer.
I tie my boat between mountain and river,
Sit early in the morning, listen to all the birds.
Overnight clouds still holding back their splendor,   5
Until the dawn sun suddenly rises with daybreak.
Being a traveler I am moved by their singing together,
A bound fugitive, I brood on how they soar lightly upward.
A long time now my tears have flowed scattering,

25. *HCLS*, p. 21.

Twisting, turning thoughts encircle me still more.   10
Go on then! Don't be like this!
Only when covered in my coffin will the matter be decided.[26]

Here we can recognize one of Tu Fu's favorite tropes, nature's indifference to human affairs, her continuing to flourish in spite of human troubles. The splendor of the dawn (nature's light of kindness) and the joy of the birds contrast with his own state of exile. His loneliness as a traveler contrasts with the birds singing together; his bound state (i.e. bound in government service and to the expiation of his guilt in exile) contrasts with their freedom to "soar lightly upward." Parallelism is used in the third, fourth, and fifth couplets, echoing the required parallelism in the middle two couplets of a regulated verse. The last couplet with its harsh exclamations is more reminiscent of Meng Chiao's poems on his failure than the controlled sorrow of Tu Fu; yet the last line here is taken almost verbatim from Tu Fu. Han Yü says, "*kai kuan shih nai liao*," to Tu Fu's "*kai kuan shih tse yi*," Han Yü's *nai liao* ("only then finished") being somewhat stronger than Tu Fu's *tse yi* ("then ended"). Tu Fu's line is from his "Singing My Feelings While Going From the Capital to Feng-hsien," which begins as follows:

There is a commoner from Tu-ling,
Growing old, how silly his ambitions.
His youthful vows were so stupid—
To become the ilk of Chi and Hsieh.
Now immobilized, I am ruined,   5
Yet, white-haired, I accept this suffering,
For, covered in my coffin, the matter will be determined,
Though always I hope my desire will be fulfilled. . . .[27]

The two poets' uses of this line are altogether different. To Han Yü it is better, suggesting that he will surely die in his exile, but that then he will be vindicated of his guilt (and it will be too late for the government to have his services); to Tu Fu the line means resignation and hope, that only time will tell whether he has achieved the greatness he longs for. In Tu Fu's lines the final determination is left in doubt (which it is not in Han Yü's poem), while Han Yü's exploits more fully the ambiguity of "then finished," referring to his vindication,

26. *HCLS*, p. 88.   27. *CTS*, c. 216, p. 2265.

his sentence of exile (finished by death), and his life. The greatest contrast, however, lies between the directness of Han Yü and the subtle balance of self-mockery, pathetic hope, and resignation in the passage from Tu Fu.

The contrast between the two following poems can give us some idea of why Han Yü cannot fully exploit regulated verse at this stage of his work.

VIRGIN GORGE

The river winds, the gorge restrains, spring's torrents wild,
Thundering wind does battle here, fish and dragons flee.
Cascades rumble, shooting into the water-god's city,
In one gush cloudlike billows are rolled a hundred miles,
Make the boat quaver and shake the stones
　　　that crack like a million tiles,   5
So close that my life seems light as a swan's feather.[28]

Though not a regulated verse, there is much in this fine little poem that resembles one: characteristic of regulated verse is the concise, objective description of a scene to which the poet responds emotionally in the last couplet. Likewise, the absence of particles, personal pronouns, and prose constructions is similar to regulated verse style. On the other hand, regulated verse has a particular tone, a formal balance and decorum, which goes against the violent energy of this poem. The disorder of the river in the gorge would be violated by the contrapuntal *order* of regulated verse. The strength of this poem lies in the contrast between the fragility of human life and the violent power of nature, a contrast of extremes that cannot reside comfortably in too balanced a form.

Fortunately, we have a regulated verse of about the same time on a similar subject. In it we can see what the regulated verse genre and the conventional tone that goes along with it can do to the power of nature.

SPENDING THE NIGHT AT DRAGONPALACE RAPIDS

Vast, wild, and rolling waters,
The more you repress the rapids' sound, the more it wells.
The rushing current seems stirred lightning,
The frightening waves are like floating frost.

28. *HCLS*, p. 89.

Waking from dream, a halo around my lamp,   5
At night's end when the rain brings on the cold.
What were the words it spoke until dawn?—
Half were of longing for home.[29]

In this poem the power of the rapids is beautiful rather than
awesome. In the first couplet Han is trying hard to suggest the power
of the gorges—but contrast "The river winds, the gorge restrains,
spring's torrents wild," from the preceding poem, in which the river
and gorge are locked in a struggle, to "The rushing current seems
stirred lightning, / The frightening waves are like floating frost."
Lightning describes the river's speed, while frost describes the whitecaps on the waves; these are the elements of the rapids' violent power,
but they lack the force of the simpler line from "Virgin Gorge." The
beautiful melancholy of the second half of the poem totally under-
cuts the power Han tried to suggest in the first couplet. Perhaps, as
they are sometimes interpreted, the words "spoke until dawn" are
those of Han Yü himself or of a companion, but I think, rather, that
it is the sound of the rapids which is speaking to him. The mighty
rapids have become a gentle friend, whispering to the poet of home.

The development of the landscape within the narrative from an
incidental position to that of a central symbol is paralleled by the
appearance of purely descriptive poems in which the description is
used for its own sake, playfully and wittily. In style, the growth of
descriptive passages in the narrative and the appearance of purely
descriptive poems are related to Han's early experiments in regulated
verse. The heavy use of particles, pronouns, and prose constructions
which characterized Han's earlier poetry is difficult, if not clearly
impossible, in the dense symmetrical parallelism of regulated verse.
But as the earlier prosaized style lent itself to reasoning, persuasion,
and narrative, the denser style of regulated verse lends itself to description. Furthermore, in Han's descriptive verse we see a change
from the hypotactic style of his earlier poetry to a paratactic one.

We first saw this delight in description in "Pien and Ssu Flow Together," where it was justified by the didactic assumptions of the
submerged *fu* form. In the following poem such didactic assumptions
are no longer present, and the primary function the poem serves is
to dispel the poet's melancholy by his delight in both the scene and

29. *HCLS*, p. 115.

in writing the verse. It is, however, possible to see hidden in the
description of the fishes' destruction a metaphor for his own political
ruin and that of his friend Chang Shu. It is significant that this first
purely descriptive poem is a long, regulated verse, a *p'ai-lü*. It was
written while Han was in Yang-shan.

FISH-SPEARING: TO SUMMON CHANG SHU

We spear fish when spring's shores are widest,
The urge to do this comes at midnight,
When great torches burn like noontime,
And long boats are bound to resemble a bridge.
Peering into the depths you can count the sands,   5
Gently rowing forward—not a tremor in the water.
From beneath the spear-blade how can they escape?
Among the waves some leap up.
When it strikes their scales, I pity the brocade shattered,
When it hits an eye, I am shocked at the pearl's melting.   10
Confused by fires, they flee by coming around nearer,
Then startled by men, they go suddenly far off.
Competing for the most, our hearts grow attentive,
When one gets a prize specimen, others shout their approval.
Since the deep pools are empty, we know few survive,   15
The boats are level with the water, so we realize the
    abundance of the catch.
Their crossed heads seem to be gathering to the bait,
Their ranged skulls are as though on the same stringer.
Though their hearts are loving, moistening each other with
    saliva,[30]
Their chance to mount Dragon Gate is far away.[31]   20
A fish big enough to fill a wagon was a deceiving legend,[32]
But there's enough to feed the dogs—it will be proven this
    morning.

30. *Chuang-tzu*, "Ta-tsung-shih": "When streams dry up, and fish are together on dry
land, they breathe on one another for wetness, and moisten each other with saliva."
31. Legend had it that if fish made their way up the Yellow River to Dragon Gate
Mountain and over the falls there, they changed into dragons. The purpose of the legend
is to account for a spawning run. This couplet can be paraphrased: "Although they try
to preserve each other, having been caught, by moistening one another, they have no
chance to survive and will never become dragons."
32. This is the traditional Chinese "big fish" story; it is mentioned in the *Lieh-tzu* and
K'ung-tsung-tzu.

Bloody waves curdle, still bubbling up,
A carrion smell in the wind blows stronger the farther it goes.
Covering the river, a veiling mist, 25
Reflections of sweeping oars are now lonely.[33]
The otters go away, sad that they've nothing to eat,
The dragon has gone off, fearing lest the blaze reveal him.
If one seeks to "go to T'ang," the name is wrong,[34]
If it's "angling in the Wei," the days will pass in vain.[35] 30
The wandering poet is startled, describes it in verse,
Before the boat-poler happily finishes his song.
As they make filets, I long for my friends,[36]
Watching the people's joy, I remember my colleagues.
This of itself can throw off the bonds of melancholy, 35
Why need I forcibly question an owl?[37]

In Han Yü's early poetry metaphors were used only sparingly, if
at all, and a plain, direct style was sought rather than elegance. Here
the situation is reversed. There is a residual hint of narrative and
philosophical meditation, but clearly the center of interest in the
poem is the poet's delight in clever description. Antithetical parallelism and various other poetic devices from the conventions of
regulated verse give the poem a tone we have not seen before in Han
Yü's work.

The function of the metaphor in the following lines is as purely
decorative hyperbole to intensify the brightness of the torches and to
make the boats seem more numerous:

33. I.e. the other boats have disappeared.

34. An excellent example of the flippant use to which classical allusion can be put. *Tso-
chuan*, Yin, V: "The duke went to T'ang to see the fish[ermen]." Since there are no fish
left in the river after the spear-fishing, to invoke this ancient example would be a mistake.

35. King Wen of Chou met his minister Lu Shang as the latter was fishing in the Wei
River. Han's use of allusion is cleverer here: on the one hand, he is saying that since there
are no fish left in the river, angling is pointless, but he is also suggesting that Yang-shan is
no place to await recognition by his ruler.

36. Although this may simply be an image of conviviality, there is possibly a pun here
on Middle Chinese *kuai°*, "fish filet," and *ruai°*, "meeting," the former bringing to mind
the latter, meaning that Han longs for his friends.

37. The Han writer, Chia Yi, was assigned as a tutor to a Han prince in Ch'ang-sha (in
Han times, the barbarian south), a post equivalent to exile. During this exile Chia wrote
the "Owl Fu" in which he questioned the wordings of fate. Han Yü is suggesting here that
by taking pleasure in such things as spear-fishing, he can dispel the depression of exile that
affected Chia Yi. *HCLS*, p. 100.

> Great torches burn like noontime,
> And long boats are bound to resemble a bridge.

Even more hyperbolic is the couplet following the one above, in which the water is so clear "you can count the sands," and the boats sail so smoothly there's "not a tremor in the water." In addition to decorative hyperbole, we find preciousness, a trait Han would have scorned in his early poetry, but which assumes greater importance in the poetry after his exile.

> When it strikes their scales, I pity the brocade shattered,
> When it hits an eye, I am shocked at the pearl's melting.

This strange blend of violence and delicate beauty is characteristic of Han's later poetry. The description of a fish eye struck by a spear as a "pearl's melting" is neither expected nor decorous.

Another device from regulated verse is the evidence trope, which follows the pattern: "from x we know y."

> Since the deep pools are empty, we know few survived,
> The boats are level with the water, so we realize the
>   abundance of the catch.

This trope is generally used to show the sensitivity of the poet's powers of observation rather than to boast of his deductive powers. Here, there are elaborate and imaginative metaphors, such as comparing the fish-heads stacked together in the boat to their gathering round the bait. There are also elegant periphrases such as: "Reflections of sweeping oars are now lonely," which simply means that most of the boats have gone back to shore. Furthermore, there is the witty use of erudite allusions (ll. 19, 21, 29–30). The significance of these devices lies in contrast with the bareness of Han Yü's early poetry. Indirect means of expression have overcome direct ones, while the poetic interest lies in the beauty and cleverness of the style and metaphors rather than in the "message."

In the next chapter we shall see this style perfected in the linked verses. Pure delight in descriptive show, the epideictic mode, is essential to the *fu*, and of the several borrowings Han Yü made from fu technique, the epideictic mode is probably the most important. The fu is a genre whose beauty lies largely on the surface, in style and structure, much as the *shih* (poetry, either "old-style" or regulated) is introspective. Han Yü, an outward poet, would naturally come to exploit the epideictic style; but since the vitality of the fu as a genre died out long before the Mid-T'ang, Han recreates many fu effects in the shih. In contrast to the Han poet Yang Hsiung, mentioned earlier, who moved from the epideictic to the didactic, Han Yü is moving from the didactic to the epideictic.

7

The Linked Verses: 806

With the succession of Hsien-tsung to the throne in 806, in late summer Han Yü was recalled to the capital from Chiang-ling, to take up the post of professor in the State Academy (*kuo-tzu po-shih*). In Ch'ang-an, Han Yü was reunited with his old friends Meng Chiao and Chang Chi. The post was not a demanding one, and Han Yü found himself with more leisure to devote himself to poetry. In 807 when political enemies again became a threat, Han Yü, having been "chastened to subdue himself," requested and received a teaching position in the branch of the State Academy in Lo-yang, the cultural capital of the empire.

The autumn and winter of 806 was a period of great poetic activity for Han Yü and an important year in the development of his own poetry and that of his friend Meng Chiao. The focus of the changes that occurred in their poetry during those months can be seen in the linked verses they composed together.

Unlike its Japanese counterpart, the *renga,* the Chinese linked verse or *lien-chü* is an ill-defined genre, having no limitations other than being a poem in which two or more poets take part. Traditionally seen as evolving from the "Po-liang T'ai" verse of the Han Dynasty,[1] the first true linked verse that has survived was composed by the Chin Dynasty poet Chia Ch'ung and his wife.[2] Although there are linked verses attributed to Li Po and Tu Fu, the real appearance of the linked verse in the T'ang Dynasty is in the hands of Yen Chench'ing, a friend of Chiao-jan. Chiao-jan took part in several of Yen's linked verses, and it is quite possible that Meng Chiao's association with Chiao-jan and his friends is one of the factors that led Meng

1. Ting Fu-pao, ed., *Ch'üan Han Shih,* in Ting Fu-pao, ed., *Ch'üan Han San-kuo Chin Nan-pei-ch'ao Shih* (1916; reprint, Taipei: Yi-wen, n.d.), p. 48.
2. Ibid., p. 415.

Chiao and Han Yü to compose linked verses themselves. However, Yen Chen-ch'ing's linked verses are not of much artistic value, and it was Han Yü and Meng Chiao who first exploited the full possibilities of the genre and gave the linked verse its witty, hyperbolic tone, which it retained in its subsequent development.

The length and complexity of Han Yü's and Meng Chiao's linked verses vary from the simple four lines of "So-cha Valley Linked Verse"—

> *HY*   From time to time the gurgle of the frozen creek ceases,
>   It's then that the wind raises high the oaks.
> *MC*   If this place doesn't break the heart,
>   Then I know for certain there's no place that does.[3]

—to the expansive three-hundred-and-six lines of "South of the City." Excluding "South of the City," the form of these linked verses consists of each poet composing one or more couplets to suit his inspiration and the other(s) responding with a roughly similar number of couplets. This series of responses continues until their inspiration ends.

The progression of Han's and Meng's linked verses through the late summer, autumn, and winter of 806 forms an excellent record of the changes that were then taking place in their poetry. Besides recording the change, there is little doubt that the linked verses themselves had a substantial influence on the change. The genre itself has a built-in tendency toward wit and hyperbole, preciousness, and violation of all norms of poetic restraint. Competition, the heart of the linked verse, focuses the poet's attention on the imaginative use of language and imagery rather than on the expression of emotion or the development of an idea. Such competition renders the verse epideictic. If these linked verses lack depth, they more than make up for it in inventive genius. However, when we consider the impact of this genre on the later poetry of our two poets, we see that the imaginative language and imagery of the linked verses is still present in more intellectually involved and emotionally deeper poems. The effect of the linked verse style can also be felt strongly in the poetry of the followers of Han and Meng.

In judging the linked verse as a genre, we must keep in mind that certain inherent qualities, predetermined by the nature of the genre

3. *HCLS*, p. 295.

itself, separate it from ordinary poetry. First, it is dialectical, based on response. Response is the only form of continuity, even in the most descriptive of the linked verses. In ordinary poetry a pattern of development is determined by the totality of the poem; individual lines and couplets ideally operate in relation to that totality. In the linked verse, on the other hand, any given line or couplet is related only to the couplet which precedes it or, at best, to the entire poem up to that point. Thus the structure of the linked verse is unique in that we do not assume it knows where it is going when it begins. The verse moves erratically from one aspect of its subject to another, and is meant to be considered as a series of responses rather than as a unified whole.

Second, linked verse is kinetic verse, poetry in action. We do not know if these verses were polished up later, and if so, to what extent; however, we may say at the very least that they are presented *as though* they were spontaneous (actually, it does not seem that these verses were altered in any way). Linked verses are not complete in themselves; rather, they are records of specific performances. They are not, moreover, records in the sense that a folk epic or ballad is a record of a performance. The linked verse is competitive innovation rather than an individual re-creation of a common story using common devices; it is an event, and its text, only the record of an event. Reading it, we feel that the poets are speaking to each other rather than to a reading audience, and thus we are constantly forced to recognize the verse as a specific performance.

The linked verses of the late summer of 806 show, in the individuated styles of Han Yü and Meng Chiao, continuity with their earlier styles. There can be no doubt that Meng Chiao wrote:

> We know your swordlike heart hasn't died,
> And your poetic thoughts still jut up solitary.
>
> ["Reunion," ll. 5–6]

Here is the moral metaphor of the "sword [like] heart" and a characteristic description of the intangible "poetic thoughts" in tangible terms—"jutting up solitary." Likewise, we can see the intellectual gymnastics and prosaic style of Han Yü in:

> Thinking on these hardships I must try hard to remember them,

> But I regret how easy it was, so I must not lightly follow
> those tracks again.
>
> ["Reunion," ll. 11–12]

There are no concrete nouns in the Chinese of this couplet, and it would require a paragraph of paraphrase for the reader to understand what this sophistry refers to. This is not Han Yü's developing descriptive style, but rather the ethical, intellectual style of his earlier poetry. The verse is from the summer of 806; by winter a strange phenomenon has taken place: not only are the linked verse styles of Han Yü and Meng Chiao indistinguishable, but this common style is different from the earlier styles of either of the two poets. In describing a battle, can we distinguish

> Fire comes out—the point that stirred it reeks of gore,
> Blood drifts down—feet that step on it slip.

from

> The river is reversed—whales and dolphins boil up,
> The mountain shakes—wildcats and weasels smash them.

"Fire" in the first of these couplets refers either to blood or to the sparks from a sword striking armor. The second couplet describes the imperial army surging to attack rebels. Both couplets are from "The Campaign Against Shu," written in the winter of 806; the first couplet is by Han Yü and the second, by Meng Chiao.

This joint style does have its antecedents in the earlier styles of both poets. We have seen hyperbolic description in some of Han Yü's exile poems, while bizarre, imaginative metaphor was present in Meng Chiao's poetry of the late 790s and early 800s. In the linked verses these tendencies have been intensified and gradually brought together. After 806 the styles of the two poets diverge again, but both bear the influence of the linked verses.

The result of this change is best summed up in the following line of Meng Chiao's from "Letting the Cool Air In," in which he shows he is aware both that a change has taken place and of its direction: "In *laboring for the unusual* we are pleased with a new form."[4] "Laboring for the unusual" is the spirit of the decade that follows. The competitive element in the linked verse, the attempt to "outdo"

4. *HCLS*, p. 191.

each other, creates this "laboring for the unusual." Wit and imagination have become dominant over "message." Their desire is to
delight, dazzle, and show their wit and creative talent. Contrast
Han Yü's moral stance in "Poem of Hsieh Tzu-jan"—"How could
what I say be vapid, elegant verse?"—with the magnificent praise
of poetry in "South of the City" (ll. 95–106):

HY   Like the valiants of Shu—Li Po and Tu Fu—they excelled,
MC   Their mountain-moving powers crashed and rumbled like
          the thunder chariot.
         Their mighty lines set rolling the mystic forces of creation,
HY   Their high diction crashed booming over the empyrean.
         The tips of their brushes caused heat and cold to interchange,
MC   The aid of the gods made their goblets overflow.
         Both immense and infinitesimal followed their cycles,
HY   Their voices, likewise, rose either rushing or sluggish.
         They outdid the flowers, nibbling the powdery stamens,
MC   Pared threads to string pearly cherries.
         Their broidered diction was washed in clearweather snow,
HY   Their charming phrases cheeped like fledgling orioles.[5]

The two poets are praising the grandeur and subtlety of poetry, with
diction appropriate to each. Though there need be no contradiction
between poetic imagination and morality, there is no doubt that
there has been a change of emphasis in Han Yü's and Meng Chiao's
poetry.

   With the shift toward wit and imagination came a complementary
abandonment of personal themes. Each of the linked verses is less
personal than the one which precedes it, for the genre is less a means
of self-expression than a means to show off one's talents. Teasing and
joking, witty repartee, come to intrude on personal notes. Thus in
"South of the City" (ll. 289–90), when Meng Chiao refers to Han
Yü's exile in the South: "In vain you offered libations to Ch'ü
Yüan's stinking reputation" (referring to Ch'ü Yüan's "sinful"
choice of suicide over enduring his suffering and waiting for a better
ruler), Han Yü responds humorously: "No—I'll live out my natural
span and long in vain for P'eng."[6] Ninth-century intellectual jokes
lose all their immediacy and humor through the differences of time,
language, and culture. "P'eng" may refer to P'eng Hsien, as at the

5. *HCLS*, p. 219.   6. *HCLS*, p. 227.

end of the *Li Sao* where Ch'ü Yüan says: "I shall go where P'eng Hsien dwells." P'eng Hsien was traditionally thought to be a loyal minister of the Yin Dynasty who drowned himself when he was slandered. Thus Ch'ü Yüan is saying he will drown himself.

On the other hand, especially in conjunction with the phrase "natural span," *t'ien-nien* (from the *Chuang-tzu*), "P'eng" may also refer to P'eng Tsu, who is mentioned in the first chapter of the *Chuang-tzu*: "Now P'eng Tsu is especially known for his longevity." Thus by the ambiguity of "P'eng," Han Yü is playfully responding in two ways. First, "I'll live out my natural span of years and in vain (because I have no intention of commiting suicide) admire P'eng Hsien for the courage he showed in committing suicide; Ch'ü Yüan's admiration, on the contrary, was not in vain." The second response is: I'll live out my natural span, and what's more, I'll even long for the longevity of a P'eng Tsu, although such longing will be in vain since I will never have such a long life as he had." Han Yü has cleverly twisted Meng Chiao's line into an ambiguous and humorous rebuttal.

As can be seen from some of the passages quoted above, there is a strong element of pure linguistic bravado in these verses. This increases as the year progresses. The verses abound in archaisms, coined phrases, and obsolete usages; frequently, violent controversy has been stirred up between the commentators as to the meanings of certain phrases, and therefore several instances arise when I am less than sure about the translation. Such linguistic bravado is closely related to the epideictic *fu* style, which we have noted Han Yü used earlier with some success.

"Reunion," by Han Yü, Meng Chiao, Chang Chi, and Chang Ch'e, is the earliest and the weakest of the linked verses.[7] Not only is the description flat, but the links between the verses are flimsy or obvious. It is easy to see that the greatest potential for rapport exists between Han Yü and Meng Chiao. Chang Ch'e cannot possibly compete with Han and Meng, and even Chang Chi, an excellent poet in his own right, has some trouble. In this verse Han Yü's and Meng Chiao's styles are quite distinct, but there are the incipient elements of teasing, wit, allusiveness, word-coining, precious description, and lines designed to shock the reader. Yet as a whole, this

7. *HCLS*, p. 185.

verse is not successful; the total rapport and immediate responsive-
ness that characterize the best linked verses have not yet developed,
and instead there is a tendency to mutual compliment and self-
deprecation.

A second linked verse of the late summer of 806, "Spending the
Night Together," shows many of the same characteristics as "Reunion," and as poetry it has even less to commend itself. Its only
bright spot is the last couplet by Meng Chiao:

> If you want to know the mutual joy of our hearts—
> It's a double cocoon spinning out floss together.[8]

As a metaphor for the composition of a linked verse this is particularly effective: the two poets are bound closely together, spinning out
distinct but intertwining threads to form a single strand. This is an
extension of the conventional metaphor for subtlety of poetic structure.

"Letting the Cool Air In" represents an intermediary stage between the early linked verses and those of autumn and winter of 806.
We can see the new style in parts of this verse, but the two poets Han
Yü and Meng Chiao are not yet able to work in perfect harmony.
Each poet displays his virtuosity in an extended passage, thus dim-
inishing the number of reponses necessary to give a linked verse
vitality.

LETTING THE COOL AIR IN

MC   We whistle in turns to get a distant breeze,
       That faintly will bring autumn's first month closer.

Whistling is a conventional response to excessive heat, but Meng
turns the convention around, saying they are whistling to get a
breeze and bring autumn closer.

HY   The Metallic Element is weak, its spirit still low,
       As the Fire Element ages, the atmosphere gets even
          muggier.
       Gleaming, a blaze of light flows,   5
       Up aloft, high cirrus clouds come out.

Han Yü responds to Meng Chiao's balance between present heat and

8. *HCLS*, p. 192.

hope of oncoming autumn by traditional seasonal symbolism. Metal is the symbolic element of autumn; fire, that of summer. Han discusses the interplay between these two elements, imposing intellectual order on the weather. The light comes from the sun, upon which high clouds are encroaching. Thus the clouds bearing autumn's rain are symbolically about to overcome the sun, the fire element representative of summer.

MC   These flashed-upon reds startle slithering,
        And hardened crimsons jut up like mountains.
        Eyeing the forests I fear they'll burst into flame,
        Earing the well I only remember its gurgle.   10
        Looking up I fear the Interweaving of Cosmic Forces
           will be lost,
        And that, untimely, icy hail will form.
        Since one gets even thirstier than the man who changed
           into Teng Forest,
        Rushing to the river is a matter of perfect ingenuousness.
        Alas, who is he who suffered sunstroke on the road?   15
        What joy to him who strikes the *shang* mode!
        Oh, to be washed by streaming rains—
        Moved by them the phoenix would sing.
        If this excellent wish is not fulfilled,
        My formerly hopeful heart will be far, far away.   20
        On the cool steps we sit a thousand times,
        And clasp cold rings of jade again and again.
        Then, however, my troubled heart grows alert,
        And again my high spirits are soaring.

With this passage we enter the real world of the linked verse. Unfortunately, it requires a certain amount of explanation to make it intelligible.

Lines 7–8: Though some commentators believe that the "flash" is lightning, and that the dragonlike "slithering" refers to the lightning bolt itself, I think, rather, that this describes the clouds flashing red in the sunlight, their forms seeming like slithering dragons. The mountains of "hardened crimson" are probably cumulus clouds upon which the sun is shining. These lines respond to Han Yü's preceding descriptive couplet. The redness of the clouds suggests the fire element of summer, but their presence suggests precipitation, looking forward to the autumn rains. It is this contradiction which portends the cosmic imbalance feared in line eleven.

Lines 9–10: These are hyperboles about the heat: it is so hot that the forest will burst into flame and the water in the well is only a lingering memory. Using "eye" and "ear" as verbs does have precedents, but these are comparatively rare. The verbalized nouns add to the shock value of the couplet, already bizarre because of the hyperbole.

Lines 11–12: The "Interweaving of Cosmic Forces," *chiao-t'ai*, is a phrase used in the discussion of the T'ai hexagram in the *Yi-ching*; it means the interweaving and balance of the male and female principles of Heaven and Earth. Meng Chiao is using it here to describe the balance of heat and cold; if the balance is lost, hail will form.

Lines 13–14: This refers to a story from the third section of the "T'ang-wen" chapter of the Lieh-tzu:

> K'ua-fu couldn't measure his own powers and wanted to follow the sun's light. He followed it to the point where the sun sinks into its abyss in the west. But he got thirsty and wanted something to drink, so he went and drank up the Yellow and Wei Rivers. When these weren't enough, he was about to go north to drink up the great Marsh. He never made it; he died of thirst on the road. He cast away his staff, and being soaked by the oils of his corpse, it grew into Teng Forest.

The hyperbole in the next line is more difficult and even cleverer. The phrase "a matter of perfect ingenuousness," *yi-ch'üeh*, here probably suggests that the people were so thirsty they cast off all restraint and rushed madly to the river. The phrase is a lofty, archaic allusion to the second part of the "T'an-kung" chapter of the *Book of Rites*, where Confucius is reputed to have said: "The Yin [Shang] Dynasty was too ingenuous (*yi-ch'üeh*); I follow Chou." The couplet thus may be paraphrased: "Since it is so hot that one gets even thirstier than K'ua-fu did, people display excessive simplicity of nature by rushing to the river to get something to drink." I hope that through my extended commentary the reader can see the erudite and burlesque humor of such passages.

Lines 15–16: Line fifteen has several possible *loci classici*, but the point is simple—another level of suffering caused by the heat. Line sixteen alludes to the tenth section of the "T'ang-wen" chapter of the *Lieh-tzu*, in which we read how the ancient lutanist Shih-wen summoned a cool wind by striking the *shang* musical mode in order to show his mastery of the instrument. The *shang* mode is associated with autumn.

Lines 17–18: Here Meng Chiao is alluding to the *Han-shih Wai-chuan*:

> The Old Man of Heaven answered the Yellow Emperor saying, "The phoenix rises stirring the eight winds; when his spirit responds to the seasonal rains, he is stirred by the streaming and sings."

Since the appearance of the phoenix is associated with the Confucian millennium, the advent of the sage-king, the coming of autumn's rain assumes almost apocalyptic importance.

Lines 19–24: The sequence of events here is not altogether clear, but it seems that sitting on the steps, clasping the rings, is a temporary solution to the heat. However, Meng has exaggerated the heat so much in the preceding lines that these lines are particularly ineffective.

HY The dragon dives, its scales boiled terribly,
   Cows pant, their horns frightfully burned.
   Cicadas suffer, their chirps grow melancholy,
   Ravens caw, hungry but not eating.
   By day the eating table is laden with flies,
   By night mosquitoes are sloshed in flesh's blood.   30
   Unable to stand it I've taken off my single linen robe,
   Tired, I still clasp the long fan.
   Fortunately I have here a good friend,
   Being in this place he is shaded by splendid rafters.
   Green and sparkling a striped mat is rolled out,   35
   And the sweet gourd is cleansed until washed pure.
   The great walls are clear and spacious,
   On them ancient paintings, strange polychromes.
   Chill as though thou wert come to the Gates of Cold,
   Glistening white like gathered pieces of jade.   40
   I cleared away a wide place to invite a fresh breeze,
   And drew from cold waters to steep the fragrant rice.
   For fruits in a basket I have the choicest of the grove,

And offer bird eggs as delicacies on the plate.
In this empty hall I happily detain you,   45
And am ashamed at the paltriness of my poor provisions.

Han Yü, rising to the challenge, takes his turn at hyperbolically describing the heat outside, then the cool within. The only reference that needs explaining is the "Gates of Cold," meaning simply the extreme north. There is a certain stylistic similarity between this passage and the preceding one by Meng Chiao; however, some differences should be pointed out. Han Yü's humor is not as elaborate as Meng Chiao's; he simply describes cows with burned horns and boiled dragons. Han prefers the tangible objects of everyday life—the room, his robe, a fan, rice, fruit, etc.; Meng Chiao tends to concentrate on his own feelings (ll. 17–20, 23–24). One prose expression occurs in Han Yü's passage, and archaisms and rare words abound. In general, Han Yü's style is stranger, while Meng Chiao is most inventive in his metaphors.

I think we can feel the playfulness of these two passages. Unlike in earlier linked verses where the participants simply compliment and defer to one another, here the poets are amusing themselves in a sophisticated, competitive game. From the didactic concerns of the early 790s when every line had to serve a pedagogic purpose, we have swung to the opposite extreme where poetry has no pretense to deep significance but is simply inventive play.

MC   You take great pains to encourage me to eat,
Your attendants are even more whetted and honed.
They have courage to spare as though just off some
    frostwhite whetstone,
Struggling to advance, their icy pikes are gleaming.   50
Then faintly a sound in the roots of the grasses,
Of which our poetic senses were early aware.
Stirred by our aging, we grieved how we'd changed from
    before,
But in laboring for the unusual we are pleased with a
    new form.
Who would say that I was an old man rejected by
    friends,   55
Since I still learn from their hearts?
One dares not lean on a high balcony,

And fears that a rotten table will collapse if one rests on it.
It is hard to advance on the road to the blue clouds,
And the feet of the yellow crane are still fettered.   60
Not yet can you drink from those deep streams,
So you stand, hindered, calling to fragrant blossoms.

Lines 47–52: Meng Chiao is describing the importuning eagerness of Han Yü's servants to feed them, in response to Han's description of food in the preceding passage. The advance of the food-bearers against Meng is compared to the phalanx of a courageous army. The imagery of sharp weapons ("ground and honed," the whetstone, and the pikes) refers both to the servants' attitude and to the eating utensils they wield. "Frosty white" to describe the gleam of metal, echoes the coolness of the food suggested in Han's passage and anticipates the cool breeze that is coming. When the breeze does come, it is first noticed by a rustle in the grass, indicating the sensitivity of observation of the two poets. The line may also be translated: "It was early awakened by our poetic feelings" (in other words, the breeze was stirred by the hyperbolic imprecations of the two poets).

Lines 53–54: The "new form" refers to the linked verse in which they "labor for the unusual." This is the most explicit comment on their new style, showing an awareness of the nature of the changes that are taking place in their poetry, changes that first occur in the linked verse.

The phrase "laboring for the unusual" is of great importance for us: it characterizes Han Yü's and Meng Chiao's poetry of the early Yüan-ho Reign—from 806 until about 812 for Han Yü, and until his death in 814 for Meng Chiao. In the Chinese critical context, "labor," *kung,* means a craftsmanlike attention is paid to the novel or precise use of words and images; it suggests conscious artistry as opposed to spontaneity. The "unusual," *yi,* or, more commonly, the "strange" or "exceptional," *ch'i,* are particularly important words. In the linked verse *yi* simply refers to originality or shock value. Each competitor in the verse strives to outdo the other in originality. Every quality must be "more"; the observation of minutiae must be more detailed and sensitive, the hyperbole must be more exaggerated. During the following years this attitude was extended and transformed into a cult of poetic specialness by Han Yü's and Meng

Chiao's youthful admirers. They view the poet as different from other men; he expresses this difference by the "strangeness" of his poetry. The transformation from the didactic to the hermetic is accomplished by the alienation, the "difference" or "strangeness" of the moral poet within society, which necessarily finds expression in the "strangeness" of his verse.

Lines 55–62: Meng declares he has something to learn from Han Yü, and describes what that is in a series of moral metaphors. First, never put yourself in a dangerous or precarious position such as leaning on rotten tables and high balconies; this probably refers to Han Yü being exiled because of his memorial to the throne. "The road to the blue clouds" refers to advancement at court. The yellow crane, a bird associated with immortals, is still in fetters, suggesting Han Yü's "bondage" in official service, from which he is unable to retire. The conventional and easily intelligible nature of these moral metaphors shows the extent to which this device has degenerated in Meng's poetry. The flatness of this part of the passage contrasts sharply with the vividness of the "attack" of Han Yü's importuning servants.

HY	Long ago I parted with you,
	And, alas, I suffered great difficulties.
	The Straight Way has been ruined by warped paths, 65
	My naïve plans were hurt by malicious deceits.
	On the blazing lake I crossed through steamy fog,
	Over hot stones I walked the crags.
	The hunger from diabetes grew awful in the summer,
	The thirst from malaria was even more frequent in autumn. 70
	I could not gaze on your face,
	I could not clasp your hand.
	Recently I have been bathed in fresh Grace,
	And hope to see the Great Simplicity return.
	In the Academy I give myself to rest and wandering in study, 75
	And am satisfied in consulting the works of the sages.
	I travel the High Way without hesitation,
	I speak honestly and avoid mocking ridicule.
	We can get to ride together in horse and carriage,

And happily guzzle strong wine.   80
I only worry that they will cast away the straw—
But do I dare hope to attend at the Imperial Pavilion?
What do you think of these ambitions?—
I hope you'll polish them up for me.[9]

Han Yü has dropped his former pretenses about wanting to give up
political life to become a farmer; he is again caught up in the feverish
search for high position. It is to Meng Chiao's discredit that he
turned from the "new form" to remarks on Han Yü's political experiences—this seems to have started Han on still another repetition
of his already familiar broodings on his exile. This passage looks back
to the earlier linked verses, just as the earlier passages in this verse
look forward to the linked verses of autumn and winter.

Lines 63–66: The unnecessary, prosaic phrase "with you," *yü-tzu*,
marks the beginning of Han's narrative, expository style in the
poem. The last two characters of lines 63 and 64 are four hexagrams
from the *Yi-ching*; again Han is seeking to interpret his experiences
in terms of cosmic order. There is some difficulty in interpreting the
lines because it seems Han first intended *k'uei-li* to mean "separated"
("parted" in the translation). However, in using the second pair of
hexagrams, the first two, *k'uei-li*, took on their specialized *Yi-ching*
meanings: "Long ago with you there was a state of Opposition and
Clinging." ("Opposition" in this context means retaining one's
individuality in the company of lesser men and has positive connota-
tions: namely, both Han and Meng were above the ordinary.) The
next line is: "And, alas, I suffered Initial Difficulties and Splitting
Apart," referring to his exile and parting from Meng Chiao. "Ruined
by warped paths" refers to a passage in the "Essay on the Five Elements" in the *Han History*: "As warped paths ruin a good field, so
slandering mouths can bring confusion on a good man." Han Yü is,
of course, referring to the slander that he supposed brought on his
banishment.

Lines 67–72: This is a swift recapitulation of his sufferings in exile,
followed by a couplet on his longing for Meng.

Lines 73–84: The "Great Simplicity" refers to the unconfused
state of idealized antiquity. In answer to Meng Chiao's warning
about leaning on a "high balcony," Han says, "I travel the High

9. *HCLS*, p. 189.

Way without hesitation." Then to mollify Meng Chiao, whose conventional admonitions about the dangers of political life Han has just contradicted with Confucian platitudes, Han points out the positive aspects of his position—he and Meng can be together in the capital. Then with a final outburst of courtesy and self-deprecation, Han fears lest they "throw away the straw" (dismiss him from his post because he is of no value), suggests hope for a high position by denying hope (1. 82), and finally asks Meng to "polish" his ambitions, to show him the proper way.

The verse ends on a disappointing note. The boisterous humor of the first part has sunk to moralizing and exchange of polite compliments. For one thing, the length of the passages destroys the immediacy of response so that the poets turn from outdoing to self-expression, which is not suited to the linked verse. By trying to be personal, they end up with a polite but hollow social interchange.

By the time of "The Autumn Rain," a month or two after "Letting the Cool Air In," the two poets are working in total rapport; this poem never slips away from what a linked verse should be, a quick-moving competition of wits. By winter not only had their verse styles merged, the inherent tendency to hyperbole and fantasy had reached an extreme.

"The Campaign Against Shu," from the winter of 806, presages the style of Han Yü's mythopoeic poems of the next five years. The styles of the two poets are indistinguishable. The violent energy that characterizes the description in this poem is reminiscent of the bloody hunting scenes of Han Dynasty hunt *fu*, but the battle scenes here go far beyond these precedents. The verse describes a campaign undertaken against the rebellion of Liu P'i in Szechwan (here called by its ancient and poetic name, Shu) in 806.

THE CAMPAIGN AGAINST SHU

HY   Ere now our prince was wrathful with their transgressions
           and impertinence,
       There were orders given which were to punish and extirpate
           them,
       Shu's strategic points have been deeply locked in and
           fortified,
       There they plot wickedness against the imperial troops as
           much as they please.

Han Yü's opening quatrain is consciously archaized, using the con-
descending manner of government edicts. He employs *jih* (usually
meaning "day") in its archaic meaning "previously" ("ere now").
"Our prince," *wang*, here refers to the emperor, though in T'ang
times *wang* usually meant "prince of the blood." In the Chou
Dynasty, however, *wang* meant "king" and is used in that sense here.
The archaic Chou title lends a moral dignity to the emperor, as does
the formal phrase "was wrathful with their transgressions and im-
pertinence." The second line is phrased with equal formality: "there
was an *x* whose purpose was to *y*," *yu* being *x*, *shih y*.

The second couplet contrasts the sinister wickedness of the rebels
plotting in their strongholds with the moral dignity of the emperor as
seen in the first couplet. It is significant that Han Yü treats the rebellion as an ethical rather than a political or purely military problem—only after the moral lines have been clearly drawn do Han and
Meng indulge in a gleeful description of the carnage.

> MC   Windblown banners circuit the land flapping,   5
> Thundering drums rumble the skies fearsomely.
> Theirs the bamboo weapons that crinkle fragilely,
> Ours the iron blades that clang sharp-fanged.

As Meng Chiao contrasts the bamboo weapons of the Szechwanese
against the metal ones of the imperial army, he indulges in a bit of
phrase-coining: their weapons are "crinkle-fragile," while ours are
"clang-sharpfang." Han Yü having drawn the ethical lines, Meng
now moves into a hyperbolic world of flags circumambulating the
earth and drums shaking up the skies. Han Yü follows him into this
world, and the result is one of the rare battle poems in Chinese literature.

> HY   The God of Punishment huffs his rage on our yak-tail
> pennons,
> The wind-quavered flame on the darkness of our hide
> armor.   10
> Waving rainbows unfurl everywhere,
> Plains filled far and wide, boundless as the ocean.

By mentioning the god of punishment, Ju Shou, Han makes a feeble
attempt to retain the moral and evaluative aspect of the campaign;
but he, too, gives way to vivid hyperbole. Han imagines that the wind

that blows their yak-tail standards is the angry puffing of Ju Shou, and that the flashing of the black, hide armor in the light is a flame blown by the wind. The army banners become oceans. Han is echoing and expanding Meng Chiao's "windblown banners" of line five. It must be remembered that even though Han Yü had had some firsthand experience with the military, our two poets' description of the campaign is entirely imaginary, probably written as they sat in the security of Han Yü's villa south of Ch'ang-an.

> MC   Ferocity incarnate, they struggle dragged out and
>   stumbling,
>   Berserkly attacking, they compete to fill the field and be
>   crushed.
>   Thirsty for combat, truly they howl and roar,   15
>   Savoring their wickedness—how they slurp and grunt.

This quatrain describes the attack of the rebels, rushing like mad beasts to the slaughter and enjoying battle as though it were a feast. Meng Chiao has invented most of the descriptive phrases in this passage; Chinese poetry lacks a large body of stock phrases to describe battle, so they must be created ad hoc.

> HY   Shouting even louder, the ranks sway against one another,
>   Hacking axes cross, both teeth are knocked out.
>   Fire comes out, the point that stirred it reeks of gore,
>   Blood drifts down, feet that step on it slip.   20

The "teeth" probably refer to axeheads that chop each other off but may refer to actual teeth getting knocked out. Likewise, "fire" may be the sparks of weapons striking armor or it may refer to blood.

> MC   Like flying apes our battle formations are never straight,
>   Like diving falcons there are slanting strikes.
>   The river is reversed, whales and dolphins boil up,
>   The mountain shakes, wildcats and weasels smash them.

Meng Chiao describes the counterattack of the imperial army in terms of animals. The battle formations "never being straight" suggests either the eagerness of the imperial army to attack or the clever changes in tactics. When they strike from the side they seem like falcons diving on their prey. The "river" of enemy troops rushing forward is turned back, and the imperial troops emerge like whales among them. Each animal metaphor is used to show a specific quality of the imperial army on the counterattack. They are nimble as apes, swift and deadly as falcons, massive and powerful as whales, ferocious as wildcats and weasels.

> *HY*   Split in the middle, they separate into two or three bodies,
>   Outside they change, mixing into seven or eight groups.
>   Rebel necks are all roped and bound,
>   We shave enemy heads and whiskers as we please.
>   Their raging beards are still in tangles,
>   Their broken arms still trying to strike.   30

Han Yü goes on to describe the crumbling of the rebel army and its defeat: their army breaks first in half, then into smaller groups. Next we see the captives with necks bound and heads shaven, the marks of prisoners. The last couplet describes the unruliness of the rebels even in defeat. Their hair is "in tangles," *cheng-ning*, Chinese word-magic, in which unruly hair suggests an unruly nature.

> *MC*   Hidden in the rocks we have set unusual ambushes,
>   Peering out of caves, we quickly make clear reconnaissance.
>   Struck by arrows they are like weird pygmies,
>   Leaping from points, their manner is that of startled
>   werewolves.
>   Running around back, they gather on wooded peaks,   35
>   Then rise up sharply into heaps of dust and filth.

Meng Chiao now describes the mopping-up operations. Since rebellion is considered an unnatural act, the rebels become "pygmies" and "werewolves"—unnatural creatures.

> *HY*   Their battle standards destroyed—many empty flagstaffs,
>   Their chariot axles broken—few linked quions.
>   Slashed flesh saturated with gashes,
>   Ruined faces shattered by flaying and branding.   40
>   Rushing off in chaos, a reckless tumult,
>   Nimbly concealing themselves, the fleet and crafty escape.
>   Hooked off peaks, they leap with gibbons and monkeys,
>   Dredged out of rivers, they're mixed with bass and snails.
>   Leaping into chasms they crash like an avalanche,   45
>   Filling up the moats, they're lumpy and hard-packed.

First, Han describes the ruined battle equipment of the rebels, then their battle wounds and punishment. The last three couplets recount the frantic flight and destruction of the remnants of the rebels, who are "hooked off peaks" and "dredged out of rivers." In desperation many rebels fling themselves into valleys—so many that it seems like an avalanche. Han Yü maintains a precarious balance between naturalism and hyperbole, between horror and humor.

> *MC* Their hard pupils don't close in death,
>   Their vicious eyes glare even more when in difficulty.
>   As we burn their parapets, a crackling conflagration,
>   We smash open their gates which creak, gaping wide.   50
>   The Heavenly Sword has not yet even broken from its
>   scabbard,
>   But the chieftains' courage grew timid, easily eradicated.
>   Lying concealed on rafters, we push them off cowering,
>   And thrash them out of their holes from which they peek.
>   We hear them being driven together, hard-pressed,   55
>   As their feet are cut off, they cry, sobbing and moaning
>   at the wrong.

Line 51 refers to the general's sword, bestowed on him by the emperor as a token of his authority. Meng Chiao is saying here that the army hadn't even begun to fight in earnest when the enemy gave up. The enemy is rounded up and punished, their fortresses burned. The violence of the language and actions of the imperial army is part of the *concordia discors*; the rebels' disorder and violence must be matched by a counterdisorder and violence, so that harmony can be reestablished.

> *HY* Their impoverished region swiftly grows clear and peaceful,
>   The malignant element of society is accordingly carved off.
>   We cut the most elegant of Ch'iung's patterned brocade,
>   Take the most luscious and tender of Pa maidens,   60
>   Bludgeon to death the fattest of lowing oxen,
>   Carrying the spoils, camels groan.
>   But His Sage Divinity pities their stubborn foolishness,
>   His Protective Shepherding equates poisonous plants with
>   normal ones.

> He sends down orders to desist from our manly roaring,   65
> Absolving crimes, he laments their blindness and bondage.

Ch'iung and Pa are districts of Szechwan, used here to represent the entire region. Han Yü begins by continuing the rampage of the imperial army. Then the emperor declares amnesty. By "equating poisonous plants with normal ones" the emperor treats those who had rebelled like those who had not. "Manly roaring" euphemistically describes the looting of the countryside by the imperial army. In contrast to western battle poetry, conquest is less important to the Chinese poet than the restoration of harmony and order.

MC   The blood from the battles gradually melts away,
> The frosty light of swords is rubbed clear by night.
> On the plank bridges by the Han, the clamor and rumble
>   has ceased,
> Splash of bodies falling into Liao's rivers has ended.   70
> The forts are cold—gone is the morning guard,
> The kettledrums in the dark have halted their nightly
>   checks.
> When they first left, the apricots were humming with bees,
> When they reached home, the willows were humming with
>   cicadas.
> Presented to the Imperial Temple, countless heads and
>   ears,   75
> The sound of music permeates from beginning instruments
>   to last.

Line 68 means that the swords are bloodless. Meng describes the calm that now reigns over the former places of battle and the feasting when the army returns.

HY   A picture in the gallery of heroes glitters with jet and
>   crimson,
> The Sacrifice to Inform Heaven is solemn with gourd vessels
>   and stalk mats.
> We think of their age and comfort the darkened faces of
>   veterans,
> Seeing their wounds, we pity the scars and gashes.   80
> Transport ended, they let animals run free or rest,

To requite their strength there are generous oats and fodder.
At official banquets the bells ring morning,
In private feasts silken strings strum at dawn.
With cups and goblets they answer toasts with strong wine, 85
From coffers and baskets belts and turbans are conferred.
We minor officials are ignorant of the military classics,
All we can do is extol their merit and hard toil.[10]

Officers whose service was particularly meritorious had their pictures painted and hung in a special gallery. Line 79 refers to the convention that men's faces darken with age. Once order is restored the remaining duty is to requite all those who have served the state. Officers have their pictures hung in the "heroes' gallery," veterans are consoled, and even the animals are given special treatment. Officials in military service are given banquets and gifts. The Chinese sense of balance comes out clearly here: violence on the part of the rebels is matched by counterviolence by the state; services rendered to the state must be repaid (including those of the animals). Only when all deviations from the mean are canceled out is complete harmony restored.

Perhaps with the exception of "South of the City," the linked verses cannot be considered among Han's and Meng's greatest work. On the other hand, their importance in fostering and bringing to fulfillment the tendencies in their poetry during the years immediately preceding their writing cannot be underestimated. In the following chapters we shall look at the fruit of the linked verse style— Meng Chiao's greatest poems and many of Han Yü's best too.

10. *HCLS*, p. 262.

8

Meng Chiao: The Symbolic Landscape, 806-814

> I wanted to climb that thousand-stair tower
> To ask Heaven a couple of things—
> I hadn't even climbed twenty or thirty,
> When heart and eyes blew like waves in the wind, . . .
> Anyway, these words from only an inch of Earth—
> How could the High Heavens hear them?[1]
>
> > [from "Climbing Chao-ch'eng Temple Tower"]

The structure of the above experience is the single most normative theme of Meng Chiao's poetry. Man seeks to rise to the good and the immortal, only to find himself bound irrevocably to a world of insignificance, ugliness, human frailty, and mortality. Faced with unacceptable limitations, man is left with only frustrated bitterness and despair. Yet this is only one pair of antitheses in a polarized world. In the ethical realm the dichotomy is good and evil; in the physical realm, immortality and death; in the political realm, success and failure; in history, the idealized past and the corrupt present. It is the dichotomized world which generates the poetry of extremes. From this simplistic view of reality, the poet tends to categorize every aspect of experience and to fix it as belonging to one extreme or the other.

Failure is the inevitable result of a limited man in a limited world, striving for the perfect. In poetic style it takes the form of an opposition between the precious and the harsh:

> I imagine words of crystal,
> But hear only a few songs of withering.[2]

Or it may be stated in personal terms:

> With my ruined twig of a body

1. *MTYSC*, p. 173.   2. *MTYSC*, pp. 65–66.

137

> In purity and ruggedness I nourished lofty peace of mind—
> Sought peace of mind, found no peace of mind, . . .[3]

Thus in Meng Chiao's poetry there is a constant tension between affirmation of his values and rejection of them:

> During my life I've woven
> A thousand poems in the diction of the Great Odes.[4]

set against:

> A poet suffers making poems—
> Better to waste your efforts trying to fly.
> My whole life a spirit of useless squawking,
> Not of remonstrating and not of admonishing.[5]

Meng sees himself alternately as a poet in the manner of the *Book of Songs* and as a "squawker." Much of the roughness in his poetry is created by the dialectical tension between striving and failure, between affirmation and rejection. In Meng Chiao's early poetry dialectical tension was to be found in the creation of a scene or suggestion of a conventional value only to have it destroyed and devalued. This same dialectical tension finds structural expression in the poem sequences of 806–14; often each poem of a sequence will turn against the one that precedes it, affirming, rejecting, then rejecting the rejection.

Through the course of Meng Chiao's poetic career has occurred real stylistic development toward greater concentration of language, greater resonance of imagery, and toward symbolism. Thematically, however, his poetry has changed very little. In his early poetry we remember Meng Chiao juxtaposing his eremite *principles* with the *fact* of his going to the capital to seek political advancement. In the poems on his failure we find the *idealized* vision of himself juxtaposed with the *reality* of his failure: "An eagle, losing its powers, sick."[6] Later, after the revolt at Pien-chou, we may remember:

> Three thousand troops that fed on imperial favor,
> For one morning became jackals and wolves.[7]

Against this Meng Chiao responds by invoking the ideal:

---

3. *MTYSC*, pp. 63–64.   4. *MTYSC*, p. 46.   5. *MTYSC*, p. 149.
6. *MTYSC*, p. 50.   7. *MTYSC*, p. 118.

On some ocean isles the troops are all upright,
But at Pien-chou the troops are not good.[8]

There can be no compromise between the ideal and the real, between good and evil. In these last years of his life the conflict between the positive and negative poles of Meng's dichotomy deepens, going beyond the occasional to the universal. Previously, the dichotomizing and evaluating mode had been a *means* by which one understood events; in Meng Chiao's last poems the phenomenal world of events and things is only a symbol of a greater conflict between right and wrong, between "what is" and "what should be."

The most important structural development in Meng Chiao's poetry between Pien-chou and 806 is the perfection of the poem sequence. Suited to the dialectical tensions of Meng Chiao's poetry during these years, the poem sequence is the lyric poet's answer to the long poem. A poet can thereby give his topic an extended treatment, while sacrificing none of the linguistic density and intensity of a short poem. The poem sequence permits the poet to reverse viewpoints, try alternatives, expand or reject an idea as he sees fit.

There is a strong tendency in Meng Chiao's poem sequences toward "discovery of meaning," Empson's fifth type of ambiguity, in which the author discovers what he is saying in the process of saying it.[9] The poet is faced with a bewildering array of events and objects in which he must discover meaning, pattern, and value. Once value is determined, the poet strives to affirm the ideal, conquer its negative, and rectify the metaphorical world by his moral purity. Only in one sequence, "Cold Creek," is the outcome positive: by discovering ethical pattern in a symbolic landscape, Meng can perform a symbolic gesture affirming his moral purity, thereby conquering evil. In "Autumn Meditations" the poet comes to understand the meaning of autumn and transience and takes his ethical stand on the side of the ideal. But in most cases, such as "Laments of the Gorges" and "Apricots Die Young" (which we do not have space to include), the poet understands evil but can do nothing to fight it. This process of discovery of meaning also involves a dialectical exploration of alternatives and rejection of those alternatives which fail to satisfy him. Read in this way, the poem sequences can be a vigorous and, at times,

8. *MTYSC*, p. 118.

9. William Empson, *Seven Types of Ambiguity* (1930; reprint, New York: New Directions, n.d.), pp. 155–75.

desperate attempt to find pattern in the chaos of reality; if read instead as a static statement, the sequences are a confused mass of contradictions.

In the poems on his examination failure we noted that Meng Chiao's metaphors and imagery were becoming obsessive. In the poems of the last years of his life, this obsessive imagery becomes a world of symbolic objects that intrude themselves on the poet. To unravel the hermetic mystery of these objects, to find their meaning and value, is part of the discovery of meaning. These symbolic objects retain their concrete identity, as the poet explores possible interpretations.

The poem sequence discussed in this chapter will serve as an example of the numerous symbolic landscapes Meng Chiao created during his last years in Lo-yang. In these there is a division between landscapes of otherworldly purity and beauty and those of horror and evil. The landscape often becomes like man, a mountain rising from the earth, striving upward.

> The spine of the earth has been pressed down into a slope,
> Then thrusts upward into the dark, dark sky.
> This building's roots are stuck into remote clouds,
> The wings of the hall soar into the high void.[10]

The mountain pushes upward but is "pressed down" on the sides in this dynamic landscape of striving. On the summit, seeking to rise still higher, is a Buddhist temple: though "rooted" in the mountain, its "wings" (as in English, a Chinese building may have "wings") seek to carry it on upward.

Late in 806 Meng Chiao moved to Lo-yang, the eastern capital, where he found a new patron in Cheng Yü-ch'ing, the governor. Through Cheng, Meng Chiao received two minor posts, which seem to have been sinecures entailing little more than receiving a salary. Meng built a house in the Li-te Ward of Lo-yang and lived there for most of the rest of his life.

The following sequence, "Cold Creek," shows Meng Chiao exploiting the poem sequence to the fullest. Two earlier sequences, "Stone Run" and "New Dwelling in the Li-te Ward," had permitted Meng to experiment in the form. As sequences both these earlier works are failures, the first because Meng Chiao had not yet de-

10. *MTYSC*, p. 66.

veloped the dialectical structure which gives his later poem sequences energy, and the second because Meng failed to go beyond the occasional, which resulted in a contradiction between actual events and the pattern Meng had been trying to give to his experience.

The "Cold Creek" sequence, one of Meng Chiao's greatest, shows the moral man confronting an evil world and, by his unswerving integrity, overcoming it. This theme, the "rectification of nature," also appears in Han Yü's poetry of this period. Imbalance in the natural world is a reflection of imbalance in the cosmic order. Confronting natural disorder, it is the duty of the moral man to take a firm and uncompromising moral stand, thus overcoming a world of disorder by his words and deeds.

COLD CREEK: NINE POEMS

I

Frost washes the water's color out,
In Cold Creek can be seen thin scales.
As I regally inspect this empty mirror,
It shines back a ruined, haggard body.
What would sink away cunningly can't hide itself,   5
Its bottom revealed, the luster gets fresher and fresher.
Now open like a good man's heart,
It was in truth a treacherous destroyer of men.
For now I see clearly its shallow common soul,
At night it froze, by dawn already fordable.   10
Rinsed pure by a handful of its emerald green,
Melting far from me the foulness of a thousand cares.
Now I know that a stream muddied by feet
Will never be a neighbor to the mountain spring.

This poem is an introduction to the sequence, chronologically probably the last; in it Meng Chiao reviews and evaluates his experience with the creek, experience that shall be explained in the following poems of the sequence. The dominant theme is one of revelation: though now the creek seems "open" (I.7) and "pure" (I.11), the truth of the creek's treacherous nature is revealed by that very clarity and openness. Like some creatures that would like to "sink away *cunningly*," the creek would seek to hide the negative aspect of its nature.

Revelation brings out the truth; and as so often in Meng Chiao's poetry, the truth is unpleasant. "Regally inspect" *hsing-lin*, is a formal and polite term used to suggest an imperial visit or being greatly honored by the visit of a high personnage. Meng Chiao's use of it here is clearly ironic: the creek repays his courtesy with the revelation of his "ruined, haggard body." The "emptiness" of the creek-mirror suggests the absence of distortion, the impartiality of the revelation. This "mirror" shows the true nature of the poet, the creatures within the creek, and the creek itself.

In the last couplet, the poet gives the unequivocal evaluation that the moral poet must make. He rejects this landscape in favor of the pure mountain stream. However, it is not simply the physical muddying which causes Meng Chiao to reject the creek. Located in or near Lo-yang, the creek is befouled by men so that it sometimes runs muddy, sometimes clear as now. Similarly, the "mirror's" emptiness, its impartiality, suggests moral ambivalence, reflecting back whatever acts upon it. These physical characteristics are extended to moral characteristics, and it is on the grounds of moral ambivalence, the creek's ability to actualize evil as well as good, that Meng Chiao rejects it.

II

The road by the shore in Lo-yang
Is the creek before Meng Chiao's village.
The boat moves, pale ice cracks,
Its sound is the screech of blue agate.
Green waters harden to green jade,   5
White waves grow into white marble slabs.
So bright in this precious mirror,
The heavens shine forth each thing equalized.
Slanting paces descend the dangerous bends,
Climb a withered branch, hear the widow's cry.   10
The sweet fragrance of the frost dissipates somewhat,
The frozen scene is vague and equalized.
Sitting dumbly I stare straight ahead and listen,
Foolishly walking I lost the traces of the path.
The bank is in layers, I suffer hacking thorns,   15
The words I say are mostly sorrowful.

This is the chronological beginning of the sequence, in which the poet recounts his experiences when the creek was first frozen. The creek is the road to where Meng Chiao is living, suggesting the human traffic which sullied it (I.13). As yet, however, the poet is unaware of the creek's evil nature. Rather, the ice is seen as a beautiful jewel-like world of agate, jade, and marble. The ice is a mirror whose reflections are "equalized," *ch'i*, a Taoist term from the *Chuang-tzu*, meaning that everything is viewed without evaluation, without distinctions between good and evil, beautiful and ugly, etc. Such impartiality is positive in the *Chuang-tzu* but negative to the Confucian moralist. On a visual level, "equalized" also means "evenly," the reduction of the landscape to a single plane of reflection. Such an "equalized" scene which lacks any values contrasts sharply with the revelation of truth in terms of values in the first poem. This is the first hint that there is something wrong with this jeweled scene.

Realizing that the ice has "equalized" the scene, the poet gradually becomes aware of the negative aspects of the creek—"dangerous bends" and the "widow's cry." The "widow's cry" probably refers to birds that have lost their mates (see III.3–4), who now cry in the branches. A positive aspect of the creek, the "sweet fragrance" (again, a physical attribute made a moral one through the organic metaphor) disappears, and the poet sees everything "vague and equalized." Vagueness, like equalization, destroys the clarity that reveals truth and allows things to be evaluated. To regain the clarity of perception which the scene has taken away, the poet "stares straight ahead and listens." Likewise, a "lost path" is a phrase traditionally loaded with ethical overtones—the lost Way. The layers of the bank and the thorns are obstructions, both off "the path," and an example of the ugly external world that has been equalized by the creek.

Without knowing Meng Chiao's earlier poetry, in which we have seen the ethical overtones of certain words and the coalescence between the physical and moral worlds, it would be almost impossible for us to understand the evaluative fantasy in which Meng Chiao is engaging here. As in "At Pien-chou: parting with Han Yü," the physical configuration of the landscape demands that the poet decipher the landscape in moral terms. At the end of the poem Meng is saying that by "equalizing" things—taking their values away—the

frozen landscape has led him astray, and by concentrating on clearing his perception, he can see the evil done by the creek. Beauty is
deceptive; the truth is ugly.

III

At dawn I drank a single cup of wine,
Treading the snow I visited the clear creek.
The waves had frozen into knives
That hacked and carved the ducks and widgeons.
Feathers that spent the night, all cut off and lost,   5
The sound of blood sinking into mud and sand.
Alone I stand—what shall I say?
Silently I brood, my heart cries out bitterly.
Frozen blood will never make springtime,
If it made springtime, inequality would be born.   10
Frozen blood will make no flowers,
If it made flowers, it would bring the widow's weeping.
Hidden away, village of thorns and brambles,
Frozen to death, there can be no plowing.

After his attempt in the preceding poem to clarify his perception of
things, here Meng Chiao sees the frozen world of the creek in entirely
different terms. Instead of "white marble slabs," here the waves become knives. Birds had tried to land on the creek during the night,
mistakenly believing that they were landing on water. The knifelike,
frozen waves cut them to pieces, so that now the creek is a scene of
blood and feathers. Thus the poet is horrified at the reality of the
creek's evil, its destructive aspect fully revealed.

The passage that follows is difficult and may be taken in various
ways. The unnatural cold spell in early spring has, in spilling the
blood of the birds over the landscape, created an unnatural kind of
spring rain. Meng Chiao fears that this rain of blood will take the
place of normal spring rain, causing the plants to grow unnaturally.
"Inequality" (*pu ch'i*, literally "not equalized") is a negative term
here, as its opposite, "equalized," was in the preceding poem. The ice
world that lacks any values will give rise to a springtime that can be
evaluated, but evaluated as evil. Having been watered by blood,
flowers, which are the usual markers of springtime, will create an
"anti-spring." Flowers, associated with sexuality, will give rise to an

unnatural kind of marriage—widowhood, which refers back to the "widow's cry" in the preceding poem, and here may also suggest birds.

The unnatural cold spell destroys the forces of life. Instead of natural crops, thorns and brambles grow in the village. More important still, the freezing makes spring planting impossible. The inability to sow crops introduces the theme of food, and unable to eat plants, men must turn to hunting and fishing, as we shall see in the next poems. Thus the freezing which kills plants and birds begins a chain of destruction, forcing men likewise to become killers. Seeing this extension of destructiveness into the human world, the moral poet is duty-bound to oppose the unnatural cold and the chain of destruction.

IV

> The boat-poler chucks jade stars behind,
> All along the path he makes scattering fireflies follow.
> The northern freezing—lament pierces to the bottom,
> The hunters are famished, chant to the sunken fish smell.
> Teeth of ice grind and gnash together,   5
> The wind's tone runs sour through hanging chimes.
> Such clearly heard sorrow cannot be fled,
> Washing out the faintest things to the ear.
> The continuous roll of emerald ripples has ceased,
> The colored floss has flown loose and fallen.   10
> When they set foot below, it's slippery and uncertain,
> Roosting above, branches broke, they couldn't stop over.
> Grunting, huffing, screeching, jabbering their grievances,
> Looking up in complaint—when shall there be peace?

The first couplet of this poem echoes the jewel-like vision of the frozen creek. Meng seems to use these passages which make the creek seem beautiful in order to bring out the duality of the creek's nature and to heighten the contrast between those aspects. The couplet describes the chips of ice being knocked loose as the boat is poled through the frozen creek, leaving a line of water that shows the boat's path through the ice. These chips of ice become "jade stars" and "scattering fireflies."

The second couplet, however, brings us back to the themes of suf-

fering and destruction. A suggestion is made of the hunting and fishing brought about by the impossibility of planting. Instead of stars
and fireflies, the ice now forms teeth that "grind and gnash together."
Just as when the ice formed knives (III.3) it brought purposeless
destructiveness, here the ice forms teeth, suggesting the themes of
eating and animals.

The creek scene in this poem is dominated by the *sounds* of violence—"lament," "chanting," the grinding of the ice together. Combined, these sounds drown out all else, building to a final cacophony
of woe in the last couplet. Lines eleven and twelve refer to animals
and birds, respectively; the landscape is treacherously seeking to
destroy them. The cacophony of noises from birds, animals, and
landscape seem to be expressing "grievances," telling the wrongs
done to them by the cold. In this condition the poet becomes the
mediator between the sufferers and the powers above. We may read
the last line either as the suffering animals looking up to the poet or
to heaven for redress of their grievances, or as the poet himself looking
up to heaven, demanding redress on their behalf. Just as an ancient
function of the western poet is as the prophet, the mediator between
gods and men, an ancient role of the Chinese poet is as a mediator
between the suffering people and their rulers. Thus it is on the model
of a political expostulation that the poet takes on the responsibility to
rectify evil and help those who suffer.

V

A twist and then a straight stretch of water,
A white dragon, how scaly!
In a frozen whirlwind the jumbled fragments cry out,
Valley and dale chafe with a vinegary tone.
My notes and memoranda stammer forceless,   5
Yet flying and walking creatures think of me even more kindly.
Once the string of the fierce bow is broken,
With their last gasps they vie to be my guests.
By establishing grand sternness here,
Such little killings will no longer occur.   10
Snowy white, how snowy white!
The gentle cosmic forces rise to fullness.
A lucky sky clears, brushed by sun and moon,
In the high azure, stars and planets appear.

Alone I stand, my two feet in the snow,   15
Reciting poetry in solitude, a thousand worries renewed.
The Heavenly Slanderer wastes its brilliance,
The Sieve's tongue rants in vain.
Yao was a sage, he gave no heed to you,
Confucius's position was humble, but he too had "subjects."   20
The remonstrance is at last finished,
But the ancient attitude is hard to tell completely.

The twist and straight stretch of the creek suggests the change-
ability of its moral character. The frozen creek becomes a "white
dragon," both in its sinuous, icy appearance and in its cruel nature.
It might be pointed out here that dragons in the Chinese tradition,
contrary to popular western opinion, are not always beneficent tutelary spirits, though they may be so. Often, as here, they are
monstrous creatures characterized by demonic power and cruelty.
The second couplet vividly describes the wind sweeping over the
landscape. The synesthesia of the "vinegary tone" (literally, "minced
vinegar salad tone") is a self-consciously strange description of the
"sourness" of the sound of the wind, and also suggests the wind's
mincing things into fragments.

In the third couplet the poet assumes his function as the mediator,
interceding with higher powers on behalf of the suffering creatures of
the landscape. "Notes and memoranda" suggest that Meng Chiao is
remonstrating with either the landscape or Heaven. The political
model the poet uses here serves to make the violence of the landscape
intelligible, to give the poet an orderly and tradition-honored means
to cope with that violence. It is likewise a natural result of treating the
landscape in moral terms, since morality is defined in terms of the
orderly functioning of society, rather than being a set of values within
itself. "Stammering" indicates the poet's inability to articulate clearly the wrong done to the creatures of the landscape, as well as suggesting a purely physical reaction to the cold—his teeth are chattering. Even though his remonstrance is "forceless," not efficacious, still
the animals of the creek see his compassionate intent.

In this scene the cold is not the only destroyer; hunters also are
participating in the destruction of the "flying and walking creatures,"
the animals and birds. Though the hunters' need to kill is caused by
the cold, were Meng Chiao to justify the hunters' actions on the

grounds of hunger, he would be tacitly accepting the unnatural cold. Thus Meng's moral stand must be against killing altogether. It is also possible that the poet's remonstrance is to the hunters. In any case, the birds and animals respond to the poet's compassion and come to him. The broken bowstring (V.7) may be his own, indicating his personal rejection of killing as a way to satisfy his hunger. Although this compassion toward animals may have been influenced to some extent by Buddhist thought, it is treated here in purely Confucian terms. The creatures are the poet's "guests," a social relation demanding hospitality and protection on the host's part, and are later to become his "subjects," over whom he is the beneficent ruler.

Meng Chiao's moral stand here does affect nature; the clearing of the sky is the first stage in rectifying the natural imbalance (V.11–14). But even though the poet's stand, actualized in his remonstrance and in his breaking his bow, has brought about a clearing of the weather, the destructive cold and hunger remain. Seeing the incompleteness of the rectification, Meng Chiao's "worries are renewed."

Elaborating on the political model used earlier in the poem, the poet imagines that the two constellations, the "Heavenly Slanderer" and the "Sieve" (part of whose stellar configuration is imagined to be a tongue), are making evil suggestions to him. From the context (see VI.1), it seems clear that these suggestions are that the poet should take advantage of the animals' trust in him and their state of exhaustion ("with their last gasps"), by eating them to satisfy his own hunger. Taking the sage-king Yao and Confucius as his examples, Meng Chiao rejects these suggestions (which more likely come from his stomach than from the stars). He sees himself as a miniature version of the "sage-ruler," and his subjects are the animals. The reference to Confucius comes from *Analects*, XIX.7: "The master was very sick. Tzu-lu had the disciples act as the Master's 'subjects.'" Although the meaning of this passage in the *Analects* is that the disciples were to take special care of the master, Meng Chiao twists the meaning to make them actual subjects of Confucius, in other words, the ruler-subject relation is the same as the master-disciple relation. Thus Meng Chiao views his relation to the animals that have come to him as one of a ruler and his subjects. In this situation is also the traditional theme that if there is a perfectly virtuous ruler, people will naturally flock to him (as the animals have to Meng).

The poet's remonstrance to the powers above or to the hunters is completed but he feels it is insufficient. The cause of this feeling of inadequacy is an important symptom of Meng's idealistic Confucianism. Because the universe is organized ethically, had the poet expressed the proper "ancient attitude" fully, the imbalance in nature would have been rectified of itself. Conversely, since the poet can see that the imbalance in nature has not yet been fully rectified, he assumes that he has not expressed the "ancient attitude" fully. If one consistently tried to deal with the empirical world in this fashion, it could doubtless give rise to a strong sense of personal inadequacy, since the empirical world rarely heeds moral pleas. Han Yü may have successfully dissipated a fog through his sincerity in "Visiting a Temple on Mount Heng," but judging from his reaction in the poem no one was more surprised than Han himself that purity actually did seem to have a magic power over nature. The roots of this belief are very old and powerful in the Chinese tradition; however, Meng Chiao's personal and sophisticated version of this belief is unusual.

VI

Because of the freezing you can eat what's dead,
The killing wind has still not ceased.
But were I to make a weapon of my virtue and kindness,
My virtue and kindness would grow on a knifepoint,
And on that knifepoint my virtue and kindness would stink—   5
Such is not to be sought by a good man.
The waves draw out their swords of ice,
Rending one another like bitter enemies.

The sixth poem begins with a counterstatement to the poet's moral position. By eating what has been killed by nature itself (rather than hunting) one can obtain nourishment. Although the sky has cleared, "the killing wind has still not ceased," nature is still destructive. The next two couplets are a powerful reaffirmation of his moral stand and extension of it to the new situation above. There can be no compromise; if he were to betray the animals' trust in him by eating what had been already killed, he would be using his "virtue and kindness" like a weapon. Throughout the sequence, weapons (swords of ice, bow, etc.) have suggested the destructive violence of the cold, against which the poet must stand firmly. Appropriately, the "stink," *hsing*, which would appear on his "virtue and kindness" is the foul smell of carrion. In the last couplet we find the ice of the creek doing what Meng Chiao has refused to do, "drawing swords of ice."

VII

Sharp-pointed snow enters a fish's heart,
The fish's heart turns bright red with pain.
In a blur a water phantom speaks,
Seeming to state the reason it was hacked up.
Who caused the spirit of some strange place   5
To enter the streams of the heartland?
It cut away the first month of spring,
Blocking up gloom in all the valleys.
Looking up, I am moved by the light of newly cleared skies,
That shines down on me making me doubt my sorrows.   10

The "swords of ice" seen in the preceding poem here become "sharp-pointed snow," which kills a fish. "Turn red with pain," *ch'iao-ch'iao*, usually refers to a flush of sorrow or anger, but here seems to indicate the red of the fish's bleeding heart. The evil creek is demon-infested, dominated by a "spirit from some strange place," which has destroyed spring. It is unclear whether the water phantom belongs with the "strange spirit" or whether it is stating a grievance to the poet, demanding the poet to explain the death of the fish. In the latter case, *su*, "state," is used in the restricted sense of "to state a plaint," and the water sprite would be acting on behalf of the dead fish. Again the poet notes the clearing skies above and wonders whether the cold might not be dissipating of itself, in which case his worries over rectifying evil would be unnecessary.

VIII

The old man of the creek weeps over the extreme cold,
The falling tears become tinkling ice.
Forms of flying creatures dead, of walking creatures dead,
The snow has split, the heart flurried.
Sword and knife frozen, won't cut,   5

Bowstring stiff, can't shoot.
Always I have heard that if a good man has a valiant spirit,
He won't eat what has been killed naturally.
Chopping in jade, I cover the skeleton and carcass,
A marble dirge, my tears of lament stream down.   10

The extreme cold transforms the poet's tears into pieces of ice that tinkle as they hit the ground. The poet is confronted with the corpses of animals all around him. This morbid hyperbole is bringing the poem to a climax. In the fourth line "flurried," *fen*, creates ambiguity, as *fen* is a word commonly used to describe a flurry of snowflakes. Thus we may interpret the line as the poet's heart being "flurried," or as the hearts of the animals in a "flurry" of snow. The third couplet makes killing by the hunt impossible, while the fourth couplet reaffirms that a good man cannot eat what has been killed by the forces of nature. In the first part of this poem many of the themes from earlier in the sequence are summed up—human suffering from the cold, sympathy for suffering animals, hunting, and rejection of eating altogether in favor of unswerving ethical principle. This summation prepares for the poet's final moral gesture in the last couplet, which will set the world aright and restore balance to nature.

The poet digs in the ice to bury the animals, his "subjects." In so doing he echoes a phrase in the "Yüeh-ling" chapter of the *Li Chi*, "cover over the skeleton and bury the carcass," *yen ko mai tzu*. The allusion heightens the ritual and moral significance of the gesture. He weeps for them a "marble dirge" of frozen tears. The dead animals have been given a proper funeral with ritual burial and dirge; the ritual significance of these deeds confirms and demonstrates to the powers above the sincerity of Meng's moral position. He has rejected the needs of his body, his hunger, in favor of his ethical principles and has acted on behalf of the animals through remonstrance and by burying them according to ritual. As the mediator who intercedes for those who suffer to the powers above, his behavior has been selfless, compassionate, and ethically correct. Hearkening back to the old Confucian principle that if one man demonstrates perfect virtue, the entire world will be rectified, we may now expect Heaven to respond to the poet's goodness, restoring the balance of nature. This is indeed what happens in the final poem of the sequence.

IX

Wind on the creek shakes the remaining ice,
The scene of the creek holds bright spring within.
The jade melts, flowers drip,
The dragon comes apart, its scales glittering.
Remote paces descend clear bends,   5
At melting time I wash at the sweet-smelling ford.
Across a thousand miles where the ice cracks.
A ladleful of water, warm and kind.
Frozen spirits bathe one another,
Rolling ripples struggle to begin anew.   10
Suddenly as though, its sword gashes gone,
There began to rise a body of a hundred battles.[11]

At last the ice is only "remaining ice," as the poet senses springtime approaching once again. The evil dragon "comes apart," a
visual description of the chunks of ice (scales) breaking loose. Instead
of thorns and brambles (II.15, III.13) we now have dripping
flowers. Instead of the "stink" of dead meat (VI.5), here we have
a "sweet-smelling ford." We have "*remote* paces descend *clear* bends,"
instead of the warped landscape in which "*slanting* paces descend
dangerous bends" (II.9). The suddenness of spring's appearance confirms its magic relation to the poet's ritual gesture in the preceding
poem. The "warm and kind" water now is associated with purification, "washing" and "bathing." The last couplet is a metaphor for
the creek and its rebirth in spring. The healing of the "sword gashes"
suggests the split snow (VIII.4) that is now melting away, as well as
the wounds the animals suffered from the "swords of ice" (VI.7).
Indeed, we might translate "body" as plural, referring to the reap-
pearance of the animals that seemed to have all been killed by the
creek. Whatever its referent, it is a powerful image of the transition
from harsh cold into the vitality and rebirth of spring.

The following poem is from a series describing a spring scene, unusual for Meng Chiao. The theme of the fundamental disharmony
between an old man and springtime is reminiscent of the seven
quatrains of Tu Fu's "Walking Alone on the Banks of the Yangtze
Looking for Flowers," and may even be modeled on those earlier

11. *MTYSC*, p. 88.

poems. Like "Cold Creek" this is a hermetic landscape, but a mild one that does not intrude itself upon the poet.

COLD FOOD FESTIVAL AT THE SOURCE OF THE CHI RIVER
[first of seven]

Wind-blown nests swaying, spring crow after crow,
A childless old man raises his face and sighs.
I spy about for willow bow and reed arrows, don't see them,[12]
High red and far-off green toil to cover them.[13]

Meng Chiao did not often write quatrains, but when he did, he was usually successful. As is often the case in the quatrain, wit is the very soul of this poem. The first line sets the theme of birth and family. Though springtime and the nests suggest family and growth, swaying in the wind implies precariousness, an insecure position. The second line relates this image to the poet himself, who is "childless" in contrast to the birds. He sighs at their joy, his childlessness, and their insecurity.

For his imaginary bow and arrows, the ritual objects for the ceremony at the birth of a son, Meng Chiao uses the plants in the scene, willow and reeds, rather than the proscribed mulberry and tumbleweed. His son having died, Meng cannot find these ritual bow and arrows—the wood that would form them, willow and reeds, are *living* plants, covered by the red and green of spring's growth. The death and bareness of willow and reeds (as the ritual bow and arrows) would mean life for his son; conversely, their life covered with leaves and flowers means his son's death. With this idea in mind, we can understand the first couplet more clearly: Meng fears that the crows may bear the same relation to the springtime vegetation as he and his son did. The suppleness of the branches threatens the young crows in the nest with death—it can spill them to earth. Thus the characteristics of life in spring vegetation—flowers, leaves, and suppleness—become enemies of other living creatures.

12. *Book of Rites*, "Household Regulations": "When a child is born, if it is a male child, you set a boy to the left of the gate, . . . a bowman takes a mulberry bow and six tumbleweed arrows and shoots them in the four directions of Heaven and Earth."
13. *MTYSC*, p. 79.

9

Meng Chiao's Vision of the Poet

During his residence in Lo-yang from 806 to 814, Meng turned
seriously to consider his own nature as a poet and as a moral man.
The poet becomes the representative of Confucian principles in a
corrupt society, and the sufferings and deprivations he undergoes as
a result of his incorruptability themselves become emblems of his
morality. In this we can see an important difference between these
later poems and the poems on his examination failure: while in the
earlier poems Meng Chiao's sufferings were something from which
he sought release, here they are requisite attributes of the moral
poet's specialness, his moral superiority. This self-conception is based
on one of the most honored Confucian principles, "resoluteness in
deprivation," *ku-ch'iung* (*Analects*, XV.1). But while the *Analects*
passage states what a good man should be *in the case of* deprivation,
Meng Chiao makes deprivation a positive value in itself.

The poet is "cold and pure" like snow or frost—but this ideal of
purity finds expression in suffering from the cold, as in "Cold Creek."
Besides being cold and pure, the poet is always hungry, and imagery
of hunger and starvation plays an even more important role in
Meng's later poetry than it did in his poetry of the early 790s. Suffering from hunger is a positive value; its negative counterpart is the
plenty of the rich and powerful. From constant hunger the poet is
emaciated, and this emaciation makes him seem "rugged" like a
craggy mountain or "gaunt" like a mountain pine. Both mountain
and pine have traditional associations of eremitic solitude and moral
purity, respectively; the traditional associations merge with Meng's
personal associations of emaciation. Poverty and old age, with their
attendant sufferings, are definite virtues. The color white brings
together many of these symbolic attributes: it is the traditional color
of autumn, old age, and death, as well as being associated with the

cold purity of snow and white jade. White is Meng Chiao's favorite color, and through it are expressed a wealth of traditional and personal associations.

In the midst of suffering and deprivation the poet emerges as the transmitter of morality. Few of these late poems are didactic in contrast to the many didactic pieces Meng wrote in the early 790s; rather, they conform to another Confucian principle, teaching by example. By being himself the exemplar of moral purity and by praising other poets who are also such, Meng Chiao maintains his strong ethical focus in intensely personal poetry. This is consonant with a central concern of Han Yü's, Chia Tao's, and Li Ho's poetry during these years—the *specialness* of the poet, his alienation from other mortals. However, it is in Meng Chiao's poetry of 806–14 that the special poet and the moral poet merge perfectly: the poet's uniqueness, his specialness and alienation, is both the natural cause and the result of his suffering and perfect morality.

This vision of the poet was involved in the cult of superior talent, practiced by the young followers of Han Yü and Meng Chiao, as shall be discussed in a later chapter. The morally superior man expresses his alienation from society in self-consciously obscure poetry written to be understood only by a select circle. Han Yü and Meng Chiao believed in this principle to some extent, though they both showed reservations about the extremities to which their youthful followers went.

One of their followers was the young priest Wu-pen, or as he was later known, Chia Tao. Chia sought to impress both Han Yü and Meng Chiao with the strangeness of his poetry and his behavior, giving rise to the following description by Meng Chiao. As well as making fun of the cult hermetic style, Meng's poem is itself an excellent example of it.

> PLAYFULLY SENT TO WU-PEN [first of two]
>
> Ch'ang-an, sounds of autumn dry,
> As the tree leaves cry out to it in sorrow.
> The lean monk lies down like an icicle,
> Hidden in his mocking songs are sword gashes.
> These sword gashes are not the scars of battle,   5
> Yet severe sickness can be in them.
> Poetry's bones jut in Meng Chiao,

Poetry's waves gush out in Han Yü.
But there are times when he walks tottering,
As though someone had startled a wise ol' crane.[1]   10
Too bad Tu Fu and Li Po are dead,
Not to see such madness as this.[2]

This poem should be read in conjunction with Han Yü's "Sending Off Wu-pen on His Way Back to Fan Yang," (p. 224), which shows similar shock at Chia Tao's affectation of strangeness. The dryness of autumn's sounds probably refers to the leaves. "It" (*hsiang*, indefinite direct object marker which may also be translated "him" or "each other") may refer to Ch'ang-an, autumn, Chia Tao, Meng Chiao, or the other leaves. The "icicle" metaphor for Chia Tao contains the positive moral attributes of leanness, coldness, purity, and suffering. Chia Tao's "mocking sounds," his satires, can wound people gravely, but if this talent is used in the proper moral way, it is a point in Chia's favor.

Having thus described Chia Tao's verse, Meng proceeds to characterize his own and Han Yü's poetry. Meng's style is poetry's "bones," the rugged solidity and bareness of his best poetry. Han Yü's style is "poetry's waves," the grand, powerful style which likewise characterizes Han Yü's best work. "Tottering," *liang-chiang*, is a confused, disjointed walk characterizing old age or madness, and suggests the theme of the virtuous man who seems mad in contrast to the decadent ways of his own age.

Meng shows a certain critical acumen in noticing the "madness" that characterizes the Mid-T'ang in contrast to the sober, classical style of Tu Fu and the free-wheeling romanticism of Li Po. But as we have seen earlier, madness can be a positive moral quality, an illusion created by an evil age. On the other hand, Meng's feeling about the "madness" of the cult hermetic is uncertain: in this description of Chia Tao he seems to see some of its more ludicrous aspects. In any case, there is a thin but important line between the personal herme-

1. This couplet is quite difficult. Meng Chiao seems to be poking fun at Chia Tao's walk or at his poetic manner. "Tottering" has been used to describe the walk of cranes as well as suggesting old age, madness, or drunkenness. It may be an affectation of Chia Tao or, since Chia Tao was known for his gauntness (see l. 3), it may just be poking fun at Chia's appearance.
2. *MTYSC*, p. 112.

tic world of "Cold Creek" and the self-conscious obfuscations of the cult hermetic.

It is unfortunate that we must omit such interesting poem sequences as "Seeing Off Tan-kung," a virtuoso display of an entire range of T'ang poetic styles. I will quote only the twelfth and last poem of the sequence; in it Meng asserts his own poetic style and makes one of his most impassioned statements about poetry.

> SEEING OFF TAN-KUNG [last of twelve]
>
> The poet suffers making poems—
> Better to waste your efforts trying to fly!
> My whole life, a spirit of useless squawking—
> Not of remonstrating and not of admonishing.
> Bare, leafless twigs hang from cold branches,   5
> Cast off as though a tiny ball of spittle.
> Step after step you shall beg
> For scrap after scrap of clothing.
> Those who have relied on poetry for a livelihood
> Since ancient times have never gotten fat.   10
> The old man, hungry from poetry, is not bitter,
> But the suffering priest's tears fall like rain.[3]

The initial disillusionment of this poem is offset by the positive qualities of leanness, suffering, and refusal to be bitter about such suffering. The first two couplets, however, see poetry not only as a futile task that leads only to suffering, it also fails in the high ethical purpose Meng Chiao has set for it:

> My whole life, a spirit of useless squawking,
> Not of remonstrating and not of admonishing.

In the course of this sequence, Meng Chiao rejected at least two other poetic styles as failing in their moral purpose. We see a genuine despair on Meng's part that his own poetry can accomplish anything. Here at least, the didactic ends of the poetic reform do not seem commensurate with the capabilities of poetry.

The "bare, leafless twigs" are another metaphor for the poet—his "bareness," gauntness, and insignificance. His vileness and lack of value make him seem to himself like "a tiny ball of spittle." This is

3. *MTYSC*, p. 149.

the common fate of all poets, including the monk Tan-kung, whose vows of poverty and begging reinforce his impotence. There seems to be an implicit comparison between the "bareness" of the twigs and Tan's begging for scraps of clothing, like leaves to cover his bareness (accepting the identification of poet with twig). Yet in this state, the poet maintains the positive Confucian value of "not being bitter," even though Tan-kung may weep for him and his suffering.

The following short poems may be considered the mature counterparts to Meng's youthful poems on his failure. In them Meng Chiao considers himself as an old man and as a poet. The themes are often the same ones raised in his poems on other poets, but insofar as they concern him directly, they are infused with that uncanny power Meng Chiao possesses when looking inward.

GOING OUT EAST GATE

A starving horse, even his bones jutting,
I drive him out East Gate.
For a youth, only a day's journey,
For a dying old man, ten days seem too hasty.
The cold shadows are not as I,   5
As they run swiftly, falling on the plain.
In the distant silence I go amid wild grasses,[4]
Terrified that the night moon will fall.
During my life I've woven
A thousand poems in the diction of the Great Odes.[5]   10
My road is as though spun from a silkworm,
Round and round as my twisted, knotted guts.[6]

The "starving horse" here suggests the traditional symbol of the worn-out horse, the Confucian scholar past his prime who is no longer employed by the government. Likewise, its "jutting bones" remind us of "poetry's bones jut in Meng Chiao," in "Playfully Sent to Wu-pen." The slowness of the old man's journey increases to hyperbolic proportions in the third couplet: the poet is going so slow that the afternoon shadows seem to be going faster than he. The poet is traveling eastward ("going out east gate") so that the afternoon shadows lengthen *in front of him.* Thus he imagines himself to be in a

4. "Distant silence," *miao-mo,* often has the association of death.
5. The "Great Odes" are the *Ta-ya,* one of the major divisions of the *Book of Songs.*
6. *MTYSC,* p. 46.

race with the shadows, whose lead advances imperceptibly—it is a
race he cannot win. Furthermore, the shadows involve the declining
sun, which is associated with impending death. From this we move
to a night scene in the wilds, with associations of the world of death.
The moon is his only companion and source of light, with its associations of life. If the moon falls, it will leave him silent and alone in
total darkness.

Three images of threads are used in the last two couplets: the
weaving of poems, the road's resemblance to a thread, and the threadlike twisting and turning of the poet's guts. The thread metaphors
unite these three elements, independently associated in the poet's
mind. As we have seen in many poems before, poetry, wandering,
and emotional suffering are mutual causes and effects. In this poem
the weaving image is separate, but the twisting of the road resembles
the twisting of the poet's emotions (the emotional feeling of being
"twisted up inside" and the actual coiling of the intestines), and
both resemble the twisting and coiling of a silkworm's spun strand of
silk.

WINTER DAY

When an old man handles a man's affairs,
Of a hundred not one reaches completion.
The four hooves of my frozen horse stammer,[7]
Climbing up and over hills I can't hold it back.
Short shadows fly past slanting,   5
Noon's sunbeams won't stay above my head.
When young and strong, the sun gave me brightness,
Now old and failing, the sun gives me grief.
Daily I grieve, imagining to make the sun abide,[8]
But they're arrows of the years, shot forth as at enemies.[9]   10
Thousands of things I haven't tasted yet,
My whole life, vainly imprisoned in myself.
I don't know of any gain from literature—
Until you die, wander carefree to no purpose.[10]

7. We may understand the "stammering" of the horses's hooves either as "faltering"
or, as I prefer, as describing the repetitious sounds of hooves on the ground.

8. "Day/daily" and "sun" are the same word, *jih*.

9. The days pass so swiftly that the sun seems to be an arrow shot across the sky and the
year becomes a flight of arrows.

10. *MTTSC*, p. 47. *Chuang-tzu*, "Lieh-yü K'ou"; "The crafty labor, and the wise are

The intensity of this and the preceding poems is reminiscent of Meng's earlier poems on his failure; however, there are significant differences. First, in these later poems the metaphors are more complex and resonant: the futile race with the afternoon shadows in "Going Out East Gate" and the days as "arrows of the years" in this poem demand more from the reader than the image of the poet as a sick eagle in "Failing." Second, the cognitive aspect of the poet's meditations have become more complex, as we shall see when we discuss the last couplet of the poem. The use of words is bolder, as in the horse's hooves "stammering." Furthermore, while the earlier poems were directed outward, these poems are internal meditations.

In the first couplet we are given to believe that an old man is somehow less than the general category of man. He starts everything, but none of those things ever reaches completion. Thus he becomes, unwillingly, like the Taoist ideal of one with no abilities, "wandering carefree." Even the use of "stammer," implying incompleteness in small matters, is placed in the larger context of his life, which seems to have passed so swiftly that there are "thousands of things I haven't tasted yet."

The sun and the shadows it casts serve as markers of time. Noon is the middle point, passing rapidly, and the swift appearance of shadows on the other side makes the poet acutely aware that time is not a stable point like noon but a constant movement. Meng projects his own emotions toward the sun onto the sun itself, making it love him as a youth and hate him as an old man. The "arrows" that are days flying swiftly overhead are meant to kill him. The ethical poet's habit of ascribing purposeful intention to all phenomena and determining blame is unconsciously operating here in a nonethical context.

A characteristic of Meng's later poetry, the intense emotional response to his sense of personal failure

> Thousands of things I haven't tasted yet,
> My whole life, vainly imprisoned in myself

leads to a philosophical consideration of the problem. The "gain," *li*, Meng might have derived from literature is a negative value in

---

melancholy. Those with no abilities seek nothing; if they have plenty, they *wander carefree*, floating like an untied boat. Vainly [here *hsü* as in l. 12, synonymous with *k'ung* used in l. 14], they wander carefree."

the Confucian tradition, something a moral man should not consider. Thus in saying "I don't know of any gain from literature—" Meng is ambivalent, both blaming and praising himself. Similarly, in the last line "wandering carefree" has a positive sense as it is used in the *Chuang-tzu*, but Meng is using it as a self-reproof. Thus, as Meng sharpens his criticism of the futility of his life, he at the same time boasts of his character—he has avoided opportunistic ambition and has maintained a Taoist freedom. This is a lie, however, for he is anything but carefree.

The following poem sequence is, I feel, Meng Chiao's greatest. As in the other sequences, the structure is a search for meaning and pattern—the meaning of autumn, whose symbolic world we have seen often in Meng Chiao's poetry. The old poet confronts the autumn of the year as the autumn of his life, and the scene becomes an array of hermetic symbols that tell him of man's relation to time and the value of his own life within time. The "autumn meditation" is a subgenre of T'ang poetry, and judging from the works of Tu Fu, Meng Chiao, and Han Yü in this subgenre, we are tempted to believe that each poet put much of himself into them in order to make a permanent statement about himself. The "Autumn Meditations" by Meng Chiao certainly present one of the most chilling visions of an old man in world literature.

AUTUMN MEDITATIONS: FIFTEEN POEMS

I

Lonely bones can't lie down at night,
The singing insects chirp to them.
No tears in an old man's sobbing,
Autumn's dew drips for him.
Departing vigor—abrupt as though cut,   5
Coming decline in a tangle, like a weaving.
I touch the thread's end, no new feelings,
Too many of the griefs that gather are memories.
How could it let me follow a southward sail
Over mountains and rivers to tread my past?   10

Often in Meng Chiao's poetry, as man and his works decay, nature replaces them and assumes human functions. One of the most beautiful examples of this theme is a line by Han Yü in the linked verse "South of the City": "White moths fly over the dancing places." Here Meng Chiao and Han Yü are walking through the ruined estates of formerly great families. Instead of the "moth eyebrows" of lovely women dancing, Han sees real moths (remember that white is the color of old age, death, and decay). In the above poem, too, nature takes on the functions of the dying poet: the autumn dew becomes his tears and the crickets are "singing," *yin*, which usually means "to chant poetry."

The absolute loss of his vigor, its having been "cut," is set against the confusion of old age, a tangle of perceptions and emotions like a weaving, the ends of whose threads the poet is touching. The implications of the "thread's end" are much like the English "to be at the end of one's rope," although in Chinese the image is original. The world of death is one of absolutes, of cut threads and thread ends—of his vigor and his potential for new experience: "no new feelings." In contrast, the world of his remaining life is a tangled confusion of twisted threads. Another image of cloth and threads is that of the "sail" in the last couplet, the "weaving" of past experiences that carry him over his past life. This review of past experience is the only kind of experience possible for him now, since there are "no new feelings."

The poet is in a tenuous in-between state, neither wholly alive nor dead, able neither to lie down and rest nor to go off and relive his past. The phrasing of the last line is quite peculiar in Chinese:

Rivers   mountains   tread   past

The above translation is grammatically the most direct and in keeping with Meng's tendency to describe intangible things, such as one's past, in tangible terms, such as "treading." However, one might also translate it as: "My treading over mountains and rivers is a thing of the past." In any case, the question posed in the last couplet is a rhetorical one, implying that he can no more return to his past than he can have new feelings.

II

In autumn moonlight the face turns to ice,
Old wanderer, the force of his spirit reduced.
Chill dew drips a dream to pieces,
A rugged wind combs the bones cold.

On the mat, print pressed by sickness,[11]　　　　5
In the heart, writhing coils of grief.
These feelings of doubt are based on nothing,
Listen in vain to things—mostly without cause.
A wu-t'ung tree, bare and towering,[12]
It's echo like plucking a lament.

In the moonlight, the poet's "face" (literally "the color of his face") becomes ice, the cold whiteness (color) so often associated with suffering and purity in Meng Chiao's poetry and with impending death in traditional autumn symbolism. It is equally plausible to construe the line: "The face of the autumn moon turns to ice," in which the moon itself takes on the deathly chill of autumn. This ambiguity is particularly meaningful in that, as we shall see, the moon is to become Meng Chiao's alter ego, as well as the instrument of his destruction. His moonlit face and the "moonface" resemble one another.

"Reduced" is *tan*, meaning "single," "simple," "thin," and a "single thickness of *cloth*." Here, *tan* refers to the solitude of the poet as well as the weakness of his spirit. Autumn is gradually stripping the poet of all he possesses: his vigor (I.5); hope for new experience (I.7); hope of reliving old experiences (I.9–10); and his will, the "force of his spirit" (II.2).

The "chill dew" not only keeps him awake physically ("drips a dream to pieces"), it also drips to pieces his dream of the past, of returning home; the dew is, we may remember, nature's version of his tears, taking over his functions because he is on the point of death. The wind's "ruggedness," *ch'iao*, is an essential quality of the moral poet, as Meng said of Lu Yin—

Poets are usually pure, rugged,
Die from hunger, cling to desolate mountains[13]

—and of Liu Yen-shih: "The poet takes loneliness and ruggedness as his legacy." Again nature has taken on a quality belonging to the poet himself. The wind is harsh just as the poet's emaciated shape is

11. I. e. the sick poet, having laid on his mat for a long time, leaves the imprint of his body on it when he gets up.
12. The wu-t'ung tree, besides being associated with autumn, was a favorite wood for making Chinese lutes.
13. *MTYSC*, p. 190.

harsh: the poet and his physical surroundings are one. His boniness is the emaciation brought on by virtue, a tangible physical quality representing a spiritual as well as a stylistic one: "Poetry's bones jut in Meng Chiao" (from "Playfully Sent to Wu-pen"). Meng Chiao's organic metaphor allows these many different worlds to coexist in one symbolic quality. Indeed, in these first four lines we find most of the spiritual-physical-ethical-stylistic qualities that Meng Chiao values—coldness, emaciation from hunger, ruggedness, whiteness (of the moon and ice), loneliness, and old age.

The next line adds yet another positive quality, sickness. The poet's bony body has pressed a contour on the mat on which he has been lying ill. "Print," *wen*, also means "writing," as though the imprint on the mat could be "read" by the viewer. "Pressed," *yin*, likewise means literally "imprinted by a seal," as though the poet's sick body had left its seal or signature, on the mat, a hermetic sign given the poet to decipher.

In the fourth couplet the poet rejects the symbolism of the autumn world: his feelings are "based on nothing" and "without cause." This denial of hermetic meaning in the scene serves only to intensify the impression that they *do* have meaning for him. Though he tries to extricate himself from this world of his fantasy, he cannot. The example he gives of his "listening in vain" is that the sound of the wind in the wu t'ung tree sounds like a lute playing a lament. The strings of the lute carry on the thread imagery, which is here associated with a "lament," a song about death.

The wu-t'ung sounds like a lute, as well as being a tree from which lutes are made. Its "bareness" and mountainlike "towering" are two more positive moral qualities, associated with the others listed above. As Meng finds these correspondences between his inner state and the external world around him (both in general and in particulars— moon, wind, and wu-t'ung), he is not only being "replaced" by nature, he is merging with it. By its sound, this tree announces the poet's death (the hermetic sign), and in its "bareness,"—its withered, dying state—it is one with the poet.

III

One foot the moonlight penetrates the door,
Intrepid, icy, like a sword's flight.
Old bones are startled by it,

And my sick strength is made even less.
Insects lust bitterly for night's beauty, 5
Birds make a high nest for the stars' glitter.
The widow arranges old silk,
The orphan weeps, drawing forth still more longing.
Floating years, not to be sought after,
Declining footsteps always return in the evening. 10

In the first couplet, the moonlight coming in through a crack in the door becomes a sword to kill the poet. The autumn moon, traditionally the primary symbol of that season of death and destruction, becomes the instrument of the poet's execution. This comes out even more clearly in the sixth poem of the sequence. We find here the association of sexuality and death, common in western literature but comparatively rare in Chinese. The "lust," *t'an-se,* of the insects and the familial "nest" made for the stars parallel the widow and orphan, respectively. The world of nature assumes human functions of life, lust, and family, while human beings find death in parallel situations, the death of a spouse or the death of a parent. The "nest for the stars" is likewise an elaborate visual image: the stars are seen above an empty nest, and it seems the birds have made the nest for them, their small, round whiteness resembling eggs. Both "beauty" (*se,* literally, "color") and the stars, the images of sexual desire and family, are things of light and life against the darkness of the night. But they mean life only to nature; for human beings they are like the moon / sword, threatening death / light.

The widow's "old silk" may be her weaving, continuing the thread imagery, with an overtone of the convention that a wife stays home and weaves clothes for an absent husband to keep away the cold. The significance of the thread imagery varies throughout the sequence, but in general it seems to be associated with the various aspects of human life, especially with emotions. When one reaches the end of a thread or a thread is cut, some part of his life is gone. "Old silk" may also mean the widow's hair, "silken threads," *ssu,* being commonly used to describe the white hair of old age. While nature, in the form of the insects, feels the lust of youth, the widow combs her white hair, a vain act of making herself beautiful for no one. "Draw forth," *ch'ou,* also means to spin out threads as a silkworm does; thus the orphan, who "draws forth" his longing, is giving up the "threads" that make up his life.

IV

Autumn has come, the old man gets still poorer,
A broken-down cottage with no door.
A slab of moonlight falls on my bed,
Through the four walls, wind gets in my clothes.
Dreams that went far no longer are distant,   5
So that a weak heart can easily return.
Shang blossoms, about to lose their green,[14]
Coil around as they vie in their remaining splendor.
Occasions are few to tread the fields,
Brooding in sickness, I go astray when confronted with things. 10
Insects hidden away in the roots of the grasses—
The meaning of their life is as insignificant as my own.

Old age and poverty, elements of the "virtuous suffering," are set
in autumn, the season proper to the old poet. The cloth/thread
imagery appears again in the poet's clothes, which cannot keep out
the wind, hinting back to the widow's weaving in the preceding
poem. Related to the theme of the merging of the autumn world
with that of the dying poet are the images of penetration, the en-
croachment of the autumn world into the poet's. The preceding poem
showed the moonlight *penetrating* the door; here the door is missing
(letting the outside *in*) and the autumn wind comes in through the
walls and the poet's clothes.

In contrast to the autumn world's penetration into the poet's
world, the autonomous world of the poet is confined; he cannot
move outward, penetrating the autumn world. His dreams that
"went far" (he dreamed of distant places) no longer can do so; they
must stay near by so that the "weak heart" (the spirit which leaves
the body in dream) can get back to body easily. Not only is his
spirit confined, he is physically confined, unable any more to "tread
the fields." The summation of this sense of confinement is found in
the last couplet, in which the poet compares the "meaning of his
life" with that of the insects—his ambitions confined by his insignificance, his body confined to a tiny spot, his time confined to the
short span remaining in his symbolic autumn.

In this context, the image of returning in the last couplet of the

14. *Shang* is the musical mode associated with autumn, and by conventional synesthesia
can describe any autumn thing.

third poem takes on special significance: with the weakness of old age he retreats from the external world into his home and into himself. In the world outside the poet "goes astray." "Go astray," *wei*, is a difficult word, and its use here must certainly echo its use in the famous couplet of the second of Tu Fu's "Autumn Wastes":

> Easy to understand the principle of this floating life—
> It is not to make a single thing go astray [from its proper role].[15]

The meaning of both poets' usages is less than certain, but Meng seems to be suggesting here the fantasy world he has been creating. Like his affirmation in the second poem that his fantasy was "based on nothing" (II. 7–8), here Meng seems to be saying that he sees things as having other roles than their proper ones in the autumn world—moon/swords, lusting insects, and nesting stars, for example. However, at this point in the sequence, Meng cannot escape this bizarre, hermetic world of autumn.

V

> Bamboo and wind speak to me tapping,
> I hear them hidden away in the darkness of my bedchamber.
> Ghosts and demons fill my declining hearing,
> Blurred and indistinct—can't distinguish them.
> *Shang* leaves follow down in a dry rain,   5
> Autumn clothes lie down in a thin cloud.
> Sick bones can cleave things,
> Even with this sour moaning I can finish a poem.
> Lean things gather, as bare as this,
> My vigor falls, following the westward brightness.   10
> Twining around, a single thread of life,
> Which, in vain they say, is tied to the mighty forces of the cosmos.

Just as the wu-t'ung/lute was trying to tell Meng Chiao something in the second poem, here wind and bamboo are talking to him. The darkness he experiences is the approach of death complemented by the departure of sunlight and his vigor (V. 10). This sensory deprivation is both the symbolic darkness of death and the physical failing

15. *CTS*, c. 229, p. 2499.

of his sight and hearing. In youth things are clearly distinguished, but in his decline everything is "blurred and indistinct," leading to his "going astray" when confronted with things. Thus in his fantasy the sounds become "ghosts and demons."

Rain is life-giving, traditionally associated with luxuriant growth of vegetation and the kindness of a superior to his subordinates. Here in autumn we have a "death-rain" of dry leaves, whose sounds seem to be in the *shang* mode of autumn. In the preceding poem there was still a little sunlight left and the vegetation was *"about to* lose its green" (IV.7–8). Now that green is gone and the leaves fall.

We find clothes imagery again as the poet compares himself lying down in his white clothes to a thin cloud. "Thin" here is *tan*, the "reduced" state of the poet's spirit in II.2; it is the "single thickness of cloth" which can let in the cold (see III.7 and IV.4). White, we remember, is the symbolic color of autumn and death, as well as being the color of funeral clothes. The fragility of the emaciated poet in his thin robes is well compared to the light insubstantialness of a cloud and is reminiscent of the following passage in the first poem of "Lament for Lu Yin":

> Since this white cloud had no master,
> When it flew off, its mind was free from care.[16]

In both passages the cloud suggests the "lightness" of the poet's life (in Chinese, meaning that one neither has nor desires to have a strong hold on life) and his solitude. There is also an implicit comparison between the poet's lying down and the falling of the leaves in the first line of the couplet: they are parallel events, suggesting death, in the autumn scene.

The poet's emaciation leaves his bones jutting, to such an extent that he can "cleave things." This is reminiscent of the moon as a sword (III.1–2) and the "cutting" of his vigor (I.5). "Poetry," *wen* ("literature") is the same word as that used for "print" in II.5; thus we might take the "also" as referring back to that earlier usage: "On the mat, the *wen* (print/writing) pressed by sickness" (II.5). Responding to that earlier passage, line eight of this poem might be translated: "This sour moaning also becomes *wen* (writing/poetry)." Sickness, which has left its "message" on the poet's bed, has also brought the poet's moaning, another kind of *wen*/writing.

16. *MTYSC*, p. 190.

As we have seen earlier, this entire image complex of hunger, emaciation, cold, etc. contains qualities that have stylistic counterparts. "Sourness" is both the real sound of his moaning and a stylistic quality he values in his poems, as is "bare."

Lines five and six may mean that the poet has shed his clothes as the tree shed its leaves, hence he can see his bones, which are gnarled and "bare" like a tree ("bare" does not mean "naked" in Chinese; it describes leafless, withered plants, and as such would only be metaphorical for his nakedness). Hence the poet is surrounded by bare, withered things—the tree, his body, and his poems.

Just as his vigor was "cut" (I.5), his "thread of life" can be cut, perhaps by his "cleaving" bones. The thread of his life is supposed to be "tied to the mighty forces of the cosmos," but such a theory is "vain," for this thread is fragile and can fall or be cut away. Meng often prefaces a traditional principle with "in vain they say"; like Meng's technique of destroying a positive scene he himself has created, this technique has particular power in the treatment of tradition and cherished principles in a bitter, ironic fashion. One fine example is in "The Nation's Dead":

> In vain they say man is the most divine.
> All around his white bones lie scattered in confusion.

This refers to a famous passage in the *Shu-ching*, V.l.i.3: "Among all things, man alone is divine." The insignificance of one human life, one "thread of life," amid the forces of the cosmos is the same insignificance he felt in comparing his life to that of the insects in the grass.

VI

> Old bones fear the autumn moon,
> The autumn moon is a sword's edge.
> Against its thin might you can't shield yourself,
> My cold spirit freezes up for no reason.
> The widowed bird makes a nest for that hollow mirror,   5
> A gale of fairies cleanses the floating ice.[17]
> I fear my startled footsteps will fly away of themselves,
> But my sickness is great—I cannot rise to the others.

17. The "hollow mirror" and the "floating ice" refer to the moon. Line six is probably a metaphor for the wind blowing away clouds from in front of the moon.

On my single sheet I awake in the gleaming whiteness,
Lying emaciated, my heart cautious and frightened.[18]   10
A washed river whose water you cannot see,
Passing through the foul, it makes it clear and pure.
Long ago when my poetry was vigorous, it was
    empty discourse,
Now my poetry declines—what can I rely on?

This poem is mostly fantasy, and as such it is the most difficult of
the sequence. The "old bones" which in the preceding poem could
"cleave things," now lie in terror of the sword of moonlight. The
"thin" line of light that first enters the room, perhaps through a
crack in the door, is an invincible killer. This moonlight is "icy"
(II.1, VI.6), so that the poet's spirit freezes. The light is spiritually
cold rather than physically cold, hence the rational voice in Meng
says the freezing is "for no reason." The "thinness," *hsien*, of the blade
of moonlight is primarily the thinness of a thread—a "strand of
light" will cut the "single thread of life."

Echoing lines five to eight in the third poem, the bird has become a
"widowed bird," whose nest is now for the moon, an "empty mirror," rather than for the stars. The autumnal barrenness that
previously reigned in the human world is now extended to the world
of nature; mateless and childless, the only thing that appears in the
hen-bird's nest is the moon, the "sword."

The wind that blows the clouds away reveals the full light of the
moon. The wind seems full of "fairies," immortals, to whose death-
less purity Meng Chiao aspires. This is the familiar conflict between
the real and the ideal: the sick body longs to "rise to" the immortals
but cannot. On the other hand, the purifying aspect of the moonlight penetrates physical foulness. Here we might point out that the
moon has two contradictory associations, one of death and the other
of purity and immortality. Immortality is a traditional association
of the moon; in it live Ch'ang-e, possessor of the secret of immortality,
and the Hare, who eternally grinds the elixir of immortality. This
contradiction, however, runs throughout the sequence in other
images: old age, ice, and sickness, for example, mean both death and
barrenness as well as moral purity.

The second episode of the poet's fantasy is his awakening in a

18. *Book of Songs*, #195: "Cautious and frightened, / As though treading thin ice."

moonlit bed: the killing sword has finally reached him. The "single sheet" of the bed is *tan*, the same word used to describe the "force of the spirit" (II.2) and the cloud of clothes (V.6). The poet now finds himself on a "single sheet" of deathlight. This deathlight is appropriately like ice, as clearly implied in the allusion to the *Book of Songs*. Thus Meng Chiao's fantasy is that he is lying on a "thin sheet" of ice (moon like ice: VI.6, II.1) and is terrified of falling through it. Extrapolating, he imagines that he is lying on the ice of a river, which probably refers specifically to the Yellow River whose turbidity is notorious. To sum up this complicated metaphor, Meng is lying on his bed covered with moonlight and imagines it is ice on a river; the ice/moonlight has purified the river by hiding the foulness beneath. It is into this mortal foulness of sickness, death, and drowning that the poet is afraid of falling. Again we have an "in-between" state: he is on thin ice above a foul river, and below flying immortals to whom he cannot rise.

Finally Meng Chiao turns to his poetry, another aspect of the organic universe, which like everything else reflects the dominant structures of the macrocosm. "Empty discourse," *k'ung-shuo*, is reminiscent of Han Yü's "empty words," *k'ung-wen* ("Poem of Hsieh Tzu-jan," p. 43), that which the moral poet seeks to avoid. In this couplet, Meng becomes aware of the contradiction mentioned above: now, as Meng attains the virtuous emaciation and suffering of old age, he is able to treat moral topics and avoid the "empty discourse" of his youthful poetry; however, in keeping with the operations of the organic universe, there has been a decline in his poetry attendant on his physical decline. As has happened often before, the correspondences in the organic universe lead to insoluble paradoxes.

VII

Old and sick, many strange broodings,[19]
Dawn and evening—heart's not the same.
Shang insects weep for the declining cycle,
Cannot unravel their tangled echoes.
Autumn grasses, frail as hair,   5
A pure fragrance joins me to distant gold.[20]

19. "Strange broodings," *yi-lü*, may refer to the strangeness of the fantasy world the poet has been creating. It may also be translated as "different worries," suggesting the mutability of an old man's emotions, as in line two.

20. "Gold" refers to chrysanthemums.

Yet how can this late fragrance last very long?
The speeding sunlight also darkens easily.
In vain I'm ashamed of my studies as a youth,
What can my knowledge undertake now in these twilight
    years?   10
Once the talent I revealed was slandered,
The wisdom hidden within me quickly deepened.
Fending off that depth, not fending off eminence
Was the attitude the ancients warned against.

In the first couplet of this poem, Meng seems to have become
aware of the contradictions in his fantasy interpretations of autumn;
he feels the instability and tenuousness of his meditations. The heart
that changes from dawn to evening cannot decide if the meaning of
autumn is to be found in the "frail" autumn grasses, autumn's
aspect of weakness and death, or in the noble chrysanthemum, a
traditional symbol of the virtue and dignity of old age. These alternatives are the poles of meaning which inform the contradictions—
all the images of hunger, cold, bareness, etc. contain aspects of death
and suffering as well as of "resoluteness amid deprivation."

This paradox is the confusion whose meaning the poet must unravel: "Cannot unravel their tangled echoes." Or, as in the first
poem of the sequence: "Coming decline in a tangle like a weaving."
And in the fifth poem:

Ghosts and demons fill my declining hearing,
Blurred and indistinct—can't distinguish them.

To understand autumn, the poet must distinguish the various threads
of the tangle.

The poet next offers an interpretation of his life. Having failed to
apply himself to studies as a youth, not only was his political
life a failure, he now lacks the wisdom to deal with the autumn
situation. (In Confucian humanism, learning is not simply an
adornment; it is the only way to become a whole man, the only door
to the tradition.) Then there follows a counterstatement; instead of
there being some failure on his part, the cause of his failure was
slander by others. Such ruin in his public life led him to inner
wisdom. Here we have another antithetical pair, parallel to "frail
grasses" and chrysanthemums. On the one hand, because of his

failures as a youth, he is now physically declining and intellectually incompetent, at the mercy of external forces, as are the autumn plants; on the other hand, the deep wisdom he has attained by being driven inward corresponds to the chrysanthemums. The last couplet is an attack on seeking public renown instead of inner knowledge; it is an affirmation of the second interpretation—inner wisdom—as the ideal of antiquity.

VIII

Year's twilight—the state of things dry,
In the autumn wind, the sounds of weapons and armor.
Weaving, weaving, they toil without clothes,[21]
Chirping, the other insects sing in vain.
These *shang* sounds stir at midnight,   5
Lame footsteps cease their forward progress.
My glossy black hair has become like an autumn garden,
Once cut, it will grow no more.
Youth like a hungry flower,
Seen in the blink of an eye, then bright no more.   10
The good man is as fixed as a mountain,
Lesser men quibble over trifles.
Quibble often, often lose long life—
By Heaven's Way you take care for its fullness.

As we suggested earlier (in connection with V.5), dryness suggests withering and death in contrast to water, which suggests richness and benevolence. While earlier it was simply a quality of the leaves, in this poem it has become indicative of the "state of things." We have seen autumn's aspect as the destroyer in the moon/sword; here it appears in the sounds of armor and weapons in the wind, suggesting both dryness and metal, the symbolic element of autumn. The poet's weakness and vulnerability to "penetration" contrasts with the strength and invulnerability of the "armored" autumn scene. The poet's clothes are only a "thin cloud" (V.6) which let in the cold (IV.4)—not the armor of the season. The crickets seem to the poet to share his vulnerability to the cold and are busy weaving clothes. If threads are aspects of the poet's life, then collectively, in woven clothes, they keep out the death-bearing cold of autumn.

21. I.e. the crickets. "Weaving, weaving" (Middle Chinese *tsiak-tsiak*) is also onomatopoeia for the sounds of crickets.

The poet's footsteps are "lame" (from his sickness) and then cease altogether; this movement is a metaphor for decline and death. The brilliant comparison of his hair, a conventional symbol for the aging process in Chinese poetry, with an autumn garden reverses the metaphor in the preceding poem, in which the grass was as "frail as hair." This reversal serves to merge the dying poet even more fully with nature. Likewise, the comparison of his youth to a "hungry flower" suggests the plants coiling upward for the last rays of sunlight in the fourth poem (IV.7–8).

Out of the hermetic maze of interlocking associations in the first six poems of the sequence, Meng's symbols and metaphors are taking on greater clarity. In face of the confusion of autumn, the poet must take a stand. Thus he affirms the moral firmness of the "good man" against his own confusion and vacillation. The mountain metaphor implies not only firmness of principles but durability as well, our first hint of Meng's solution to autumn's message of transience. The "quibbles" and worries of lesser men, like his own worries and concentration on the minutiae of autumn, only serve to make one's life shorter. The "trifles" are literally "strands of silk and hairs," *ssu-hao,* the images we have seen used so often to suggest the fragility of life.

IX

The cold dew is always sickly, pale,
Wind through bare branches breathes out in the morning.
As autumn deepens, the moon grows clear and bitter,
Insects grow old, their voices rough and harsh.
Crimson beads are strung upon the branches,   5
The fragrant gold creeps slowly and leisurely.
Trees and grasses also respond to the season,
Blooming in the cold as though it were the remnant of spring.
I grieve for my life that falls like the leaves,
Within me—what state of mind?   10

In response to his affirmation of moral firmness in the preceding poem, this piece is perfectly clear and closely resembles conventional autumn meditations. The decline of things in autumn is clearly pictured in the first two couplets; these characteristics of the autumn scene, moreover, apply equally to the poet himself. But amid the decline there is a "late flowering" of the berries and chrysanthemums. This late flowering and the symbolic chrysanthemum (gold, l. 6), both suggesting dignity and beauty in old age, are the positive aspects of the autumn world. However, this image of late flowering amid general decline is a much clearer statement of the autumn paradox. Unfortunately, from this tentative understanding of the season's meaning, Meng Chiao falls back into the nightmare world in the course of the following poems.

X

An old man is different from dawn to evening,
He may live or die in each single day.
Sitting, I seek the calm of a single meal,
Or lie down with the emptiness of a million scenes.
My eyesight short, can't see to the door,   5
My hearing coarse, can't pursue sounds in the wind.
Still it's like being a carven image,
Which lacks even the least perception.
With streaming tears I left any inception,
Yet I hope to meet my end, pure and white.   10
Lonely, isolated from my literary friends,
But especially close to old hermits in the wilds.
The year's green mourns that it yellows,
By autumn time the scattering is already finished.
Since the four seasons press closely on one another,   15
A million broodings naturally gather.
Carefree in the South, by the boundaries of vast floods,
Now, poverty in the North in the rocky soil.
Feelings of yesteryear, sunken in remote rivers,
Longings of a man in decline, tied to autumn's Mount Sung.   20
The food I've hoed can't fill my belly,
Clothes of leaves always make the body ugly.
My dusty threads won't straighten themselves out,
And who will understand my ancient poems?
Ghosts and demons whistle, hidden in bamboo,   25
Ch'u's sharp iron turns into dragons.[22]
An ambitious scholar has many different emotions,

22. "Ch'u's sharp iron" may refer obliquely to a pair of buried swords found by Lei Huan in the Chin Dynasty. The two swords were separated but later found each other again and turned into dragons. The point of this image seems to be that what is harsh, rugged, and sharp (the poet in his present state) can be transformed into a transcendent being.

But fated misery occurs from internal evil.
Always I've brooded that writing has broken my clothes,
Until I die, I'm like a boy just beginning his studies.   30
Practice true music, don't practice more noise,
If you practice only noise, you'll always be thick-skulled,
    deaf to the Way.
The words in my breast are gleaming bright,
I wish to copy them out into the high peaks of poetry.

Despite its apparent complexity ("And who will understand my
ancient poems?" X.24), this poem is an affirmation of the positive
characteristics, the "late flowering," which can grow out of autumnal
decline. The problems lie in the complexity of its argument rather
than in a maze of ambivalent symbols. In the first couplet, the poet
states the insecurity of old age without the images of terror seen in the
earlier poems. Autumn no longer intrudes on him, threatening him
with death; he accepts his transitoriness. He turns inward, the direction in which he had been driven in the earlier poems, and there
finds "the calm of a single meal." There is a new dignity in life
reduced to its bare essentials. Likewise, he can step back from his
fantasies, the "emptiness of a million scenes," seeing them for what
they are.

    As he turns into himself, contact with the external world is lost;
his perception dulls and he becomes like

    . . . a carven image,
    Which lacks even the least perception.

Lines nine and ten are difficult and can be interpreted in several
ways. Meng may be saying once again "no new feelings" (I.7), that
he has no longer any chance to begin again, but that ancient purity
will grow naturally from his present state of decline. He may be
referring to the begining of his life, the suffering he experienced, and
now the virtuous old age that has resulted from it. Or he may be
speaking of the sequence, of the distress he felt in the first poems, and
of the resolution which is growing out of that distress. He reaches this
inner purity through a process of reduction to poverty (X.18) and the
loss of external goods, to decline and confinement (X.20), the loss of
his ability to go out into the external world, and finally to hunger and
poor clothes (X.21–22). These reductions bring him to an awareness
of the purity of his own nature.

His ancient-styled moral poetry and his "iron" will, which may be transformed into a dragon, will bring him inner victory just as they have brought him external suffering. Meng vows to pursue his studies, to strive for moral perfection. This newly found morality, the "words in his breast," will become his finest poetry. Since "fated misery occurs from internal evil," the essential good in his heart will transform the world around him and bring him happiness. In this we can see the fundamental assumption of the ethically organized, organic universe: by putting the inner, spiritual world in order, the outer world will be rectified and find a similar order. Inner wrong has caused the poet's misfortunes; having turned inward, he can correct the wrong and affirm the proper attitude, thereby getting rid of his misery.

XI

My hidden bitterness gets stronger day by day,
My old man's strength gets fainter step by step.
Always I fear that, getting out of bed for a while,
If I reach the door, I'll never come back.
The hungry value a single meal,   5
The cold value a single robe.
If floating on broad waters, there would surely be shores,
Even if seeming to walk to no purpose, you're still headed
     toward something.
In my speech I'm losing coherence,
On the outside of my body, scars of sickness appear.   10
Since cassia grubs are a hidden impurity,
They ruin the beauty of cassia flowers.
A rebuke and you've lost your reputation utterly,[23]
For all time, reeking words will be heard of you.
About to die, I regret it but still can't pursue and change it.   15
Alas, my frivolous deeds—
I end my days galloping with a four-horse team.[24]

As in "Cold Creek" the sequence here turns from tentative resolu-

23. "Reputation" is literally "fragrance," one's good name. This hearkens back to the cassia flowers.
24. *Analects*, XII, 8: "A four-horse team can't keep up with the tongue," i.e. when something is said, it cannot be taken back. Besides suggesting the lies Meng feels have been told about him or the wrong things he himself has said, this may also refer to the swiftness with which he is approaching the end of his life.

tion to despair; Meng seems always to half resolve a problem, lose the resolution, and finally find it again. This poem also begins with a process of turning inward. As his outer strength wanes, the intensity of his emotions grows. By exerting himself, outward ruin would come (XI.3–4, 7–8). By such inner concentration and deprivation, simple things take on special value: hunger makes one value food, cold makes one value clothes.

In contemplating his outer ruin, Meng Chiao returns to the principle stated in the preceding poem: "Fated misery occurs from inner evil." Here, instead of suggesting the potential to perfect oneself, it leads the poet to regret and despair. An internal "cassia grub," a flaw in his nature, has brought on this external ruin. Though he regrets the errors of his youth, nothing can be done about them. In a frenetic "galloping with a four-horse team" the poet ends, rushing toward the end of his life and chasing his errors. This mood of despair leads him into the next poem.

XII

The flowing cycle, a flash almost gone,
Bare branches snap, all call out to me.
In thorny jujube branches the wind weeps sourly,
Wu-t'ung leaves, high frosty faces.
Old insects sing like dry iron,   5
Frightened beasts roar lonely like tinkling jade.
Shang-toned air washes the sounds thin,
Evening shadows drive off the light, press on it.
You cannot block out what gathers in your ears,
You cannot flee what chokes your soul.   10
I walk limping, strewing an excess of melancholy,
Or sit hidden—who is there to join me?
Not a single thread of vigor to spin out,
If I cut my feelings, they would fill a thousand measures.[25]
For lucid poetry we have the name T'iao,[26]   15
For golden chrysanthemums we have the name T'ao.[27]
When I gather up the poems I had cast away before,
I sigh that they're but a hair's-worth compared to those.

25. "Measures," *tao*, puns on an alternate meaning of the word "knife."
26. The poet Hsieh T'iao, 464–99.   27. The poet T'ao Ch'ien, 365–427.

Hidden and melancholy, these words of the year's end,
Falling like leaves, cannot be grasped.   20

The flash of light which is man's and nature's span of life is almost
gone; shadows gather and "drive off" the remaining light. The first
eight lines of this poem are a terrifying vision of autumn—breaking,
weeping, and freezing. The "iron" Meng had previously hoped
would turn into a dragon now characterizes the cries of dying insects.
The interlocking associations between this poem and earlier poems in
the sequence identify the old man and the autumn scene; for example, in IV.11–12 Meng identified himself with the insects and in
X.26 used iron as a metaphor for himself—now the cries of the insects
are "iron."

Most disturbing to the poet is the fact that his poetry, the "bright
words in his breast," offers him no hope of eternal fame, since he
feels it cannot compare with the great poems of the past. The "hair's-
worth," *mao* (no value) is reminiscent of the "trifles" (VIII.12) that
shorten a man's lifespan. The thread imagery in these cases does
indicate an aspect of his life, but suggests pettiness and insignificance
rather than fragility.

XIII

Frosty air enters my sick bones,
Ice grows on the body of an old man.
Declining hairs jab me in darkness,
Chill pains I cannot endure.
Squawking, I stretch to the light,   5
Forcing myself ever more, I grasp what I lean on,
Then sit down emaciated, frame about to snap,
Belly starving, mind on the point of collapse.
Those fools around me encourage medicine,
In their words it seems like I'm despised.   10
I prick up my ears, my choked spirit opens,
Now realizing the possibility of a good outcome.
In the daylight I gaze on my remaining sores,
And when darkness locks me in, I hear buzzing flies.
How sharp their sense of smell is!   15
The boils they scent are half scabbed over.

> You, flies, never satisfied with your hidden poisons—
> I can vaunt what life I've got left.
> Their frozen flights fortunately can't go far,
> But my reflecting heart warns of winter ordinances.   20
> Each has his time to live and perish,
> Heat and cold advance bitterly on one another.
> Looking up, I thank the Old Master of Fate,
> I asked for my life, and my wish has had a sign.

The proposition in the tenth poem (X.33–34), that poetry might lead the poet out of misery, and the failure of that proposition in the twelfth poem, leave Meng Chiao hopeless. The body, deprived of its senses and on the point of death, begins to merge with nature:

> Frosty air enters my sick bones,
> Ice grows on the body of an old man.

Against this state, Meng "stretches to the light," toward life, and makes exertion *outward*. This exertion is a failure, and when he sits back down he is on the point of "snapping" like the branches (XII.-2). This final exertion having failed and his "mind on the point of collapse," the poet is given medicine. With this, perception is restored: "I prick up my ears, my choked spirit opens." The setback in his spiritual recovery which occurred in the two preceding poems is overcome.

"Flies," traditional metaphors for slanderers and petty enemies, attack the poet as he recovers, but in vain—his sores now are only "remaining," and the poet can defy the "hidden poison": "Yet I can vaunt what life I've got left." The status of the flies in this poem is difficult but characteristic of Meng Chiao's metaphors: they are probably real flies, which Meng sees as playing an important part in the symbolic struggle between the forces of mortality and evil and those of immortality and good. Having defeated his disease, Meng can now experience the "late flowering," the dignity and wisdom that comes with autumn and old age. The recovery from his sickness is the "sign" given him by the "Old Master of Fate," a sign that Meng will live, and of the true meaning of autumn.

As we mentioned above, in Meng's sequences the first attempt at resolution and understanding is usually a partial failure. The second attempt, the ritual gesture in "Cold Creek" and the medicine in this sequence, is successful. In contrast to the crucial gesture in "Cold Creek," the resolution of Meng Chiao's sickness by medicine is ex machina. But "Autumn Meditations" goes beyond "Cold Creek" in that, following this restoration of life, Meng Chiao goes on to explain fully his understanding of autumn and to treat in universal terms the relation between man and time.

XIV

The Yellow River will flow inverted back to the skies,[28]
For all waters there is a coming back.
The human heart doesn't equal the waters,
Straight off it goes and never turns back,
Straight off it goes and some are clever,   5
But can never reach P'eng-lai.[29]
Straight off they go, not knowing exhaustion,
You only hear of them reaching some board or ministry.
Hold with the past, don't lose the past,
If you lose the past, the will easily crumbles,   10
If you lose the past, the sword also breaks,
If you lose the past, the lute also laments.
The Master had tears for the loss of the past,[30]
At that time they fell in streams.
This aged poet has a heart concerned with loss of the past,   15
By now it's cold and snowy white.
Bones of the past without corrupting flesh,
Clothes of the past like moss.[31]
I urge you, try hard to hold with the past—
If you hold with the past, all foulness will melt away.

In this poem all confusions have disappeared and the poet can make a firm and authoritative statement of the relation between transience and death in the world of autumn and the meaning of

28. This probably refers to the belief that at some point the ocean joins with the heavens, so that the Yellow River would flow into the ocean, up over the world, and down again in the form of rain.

29. P'eng-lai is fairyland, the dwelling place of the immortals, which no mortal man ever reaches.

30. I.e. Confucius.

31. "Of the past" is also used in the sense of simply "old," by word-magic uniting antiquity and the old man.

old age. In face of absolute and inexorable transience (XIV.1–8), man has only one thing that makes him eternal—the tradition, the knowledge of the collective human past. Thus the collective human past is eternal only as long as the tradition is preserved—"hold with the past." Furthermore, as we shall see more clearly in the next poem, the tradition can confer immortality on individuals. The preservation of the past is an affirmation of the eternity of mankind: the loss of the past renders individual life meaningless—the will to achieve great deeds (to be accorded a place in the tradition) is lost, deeds of valor ("the sword") are unremembered, and the lute laments because death then has real meaning. This is about as eloquent and impassioned an affirmation of *fu-ku* beliefs as one will find. Even though such a feeling for tradition is alien to the modern West, we can perhaps feel here some of the beauty and importance it held for the "Confucian" reformers of the T'ang. Though less intellectually adept than the Sung Confucian philosophers, these T'ang reformers more than made up for this lack by their depth of feeling for the tradition.

The word-magic that brings together the "ancient," that which belongs to the tradition, and the "oldness" of an old man is central to Meng Chiao's affirmation of the positive aspects of an old man's sufferings and autumn. By his very closeness to death, possessing "bones . . . without corrupting flesh," he is closer to the purity of the tradition, and about to enter the collective memory of mankind. All that is old, pure, white, cold, bony, etc. is characteristic of the old man as well as the tradition, affirming his closeness to the ideals of antiquity. But a place in the tradition is guaranteed only in writing, and it is concern for this which appears in the last poem of the sequence.

XV

By vile slander you see no blood,
But it kills people in droves.
Its sound is like the dog of some poor family,
Barking in its den so "morally."
Slander pains hidden ghosts to weeping,   5
Where slander creeps in, gold becomes worthless.
And what need that the words be many?—
The misery of ruin resides in one hearing.

The tongues of past slanders never cease,
Even now the books are full of them.   10
When a man of today reads the books of the past,
He must distinguish good and evil.
The fires of Ch'in couldn't burn the tongue,
So Ch'in's fires burned the books in vain.[32]
Thereby slander came into being once again,   15
And by now it stretches across the universe.[33]

Just as tradition, the collective memory of the past, preserves the
renown of virtue, slander destroys the reputations of those it strikes.
Slander represents evil and falsehood, and the transmission of such
falsehoods in the tradition corrupts and destroys the truth and purity
of idealized antiquity. Slander, appearing within the tradition,
destroys men for eternity, it "kills . . . in droves." Though slander
pretends to be moral, it is really no more than a dog's barking; its
power to destroy a man among the living and make the dishonored
dead weep is far out of proportion to what it actually is.

It may seem incongruous that Meng Chiao chooses to make an
attack on slander the climax of his greatest sequence; indeed, the
importance of slander in Chinese literature often puzzles the western
reader. Having described the good in the preceding poem, it is
natural here for Meng to talk of its antithesis, evil. As the pure
tradition means eternity for most worthy men, slander threatens to
destroy the meaning of men's lives forever. An omniscient God
ensured the Christian that his virtue would be rewarded with eternal
life; the Confucian tradition was more fallible. From the concept of
an omniscient god evolved the concept of personal morality—the
good one does and the purity of one's heart are known no matter
what other men may believe. In the Confucian tradition, good is
bound up inextricably with one's reputation, for it is society's judgment of a man which confers or witholds "paradise," a place of
honor in the tradition. Thus slander can ruin both a man's life on
earth and deprive him of a place in the tradition; it alone can make
a great man's life meaningless.

In the end of his life the old poet is considering his own future in

32. This refers to the attempt made by the first emperor of the Ch'in Dynasty to "unify"
thought by burning all books other than those of his own Legalist school.
33. *MTTSC*, pp. 58–62.

the tradition. Whether it will tell of his virtue or leave him destroyed eternally by slander is a very real question to him. Thus to Meng Chiao slander occupies a place of at least equal power and dignity to that of the devil in the western tradition.

It is not difficult to see why later poets and critics did not react to Meng Chiao's "Autumn Meditations." It represents the limit of hermetic symbolism in Chinese poetry, equaled only by Li Shang-yin's (812–58) more difficult poems. At times the sequence seems like mere raving, and, were it not for a familiarity we have gained with Meng Chiao's associations of symbols, his techniques of metaphor, and his structural eccentricities, the sequence as a whole would be incomprehensible to us. When we come to this tentative understanding of it, however, we see that its intensity and depth of vision make it Meng Chiao's masterpiece.

Despite the dignity of affirmation of the tradition in the last two poems of "Autumn Meditations," the Meng Chiao who remains most clearly in our minds is the doubter, the disillusioned and bitter poet for whom no resolution of the conflicts that plague him is possible. The following is the last poem by Meng Chiao we shall look at, a poem built around the familiar pattern of striving and failure.

> TRYING TO CLIMB CHAO-CH'ENG TEMPLE TOWER, BUT
> NOT MAKING IT TO THE TOP: I SIGH IN THE CELL OF
> MY NEPHEW, THE MONK "AWARE OF THE VOID."[34]

> I wanted to climb that thousand-stair tower
> To ask Heaven a couple of things—
> I hadn't even climbed twenty or thirty,
> When heart and eyes blew like waves in the wind.
> Hand after hand, clasping a frightened spirit,   5
> Footstep after footstep tramples a falling soul,
> Then back it flows into its former hand,
> I clasp at my side, it's still on the point of slipping away.
> Old and sick, I can only feel sorry for myself,
> From ancient worms, a tree with a thousand scars.   10
> How can I be proud of my old man's strength?—
> It's only a single root of duckweed on autumn seas.

34. Chao-ch'eng Temple is in Lo-yang. Anyone with the least bit of acrophobia who has ever climbed a Buddhist structure can sympathize with Meng Chiao in this experience.

Lonely, decrepit, where shall I turn?
At daybreak my eyes are as if at twilight.
Always I fear I'll lose my firm footing,   15
And then down into the gate of well and market.[35]
For feelings of kinship I have befriended this monk,
But my bamboo staff will be my descendants.
How intense this sincerity is and in vain,
For no purpose my will survives and survives.   20
Anyway, these words from only an inch on the earth—[36]
How could High Heaven hear them?[37]

By climbing the high tower, Meng seeks to be closer to Heaven, so that he might question Heaven why events on earth occur as they do. But hardly having started up the staircase (probably on the outside of the building), Meng Chiao grows frightened of the height. He feels his soul is slipping away from his body, and he clasps his chest to hold it in. From his inability to climb, both in the literal and spiritual sense, Meng realizes his own decrepitude: "From ancient worms, a tree with a thousand scars," and his fragility: "a single root of duckweed on autumn seas." Having no sons to support him in his old age, his only "support" (the pun on the two implications of "support" is in the Chinese too) is his bamboo staff.

All the inner goodness the poet has, his intense "sincerity," and his will that survives in vain—these are wasted by his lack of outer success and of descendants to whom he might transmit his values. His failure to climb the tower has given Meng the answers to his questions, and the poet is left only with disillusionment. Heaven would not hear him even if he did reach the top of the tower, for his heart is tiny in the vastness of the universe.

35. "Well and market" is a traditional metaphor for the vulgar world. Here, in addition to the traditional figurative sense, there is also the fear of really falling into the marketplace.
36. The "inch" speaking to Heaven is the poet's heart.   37. *MTYSC,* p. 173.

10

The Poet and the Symbolic Landscape: Han Yü

The first year of the Yüan-ho period (806), also the year of the linked verses with Meng Chiao, is the culmination of the transition begun in Han Yü's poetry during his exile. One aspect of these changes is Han's new attitude toward poetry. Although he was already a major poet by 806, Han Yü had had relatively little to say about or in appreciation of poetry. In his rather dour "Preface on Seeing Off Meng Chaio" (803), he elaborates on the orthodox expressionistic theory of verse, saying that poetry is generated by some imbalance within the poet.[1] In "Recommending a Man of Letters" (806), also for Meng Chiao, we have the following appreciation of Meng's poetry in addition to the accepted fu-ku history of Chinese poetry and a tribute to Meng Chiao's character:

Our Dynasty has excelled in literature,
Ch'en Tzu-ang was first to stride to the heights,
Then bursting upward, there came Li Po and Tu Fu,
All things suffered their bullying might.
Those men, coming later, who followed them
Each reached the darkest recesses.
There is one who goes beyond them all—Meng Chiao—
The talent he has received is truly bold and unbridled.
Gazing into mysterious darkness, he penetrates past and present,
Beyond the phenomena, he pursues desires for seclusion.
He coils adamantine words across the skies,
Yet they go well together, and their force is more than
    herculean.
Displaying gentleness, he winds and meanders at will,
Then in a burst of ferocity, he rolls back ocean swells.

1. *HCLW*, pp. 136–37.

Like Heaven's blossom in his flowering splendor,
Nimble to answer, swifter than an echo. . . .[2]

The last line of the passage probably refers to Meng's ability in
the linked verse. Besides the above, we also have the praise of poets
quoted earlier from the linked verse "South of the City." Though
they are phrased in the vague, impressionistic rhetoric of T'ang
poems on poetry, these passages at least show a new sensitivity on
Han Yü's part to the power and beauty of poetry. The following
poem, also from 806, shows a similar view of poetry as an art, di-
vorced from its social, ethical, and political context.

DRUNK: TO CHANG SHU

Everyone urges wine on me,
But I act as though I haven't heard them.
Today I come to your house,
Call for wine and urge *you*, to drink
So that the guests at the table　　　　　　　　　　　5
And I might be able to write poems.
Your poems take on many aspects,
Clustering in formations as clouds on a spring sky.
Meng Chiao is prone to shock the conventional,
Heaven's blossom exhaling a strange perfume.　　　　10
Chang Chi imitates ancient limpidity,
A noble stork he avoids flocks of chickens.
My nephew, A-mai, doesn't know his characters yet,
But can write stone-inscription script quite well.[3]
When a poem is finished, we have him copy it,　　　　15
So he too can increase our troop.
The reason I want to get wine
Is to wait on tipsiness to write a poem.
The wine's taste is cool and clear,
The wine's spirit too rises, spreading through me.　　　　20
My disposition gradually grows exuberant,
Then a tumult of jesting and laughter.
This is really the purpose of wine—

2. *HCLS,* pp. 233–34.

3. "Stone inscription script," *pa-fen,* was a special style of writing used in the T'ang
primarily for inscription on stone. A-mai is a child and is trying to copy the poems the
adults are composing. Han Yü jokingly calls his inept squiggles *pa-fen* script.

Anything else is a purposeless muddle.
The crowd of rich kids in Ch'ang-an   25
Have plates of delicacies, smelling of lamb and garlic.
They can't understand drinking for poetry—
All they can do is get red skirts drunk.[4]
Though they have a brief meal's-worth of pleasure,
They're a bit like a swarm of gnats.   30
Now I and these several friends of mine
Have nothing that stinks amid our sweet fragrance.[5]
Our complex phrases shock and frighten even demons,
Our lofty diction is like unto the Three Monumental Books.[6]
Or the uncarved state of the perfect gem,   35
A natural accomplishment, turning away from hoe and plow.[7]
Now we are coming into an age of great peace,
When worthy men assist a venerable ruler,
Fortunately having no problems to attend to,
We hope to spend dawn to dusk with pastimes like this.[8]   40

The poem concerns the relationship between wine and poetry:
Han accepts wine from his friends only as a stimulus for writing
poetry, considering the use of wine as a stimulus for sensual pleasure
to be decidedly inferior (ll. 25–30). In itself this would be nothing
unusual, but the contrast between the poet's use of wine and the
wastrel's use of it is treated as a moral evaluation, similar to the
contrast between the virtuous poor and the foolish rich in "Those
Who Make Friends in Ch'ang-an" (p. 41). As in the earlier ethical
poems, there is a small, virtuous "we"-group opposed to a larger,
inferior "they"-group. However, unlike in the early poems, the
"we"-group is defined in terms of poetic talent rather than morality.
The "they"-group, the rich youths of the capital, shows its inferiority
by a failure to put wine to its proper use—as a stimulus to poetic
creation. The forms of ethical judgment survive, but poetry has re-

4. "Red skirts" are prostitutes.

5. As we have seen before, good and bad odors refer to moral qualities.

6. These are three mythical writings attributed to the Yellow Emperor, Fu Hsi, and
Shen-nung, mentioned in the "Great Preface" to the *Shu-ching*.

7. I.e. the poem comes forth naturally, not requiring special labor. This contrasts with
the style described in the preceding couplet, and together this antithetical pair of possible
styles parallels the contrast between the style of Meng Chiao and that of Chang Chi from
earlier in the poem.

8. *HCLS*, p. 177.

placed ethical principles as the standard of judgment. Furthermore, we can see the exclusiveness of the ethical "elect" turning into consciousness of a poetic group, a poetic "elect."

Dismissing the lukewarm compliment to Chang Shu's poetry, we can see that two positive poetic tendencies in the group interest Han Yü. The two are antithetical, defining a conflict within Han Yü himself as much as the difference between the styles of Meng Chiao and Chang Chi. On the one hand, there is the self-consciously "strange" style that characterizes Meng Chiao's and Han Yü's poetry during the early Yüan-ho period (ca. 806–12):

Meng Chiao is prone to shock the conventional,
Heaven's blossom exhaling a strange perfume.

[il. 9–10]

Our complex phrases shock and frighten even demons,
Our lofty diction is like unto the Three Monumental Books.

[ll. 33–34]

On the other hand, there is the neoclassical balance and ease to which Han Yü will turn in his last years:

Chang Chi imitates ancient limpidity

[l. 11]

. . . the uncarven state of the perfect gem,
A natural accomplishment, turning away from hoe and plow.

[ll. 35–36]

Although Han Yü eventually achieves a certain limpidity, he never succeeds in creating anything that could be called "uncarven."

Han does feel the need to justify his new concern for poetry at the expense of moral and social values. He does so by invoking a traditional principle that good government leaves officials with nothing to do. That the group devotes itself to poetry is thus a compliment to the reigning emperor and his ministers. It is no longer necessary to "distinguish between sage and fool," as in "Those Who Make Friends in Ch'ang-an"; now it is appropriate to distinguish the sensitive and talented from the conventional. The consciousness of an exclusive group of poets who display their superiority by "shocking the conventional" is beginning to take form.

Despite the new values manifest in this poem, the style and structure are prosaic and rambling. It is important for us to remember that as Han Yü developed a new style, he rarely discarded the older one entirely. Indeed, he wrote rambling, chatty poems like this one throughout his career, and it is probably the kind of poetry that came most naturally to him. This manner, perfected in the late 790s, changed little through the remainder of his life.

Before his exile Han Yü's poetics were simple: one explained an idea or told a story with a maximum of clarity. What was important was the "message," the pattern of events, or the successful achievement of a suasive purpose. In the landscape narratives of his exile, we saw how the landscape took on meaning within the framework of the narrative and actualized certain aspects of the cosmic pattern. This was an intermediary stage between the earlier poetry of statement and the ultimate metaphorical poetry, in which one thing can actually "stand for" another. This change goes against the implicit assumptions of his early, fu-ku poetry, assumptions that were retained in his humanistic narratives. The new mediation between the bare essentials of experience and the expression of them goes hand in hand with Han Yü's growing understanding of poetry as more than a vehicle to carry a "message."

The development of this metaphorical poetry is interesting: from the perception of a pattern within events (for example, "How Sad This Day"), Han moved to an awareness of the organic universe, a cosmic pattern that determines not only individual experience but other aspects of the phenomenal world as well. The next stage of this development can be seen in "Answering Chang Ch'e," in which the landscapes become a series of portents of Han Yü's personal experiences. Though it is difficult to draw a line, I feel we can call this poem a symbolic landscape, in that the landscapes contained in it stand for complex conditions and the development of the poem consists in the change from landscape to landscape. The little narrative that is left only confirms what is already known through the landscape. The end of this development will be "South Mountains," in which the symbolic mountains are sufficient in themselves to stand for Han Yü's meditation on cosmic changes.

ANSWERING CHANG CH'E

I'm unable to requite what you graciously sent me,
But listen to my song all the same.
In the beginning I'll narrate how first we met,

Then tell later how our forms parted,
How the road between us stretched thousands of miles,   5
How the passing days and months neared ten years.
From the moors of Chün I fled the troops' rebellion,[9]
To the Sui's banks where we resided gate to gate.[10]
Our hearts were as a single ancient sword,
A pair of duckweeds floating in the waves.   10
Dipping brushes in ink, we corrected the old histories,
Grinding cinnabar, we commented on the past classics.
From the garden of meaning we laid hands on secret
    treasures,[11]
In the hall of culture, we eared startling thunderclaps.
On warm, genial mornings we trod in dewy sandals,   15
On sultry evenings we slept by breezy windows.
In forming a friendship you were lenient to your Lu K'ang,[12]
Asked to be your teacher, I was shamed before a Kung-sun
    Ting.[13]
The first taste was like munching sugarcane,
Our subsequent rapport came as freely as water flows from a
    jug.   20
We sought the exceptional and each day found abundance,[14]
Our hearts, never at peace in yearning for the good.
Across stone bridges, long and level,
Over sands and waters, bright and chill.
Riding a log raft, we culled the charms of the field,   25

9. "The moors of Chün" is a poetic, archaic reference to Pien-chou.
10. "The Sui's banks," i.e. Hsü-chou.
11. "The garden of meaning" seems to refer to the philosophical and occult commentaries on the classics and philosophers.
12. On one level this refers to the famous friendship of Yang Hu and Lu K'ang; however, the commentator Fang Ch'eng-kuei has intelligently pointed out the pun on K'ang's name, meaning "to face" and implying here, "to be together as equals." Therefore, we could also translate it: "In forming a friendship, you allowed me to face you as an equal."
13. Here too we have an allusion combined with a pun on the name. *Tso-chuan*, Duke Hsiang XIV, tells how Yü-kung Ch'a was in pursuit of the evil duke Hsien of Wei, but could not bring himself to shoot his bow at the duke's chariot because the duke's charioteer, Kung-sun *Ting*, had been his archery teacher. Therefore, Yü-kung Ch'a shot only at the yoke of the chariot. The point of this story is simply the faithful relation between teacher and pupil. However, *ting* can mean "to be in the position of," so Han Yü could be saying that he is ashamed to "assume the position of teacher."
14. "Seeking the exceptional," *sou-ch'i*, may refer to literature, in which case it is reminiscent of Meng Chiao's "laboring for the unusual."

Sinking thin lines, we drew forth the submerged fishsmell.
Visited temples, went off to climb mountain peaks,
Hiked on trails and, turning back, came through to shores,
Followed the clouds where the bamboo thrusts high,
Lost our path in the darkness of hemp vines.   30
Torrential floods suddenly spread over the plains,
A black ocean appeared, boundless on the grassy wastes.
To keep it from leaking in, they blocked the moats that night,
Bolted walls at daybreak, fearing it would burst through.
Then it came that I went off to serve with a cavalry bridle,   35
We met amid the martial music of a feast.
An autumn of drinking horns—we got drunk as we pleased,
Mornings of hunts, galloping sturdy steeds.
Our hands first parted when you went to the examination,
But I went to court and we found ourselves on the same
    galley.   40
When pressed for time, they urged the oars on in the darkness,
Or, fond of the moon, we'd linger in a deserted pavilion.
When my business was finished, I rode away on a posthorse,
While you stayed settled, keeping a window of fireflies.[15]
Among plum blossoms we parted by the Pa's waters,   45
As they awoke on Li Mountain, palace candles still burning.[16]
When it came time to set foot in the Rites Examination,
They crushed the wings of this provincial.[17]
Once again I clasped your dusty sleeves,
And teary eyes again held a double sparkle.[18]   50
Asking for leave, I got to go to Lo-yang,
And went all over the steep chasms of Hua Mountain.
From the pinnacle I glimpsed the ocean's waves,[19]
Lifting my sleeves, I brushed the stars in the heavens.
Here the chariot of the sun turns downward its axle,   55

15. "A window of fireflies" is a cliché for the poverty of a student. There is a story of a
certain Ch'e Yin who was so poor that he could not afford oil for a lamp, so at night he
used the light of the fireflies at his window to study by.

16. I.e. they parted early in the morning. There was a detached palace on Mount Li;
the scene here is of the palace attendant waking before dawn in preparation for morning
court.

17. Failure in the examination is often described as having one's wings clipped or broken

18. The tears are for Chang's failure, but the sparkle is for their meeting again.

19. This is hyperbole, the ocean cannot be seen from Mount Hua.

To where the god of metal has charge of punishment.[20]
Ribbons of streams, trailing and white,
Stony swords clustered, high and green.[21]
On mossy steps of stone slippery, inched forward, hunched and
    cautious,
Gales on plank bridges swaying in the wind, tilting.   60
Insane with regret, I was gnawing my fingers,
There is still a graven inscription to leave behind a warning.
With tall censor's cap I increased the court ranks,[22]
Lying prostrate on the rushes, I was shamed to distinguish the
    Ching.[23]
My meager loyalty longed to lay flat the grasses,   65
But my insignificant strength was ruined ringing bells with
    grass-blades.[24]
Through the layered snow I walked the summit of Mount
    Shang,
Through flying waves I boated over Tung-t'ing.
I descended into danger as though falling down a well,
Holding my office was like being locked in prison.   70
As rude dinners, I'd sup the poisonous insects of barbarians,
I was stirred by the goddess of the Hsiang, hidden in dreams.[25]
The governor performed serious divination for the crops,
While his subalterns bubbled out like caterpillars and
    locusts.[26]

20. Hua Mountain is so high that Han Yü imagines this is the point where the sun
reaches its apex and begins its descent toward the west. The west, in the symbolic arrange-
ment of the four directions, is associated with metal, punishment, and destruction.
21. This couplet refers to waterfalls and mountains, respectively.
22. The censor's cap is literally "the high *chih.*" The *chih* is a mythical animal that can
supposedly distinguish between good and evil, and therefore was an appropriate symbol
of the censorate.
23. This is a highly elaborate way of saying that he remonstrated with the emperor.
"To lie prostrate on the rushes" means to prostrate oneself. "Distinguishing the Ching
River" means to distinguish the clear-flowing Ching River from the muddy Wei—hence
to distinguish good from evil.
24. "To lay flat the grasses" means to affect events. To beat a bell with a blade of grass
suggests engaging in futile effort, trying to do something "resounding" without having the
capacity to do so.
25. The appearance of the Hsiang goddesses, Shun's wives who committed suicide on
being widowed, suggests that Han's despair made him suicidal.
26. This is a difficult couplet, but it seems to suggest that while the governor was asking
for divine aid for the crops, the real "plague" on the province were the corrupt, greedy

They carefully corrected the characters on the registers,   75
And rushed to and fro when the office bells rang.[27]
Fortunately the place was full of mountains and rivers,
So I found something to please sight and hearing.
Purple trees, graven in joined layers,
Emerald streams dripping with the tinkle of jade.   80
Shining waves unrolled their brocade into the distance,
A long screen was set, stuck into the earth.[28]
From mournfully howling apes, bitter bones died,
And from weird flowers, an odor that intoxicated the soul.
Crimson fruits split, sprouting deep in the rinds,   85
Kingfisher feathers fell from secluded fledglings.
With an amnesty, I traveled five hundred miles,[29]
Until the moon had changed the *ming* leaves thirty times.[30]
I advance slowly up the stairs to flock with flapping egrets,[31]
Entering the academy I instruct the caterpillars.[32]   90
The artemesia is sweet, I thank the singing deer,[33]
But though the jug is full, it's shamed by the pitcher's
   emptiness.[34]
May the bright sun through the window embrace this rare
   vessel,[35]
May you go flying, joining the pied wagtails.[36]

---

office underlings.

27. Another difficult couplet. Office bells rang at important arrivals. Han Yü may be suggesting that the office workers busied themselves with the niceties of punctuating and correcting official documents instead of attending to real problems, but that they made a big show of being busy when someone important arrived. However, it may refer to Han himself, stating how busy he was while working there.

28. This refers to the mountains.

29. I.e. to Chiang-ling.

30. The *ming* was a legendary plant whose leaves grew and fell once a month, hence thirty months passed in exile.

31. "Flapping egrets" is a cliché for court officials.

32. "Caterpillars" refers to the youths in the State Academy.

33. This refers to the *Book of Songs,* #161: "The deer sing, / Eating the artemesia of the moors." Deer are a conventional metaphor for friends who respond to one another, hence: "I like being at court [eating artemesia] and thank my friends [deer] for helping me get back here."

34. I.e. Han Yü is ashamed to face Chang Ch'e, who hasn't met with equal success. See *Book of Songs,* #202.

35. I.e. may imperial grace shine on you since you have rare talent.

36. The pied wagtails are symbols of brotherly friendship. See *Book of Songs,* #164.

The fish-fins will fall from your back,[37]   95
For the dragon-light shone earlier on the whetstone.
Do you think you will stand out only among your companions?—
Soon I think you will shake the entire court.
Try hard to come so we may talk face to face,
Don't dread to stay the night in this cold hall.[38]   100

Each of the landscapes in the above poem has a unity and integrity all its own, standing for and foreshadowing moments in the poet's life. The narrative, though still present, is greatly diminished in importance. The first event is a flight from disorder to security and harmony:

From the moors of Chün I fled the troops' rebellion,
To the Sui's banks where we resided gate to gate.

"Rebellion," *luan*, also means "disorder." Out of disorder Han Yü flees to the peaceful world of Hsü-chou. "Gate to gate," *lien-men* (literally, "joined gates"), suggests both contact and openness. Likewise, the *banks* of the Sui suggest order, water contained in its proper course, in contrast to the disorderly waters, the "floods," later in the poem, which portend parting and tragedy. The image of the sword suggests the two men's common opposition to the rebellion and their loyalty to the empire. This unity and firmness of spirit contrasts with their bodies, fragile as "a pair of duckweeds floating in the waves."

Han Yü's experiences with Chang Ch'e in Hsü-chou consist of scholarly and literary pursuits, followed by excursions into the landscape. This paradisiacal world involves the proper Confucian relationships, those of friend to friend (l. 17) and of teacher to pupil (l. 18); these relationships are both sweet (l. 19) and natural (l. 20). This is a world of order, of balanced and natural relationships, and of "civil" pursuits ("civil," *wen*, being the antithesis of "military," *wu*; *wen*, of course, means "literary" as well as "civil").

The landscape through which the poets pass is likewise one of brightness and clarity. This tranquil appreciation of the landscape continues until "we lost our path in the darkness of hemp vines."

37. Chang Ch'e's future success is here described by the conventional metaphor of a fish turning into a dragon. This metaphor is mixed with another, the sword that turns into a dragon, the sword itself being a cliché for a useful official.
38. *HCLS,* p. 180.

This "loss of their way" portends the impending loss of the paradisiacal world. The brightness (l. 24) becomes the darkness of the hemp vines, and the "black oceans" (l. 32) of the subsequent floods. (Hemp is traditionally described as *luan*, "disorderly.") Instead of their earlier freedom of movement through the landscape and their open gates, now with the flood the "moats are blocked up" and the gates of the city walls are bolted (ll. 33–34). From brightness, order, and openness, we move into a world of darkness, confusion, and closedness.

The next scene takes place in the army, and although the two men are still together, the dreamlike world of leisure is lost: here, images of speed (ll. 38, 41, 43) contrast with their earlier tranquillity. Though the first hints of their parting are only false alarms, the poem is building up momentum toward disaster. Associated with Chang's failure in the examination and his parting from Han Yü are the images of studying by firefly-light and the palace candles in the darkness. The happiness they shared in Hsü-chou was characterized by brightness; the above images are faint spots of light enveloped by darkness, just as the last of their joy together is sinking away.

The next landscape, that of Hua Mountain, is truly ominous. Han is at the peak of the mountain, the point at which everything goes downward. Not only must the climber descend at this point, here too the sun turns its chariot downward and the "steep chasms" threaten him with falling (l. 52). The "ocean's waves" he sees in the distance are reminiscent of the floods earlier in the poem but represent an even greater body of disorderly water. The mention of the god of the west, the god of punishment, is another foreboding sign. The precariousness of this landscape (ll. 59–60) contrasts with a similar situation in the Hsü-chou landscape (ll. 15–16): the pleasant moisture of the dew in the earlier landscape has become the dangerous, slippery wetness of the mountain; the breezes of the earlier landscape are gales on Hua Mountain, which threaten to make him fall. Furthermore, the mountains are described as "swords," another metaphor portending destruction.

This landscape symbolizes Han Yü's hubris in accepting "high" office and his terrible "fall" from that position. Parallel to the high mountains is the "*tall* censor's cap." Waterfalls are described as "ribbons" of streams, hinting at the badges of office. Han Yü shows his hubris in the parallel activities of "Lifting his sleeves and brushing the stars in the heavens," and of remonstrating with the emperor: for these he is punished. Likewise, he feels regret both at climbing the mountain (l. 61) and at his remonstrance.

Rather than the ominous, threatening landscape of Mount Hua, we next have the terrible landscapes of Mount Shang in the snow and Lake Tung-t'ing in a storm. Han Yü falls from his high position "as though falling down a well": this is paralleled by his passage over Lake Tung-t'ing on his way into exile. Later, at his place of exile, Han Yü has thoughts of suicide by drowning (l. 72). Throughout the poem water suggests destruction unless it is well contained—the duckweeds at the mercy of the waves (l. 10); the flood (ll. 31–34); the ocean seen from Mount Hua (ll. 53)—and here, falling into a well, Lake Tung-t'ing, and death by drowning. Rather than the precariousness of Mount Hua and the censorate, Han now feels as though he were "locked in prison" (l. 70), foreshadowed earlier in the poem by his loss of freedom when the city was locked and bolted against the flood (ll. 33–34).

In the southern landscape we see both the depths of despair and the hope of redemption. At first, the landscape is oppressive: the mountains are a "screen" separating him from return to the north, another image of closedness, of being locked in. However, hope appears in the following couplet:

> Crimson fruits split, sprouting deep in the rinds,
> Kingfisher feathers fell from secluded fledglings.

The first line combines both destruction and rebirth, as sprouts appear from rotten fruits. The cycle of Han Yü's fortunes has reached the very bottom and an upward movement begins. Fledgling birds learning to fly likewise symbolize a positive change.

Han Yü is then pardoned and returns to court "to flock with flapping egrets"; the earlier image of baby birds becomes one of adult birds that can fly, and good fortune likewise returns swiftly. The only thing still lacking is Chang Ch'e's presence and success in the examination. Echoing a number of earlier themes in the poem, Han Yü elaborately and allusively assures Chang of success.

Han handles these symbolic landscapes with great skill, so that they complement every element of what narrative there is. The narrative serves only to fulfill the prophecies of the landscape and to carry the poet from one scene to another. In the following poem,

Han Yü's crowning achievement in symbolic landscape, the narrative
has all but disappeared in his experience of the range of mountains
south of the capital.

Han Yü's "South Mountains," influenced by and influencing in
turn the style of the linked verses, is his most ambitious long poem.
In it he experiments with assimilating the diction and devices of the
then moribund *fu* into poetry. As Jao Tsung-yi suggests, it may also
show the influence of a Chinese translation of Asvagosa's *Buddhacarita*.[39] Both of these influences on "South Mountains" are consonant
with a general trend in Han Yü's poetry toward assimilating into
poetry a wide variety of elements hitherto considered to lie outside
its scope (for example, prose diction and logical reasoning in Han's
poetry of the early 790s).

"South Mountains" is one of the most objective descriptive poems
Han Yü ever wrote, although it can hardly be called objective by any
standards other than comparison with his other poems. As such, it is
the culmination of the trend toward descriptive poetry evident
throughout the years of Han's exile. All the same, the complex and
exotic arabesques performed by these mountains betray an energetic
and eccentric talent manipulating the "objective" scene and transforming it in his imagination.

SOUTH MOUNTAINS

I have heard that south of the capital
There is a corral for a drove of mountains.
East and west they stretch to both seas,[40]
Immense and tiny ones, impossible to examine all carefully.
The Landscape Classic and the Geographical Treatises   5
Are vague and abstruse, not carefully transmitted.
When I try to take their lumped-up phrases in hand,
I find one holds, while thousands fall through.
I'd prefer to stop here but really can't,
So I'll tell roughly what I passed through and viewed.   10

I ascended a lofty hill and gazed at them,

39. Jao Tsung-yi, "Han Yü Nan-shan-shih yü T'an-wu-ch'an yi Ma-ming Fo-so-hsing-
tsan," *Chugoku Bungaku Ho*, 19 (October 1963), pp. 98–101.

40. Believing as they did in geographical symmetry, the Chinese postulated an ocean
to the far west to match the one in the east, This may, however, refer to the Caspian Sea
or the Indian Ocean.

Saw them mass together in clusters.[41]
When the weather is clear, angles and corners emerge,
Threadlike ridges shatter from dividing broideries of mist.
Vapors, steaming upward, interpenetrate,   15
What's inside will suddenly pierce through outward.[42]
Though there's no wind, fog floats and winnows by itself,
Then condensing into moisture, it warms lush vegetation.
The clouds athwart them often harden to a level surface,
Then, spot after spot, several pinnacles are revealed.   20
Like long eyebrows floating in the sky's emptiness,
Painted deep green, freshly made up.
Or sharply dropping crests like lone slanting buttresses,
The beaks of rocs, thrust upward as they bathe in the sea.

Sunken beneath spring's Yang force is sodden dampness,   25
Shimmeringly exhaling splendid grain from deep under.
Though the sharp bluffs be craggy,
They grow languid as though full of strong wine.
In summer's blazing heat all manner of trees flourish,
Luxuriant foliage covers and buries them more and more.   30
Mountain deities daily breathe upward,
Vying to build structures of their cloud-breath.
Then autumn frosts delight in punishing them harshly,
Ripped open, they stand high and alone, lean and wasted.
Uneven and layered upon one another,   35
Hard and aloof, they look down on the universe.
Though winter's element is ink-black gloom,
Snow and ice skillfully cut and polish them.
Fresh sunlight shines on the high crags,
A million yards across, high and broad.   40
From dawn to dusk, their appearance never ceases to change,
At every instant a different form.

To the southwest Mount T'ai-po stands valiant,
Thrusting upward, nothing blocking or seconding it.

41. *Chi-chi* is used to describe the "clustering" of rams' horns in *Book of Songs,* ♯ 190.
Here it may hint at the animal-like variety of the mountains, suggested in line two.
42. This describes the mists moving over the mountains, sometimes hiding them, sometimes revealing part of them.

The capital's protective barrier, suiting our Cyclic Virtue,[43]   45
Residing separate, occupying south of the center.[44]
Rambling freely, it passes the position of *k'un*,
Attacks cruelly, sinking into the hole of *ch'ien*.[45]
There in the emptiness, it shivers from the cold,
As windy air struggles to blast and scour it.   50
Toward the Vermilion Direction, where the sun is set aflame,[46]
The Yin forms hail, blowing in flurries at will.

North of the great K'un-ming pool
Going sightseeing, I chanced on a clear day.
I gazed downward and it stretched as far as the eye could see,   55
The mountains lay upside down, trapped in a clear immersion.
Tiny ripples moved the water's surface,
As excited apes and monkeys leapt around.
Screamed in fright, pitying their shattered, broken forms,
They looked up in joy, agape that they hadn't toppled down.[47]   60

Hiking ahead, I passed the barns of Tu-ling,
Covered in dust, Pi-yüan seemed lowly.
Over rocky paths I rose to the heights,
Only then getting the full wealth of the view.
On and on, almost reaching the road's end,   65

43. "Our Cyclic Virtue": the symbolic element of the T'ang Dynasty was Earth, whose symbolic direction is southwest, the direction of Mount T'ai-po from Ch'ang-an.

44. T'ai-po was separate from the other peaks of the range.

45. There are a number of problems involved in this couplet. An old note identifies "Rambling Free" as the name of a valley, but Wang Yüan-ch'i opposes this on the grounds of parallelism. Another reason for suspicion is that whenever commentators have difficulty understanding a line, they often postulate a place-name to resolve their difficulties. The usual interpretation is of rivers pouring out of the southwest (*k'un* hexagram: earth element, southwest direction) into the basin ("hole") in the northeast where Ch'ang-an is situated. I believe the couplet is cleverer and more complex than this. Han Yü has just suggested that T'ai-po occupies the *k'un* (earth/southwest), but the height of the mountain makes the poet aware of a paradox in having T'ai-po represent the earth. Therefore, he suggests that the mountain, "rambling free," unfettered to the earth, rises from the *earth* (*k'un*) to the *sky* (*ch'ien*). "Attacks cruelly" suggests the rugged shape of the mountain thrusting up into an alien element.

46. The Vermilion Direction is south.

47. I.e. the monkeys, seeing their reflections in the pool, imagine that they have fallen into the water, and are surprised to find out that they actually haven't.

When crags and plateaus annoyingly ran from each other.[48]
In a burst of rage, I longed to smash them open,
Hard to generously forgive how they cover and conceal.
The River Titan and the Kua O Brothers
Bartered from the far past—I wished they would sell their might.[49]	70
But then I wondered if it wasn't the Creator's intention
To gather demiurges here so as to hold it firmly;
Though their force could turn me away,
I cower at their chiding rebukes of thunder and lightning.
As I scale it, my hands and feet lose their grip,	75
Then, staggering, it's as though beneath a smooth tile wall.[50]
All confused, when I try to lift my head,
I'm hemmed in by walls, lost as to what to do next.
But its awesome face destroys my melancholy,
And what's near and new leads astray what was far and seen
	before.[51]	80
When I reckon up the days and months bound to my post,
I want to go on, for I won't be able to come here again.

Thereupon, I peered at the tarn there,
Brimming with clear waters, it conceals a dark creature.[52]
Bending down, you could gather up fish and shrimp,	85
But who would dare plunder this godlike beast?
It happens that leaves fall from the boughs of the trees,
Yet, about to drop in, birds fly up startled to protect it.[53]
Vying to take them in their beaks, they fly wheeling in circles,
Then, casting the leaves away, they rush to feed fledglings.	90

48. I.e. the road is gone and the climbing gets hard. Perhaps, as Shimizu suggests, the mountain blocks his view.

49. Here Han Yü is wishing that these mythical figures would clear away the obstructions to climbing and sightseeing. The "River Titan" was supposed to have split Mount Hua with his feet in order to let the Yellow River through it. The other myth is of the "Foolish Old Man" who wanted to move two mountains that bothered him, so he ordered all his descendants to carry bits of the mountains away, assuming that after generations they would gradually disappear. Heaven sympathized with his dedication and sent two titans of the Kua O clan to move the mountains for him.

50. I.e. the poet has come to a sheer cliff.

51. I.e. the splendor of this landscape makes Han Yü forget the beauty of fine landscapes he has seen elsewhere.

52. This refers to the dragon of the mountain.

53. The birds are trying to protect the pond from being defiled by falling leaves.

Turning homeward, I looked back from the road
To where it towered skyward, robust and piled high.
I heaved a sigh—how truly wondrous it is
That its lofty substance can so transmute!

The year before last I met degradation and banishment,   95
And got an unexpected chance to pass through here sightseeing.
Coming in first through Lan-t'ien,
I peered all around me till my neck hurt.
The sky in that season was dark with great snows,
My teary eyes suffered, hazy and blinded.   100
The steep trail stretched long and icy,
Straight up as though a waterfall.
Lifted my robes, paced forward, pushing my horse along,
Slipped, fell backward a little, then came back.
I was in such a muddle I forgot to gaze afar,   105
I just kept my eyes on what was right around me.
Fir and bamboo menaced me with great spears,
All sparkled and glistened like grouped armor and helms.
My heart's sole concern—the memory of level roads,
To escape these dangers was more urgent than avoiding stink.   110

Since yesterday there has been a perfectly clear sky,
I rejoice that abiding desire has first been matched by fact.[54]
Up craggy cliffs I mounted to the very summit,
Mice and weasels mingled darting past.
In front of me it dropped off, space rived open,   115
Scattered far and wide, crowds of wrinkles lain in heaps.
Some joined as though following one another,
Some crinkled up as though in combat,
Some immobile as though prostrate in defeat,
Some stretching upward as though frightened pheasants
    screeching.   120
Some strewn as though tiles come loose,
Some heading in one direction as spokes to the hub,
Some rolling as though ships on a voyage,
Some headlong like galloping horses,

54. This is an elaborate way of saying that this is the first chance he has had to fulfill a
long-time desire to visit the mountains.

Some turning their backs as though hating one another,   125
Some face as though to aid one another,
Some in confusion like sprouting bamboo shoots,
Some heaped up like moxa applied to a wound,
Some in mixed colors like a painting,
Some coiled like seal script,   130
Some patterned like the constellations,
Some blossoming luxuriantly like motionless clouds,
Some flowing onward like waves,
Some shattered as though hoed and spaded,
Some, of the principles of Meng Pen and Hsia Yü,[55]   135
Who, gambling for victory, sold their prowess beforehand;
The one in front is stronger, his might has come forth,
The one in back, blunter, he rages mumbling.[56]
Some are exalted as an emperor or prince,
Gathering to his court the lowly and young: 140
Though they be close, he is not overly familiar,
Though they be far, he is not estranged.
Some as though looking down on a dinner table,
Heaped to overflowing with the finest delicacies.
Also there are those as though visiting a graveyard,   145
Where tomb and mount enwrap the coffins.
Some piled on top of one another like bowls and bottles,
Some lifted high like flagons and goblets.
Some lying overturned like terrapins sunning themselves,
Some collapsed like sleeping animals,   150
Some undulating like hidden dragons,
Some with wings wide like an eagle on its prey,
Some standing equal like friends,
Some following as though observing the rules of precedence,
Some scurrying off like vagabonds,   155
Some gazing as though having spent the night together,
Some embittered as enemies,
Some intimate as though married,
Some grave and stately as high-capped courtiers,
Some fluttering as dancers' sleeves,   160

55. These are two famous warriors of antiquity.
56. The "bluntness" refers to the height and shape of the "weaker" mountain, as well as suggesting that its spirit is less "sharp," more passive.

Some towering as though in battle ranks,
Some encircling as though on a hunt,
Some gush eastward streaming,
Some face north, lying prostrate in death,
Some like fire blazing under the rice pot,   165
Some like the steam puffing out,
Some go and halt not,
Some leave behind and gather not,
Some slant but lean not,
Some a slack bow that is stretched not,   170
Some bare as though bald and clean-shaven,
Some smoking as twigs burnt in offering,
Some cracked like the omens of a tortoise shell,
Some as though illustrating the meaning of the trigrams,
Some ☲ flat up front like Po,   175
Some ☷ broken in the back like Kou.

Stretching—apart and together again,
Calling it quits—oppose and meet once more,
Bubbling—fish poking heads between waterweeds,
Sparse the stars—the moon passes through constellations,   180
Majestic—they plant a wall,
Towering—erect granaries and warehouses,
Long and thin—pared sharp, swords and pikes,
Dazzling—agates and jades in their mouths,
Unfolding—blossoms spreading out their petals,   185
Pitter-patter—raindrops crashing on roofs,
Calmly, calmly—they unroll and are still,
Brooding fixedly—mad and malevolent.
Upward and beyond—still rushing outward,
Spirited—they rear up without effort.   190

Mighty they stand between Heaven and Earth,
In perfect order like the body's ducts and veins.
Who was he who first laid out their origin?
Who, in the striving and labor, urged it on?
Creating in this place the simple and artificed,   195
By joining forces with others, he endured long-suffering toil.
Could it have been accomplished without applying axe and hatchet?

Could it have been done without using spells and incantations?
Nothing survives in tradition from the Age of Chaos,
But the achievement is mighty—none can repay it. 200
Yet I have heard from the priest in charge of sacrifice
That the god descends to take the offering's sweet fragrance.
Finely wrought, I made this poem.
By which I may join in requiting him.[57]

The very length of this poem demands an architectonic complexity
more characteristic of the *fu* than of poetry, and Han Yü resolves his
structural problems with unusual success. The central theme is the
mountains as a microcosm exhibiting all the variety of change in the
universe. The treatment is epideictic and extensive but not rambling;
indeed, the orderly structure makes the broad treatment intelligible
and itself reflects the ordered patterns of cosmic change. An outline
of this structure follows:

Exordium: ll. 1–10
View from a distant hill: ll. 11–24. Han describes the mountains
    changing in the mist, followed by a pair of couplets, each contain-
    ing metaphors for the peaks above a layer of clouds. These two
    couplets represent the polarities of the mountains' aspects: the
    first, lush vegetation and feminine beauty, the second, harsh and
    jagged rocks.
The four seasons of the mountains, ll. 25–42:
    Spring: ll. 25–28, growth
    Summer: ll. 29–32, flourishing
    Autumn: ll. 33–36, destruction
    Winter: ll. 37–40, light and dark
    Summation of changes: ll. 41–42
T'ai-po: ll. 43–52, the cosmic mountain, representing earth, south,
    fire, and the T'ang Dynasty
K'un-ming Pool: ll. 53–60, the microcosm in reflection, representing
    north and water
The ascent: ll. 61–82. Han struggles up the symbolic mountain,
    permitted to do so by the mountain gods.
The tarn with its dragon: ll. 83–94, the most sacred and purest spot

57. *HCLS*, pp. 194–204.

in the mountains, the symbolic center, and the attainment of Han's
goal
Experience with the mountains while going into exile: ll. 95–110. At
that time the mountains actualized Han Yü's personal experiences
and the cosmic state by their harshness.
Present state: ll. 111–16
Variety of resemblances: ll. 117–76
Variety of ways to describe the mountains: ll. 177–90
Praise of their perfect order and of the one who created them: ll.
191–204

The exordium states Han Yü's reasons for writing the poem—the
failure of traditional geographical sources. The poet then promises to
write from experience; and indeed traditional geographical material
plays a small role in the course of the poem. In the initial view of the
range from a distant hill, the theme of changes begins: the mists passing over the mountains bring forth different aspects of them. The last
two couplets organize the changes into two polarities: first, there is
the soft and yielding lushness of the mountains covered with greenery,
and second, the rugged forms of the bare rocks, "lone slanting buttresses" and the "beaks of rocs."
    Han Yü sees the four seasons of the mountains through the tradi-
tional associations of each season. Spring is moisture and the ascendant Yang, growth and sexuality (in the languid drunkenness,
l. 28). Summer is characterized by heat and lush vegetation. Autumn
traditionally the season of destruction, is characterized by "punishing
harshly" and the endurance of hardships. In the winter scene there
is the paradox of light in darkness (sunlight on ice, shining through
the gloom of winter), of the Yang growing out of the Yin at its apex,
of life growing out of death. The general view of the mountain range
has progressed from general changes, to the polarities of softness and
hardness, to a further organization of change in the cycles of the
seasons.
    Besides Yin-Yang and seasonal symbolism, the traditional sym-
bolism of the *Book of Changes* and of the cyclical elements is important. T'ai-po and K'un-ming Pool form an antithetical pair:
T'ai-po represents the south, the "Vermilion Direction," while K'un-
ming Pool stands to the north, symbolized by water. Han Yü must
stretch his point in order to make Mount T'ai-po also stand for the

southwest, the direction of Earth (the K'un), thus serving as a symbol for the T'ang. But despite this contradiction and several others, Han is still trying to set the mountains within the cosmic order.

As the *K'un*, the Earth hexagram, T'ai-po has a special relationship to the dynasty, guarding it by its position in the southwest. Even more than this, the mountain is the K'un in action (though the K'un is the hexagram of passivity), rising up to its antithetical hexagram, *Ch'ien*, air; it is the substantial penetrating the empty. Through the union of these two primary hexagrams, all cosmic changes are produced. In terms of the weather, a similar union occurs, Yin cold mixing with Yang heat to form hail.

In addition to the changes generated by this cosmic union, there is another aspect of the microcosm, that of *reflection*. This is seen in the K'un-ming Pool to the north of T'ai-po—water in the direction associated with water. The pool reflects the mountains, "trapping" them. The reflection is so real that the monkeys believe it actually *is* what it reflects. Thus the landscape not only symbolizes cosmic change, it also reflects it. Although Han Yü's treatment of the mountains in cosmic terms is not consistent, it is still evident that he is trying to make it appear so, trying to make the mountains into a perfect example of cosmic *order*.

Moving into this symbolic landscape, Han Yü begins his ascent of the center mountain, Mount Hua. Again using traditional directional symbolism, Han eventually meets the animal of the "center," the dragon, the focal point of the generating magic that created the thousands of forms of the mountains. But, as in any good quest, Han Yü must first undergo hardships before he attains his goal. Rising from the lowly dust of Pu-yüan, Han encounters obstacles as he climbs to the heights. To overcome these he calls on the aid of the titans, but then he realizes that the gods of the mountain have purposely made the climb difficult in order to keep out intruders and preserve the sanctity of the place. Though they disapprove of Han's climb, they show their assent simply by not hurling him back down. When Han Yü finally reaches an impasse (1. 78), he turns from resentment at the obstacle to appreciation of the mountain's majesty. Next, he explains why he will not be able to come at another time.

It seems that it is in response to his appreciation and to his excuse that he cannot come again that the gods permit him to reach the tarn (in l. 83, *yin-yüan*, translated temporally as "thereupon," may also be translated as "for this reason"). In the tarn Han Yü finds the dragon, the symbolic beast of the center. The dragon is treated with great reverence, both by Han, who would not dare "plunder" the fish and frogs of the magic creature, and by the birds, who prevent falling leaves from defiling the pool. That the leaves, traditional symbols of transience, are kept from falling suggests that the pool and its inhabitant are protected from the passage of time. Birds feeding their fledglings is an unexpected sight in autumn, and this world of birth, creativity, and nurturing suggests the magic power of the mountain's center, whence are generated all the cycles of life.

Han's description of his earlier passage through the landscape on his way into exile is the kind of symbolic landscape we have seen in his earlier poems. The landscape embodies some specific cosmic state, some mood in the one who experiences it. Significant in this description is:

> I was in such a muddle I forgot to gaze afar,
> I just kept my eyes on what was right around me.

This suggests that, as he endured such hardships, Han Yü did not understand the full range of changes within the mountains but saw only the aspect that reflected his own suffering. The landscape becomes "great spears," "armor," and "helms." But now Han has come to understand it for what it actually is—not simply the reflection of one aspect of his life, but the microcosm of all potential changes.

Out of his recognition of the limitations of his earlier view, Han Yü turns to describe all the different forms the mountains take, as "space rives open," suggesting instant revelation. Although the descriptive style of the long passage that follows (ll. 117–90) is often compared to that of the *fu* (and rightly so), the description of the mountains is violently active in contrast to the tendency toward static description found in the fu, with the notable exception of fu descriptions of hunts. Moreover, Jao Tsung-yi has pointed out the formal similarities between the first part of this descriptive section (ll. 117–76) and T'an-wu-ch'an's translation of the *Buddhacarita*.[58]

Whatever their formal antecedents may be, each of these antithetically paired descriptives is representative of a kind of action or

58. Jao Tsung-yi, see n. 39.

relationship. The epideictic, enumerative structure pretends to completeness, so that the passage is like a catalog of all possible forms of behavior. Like the archetypal concepts of the *Book of Changes*, these pairs of descriptives, arising from the structure of changes in the mountains, pretend to account for all the possibilities of change. The ordered variety of the mountains is like a series of hexagrams, of which the two described directly as hexagrams (ll. 175–76) are only the most obvious examples. Thus, by viewing these mountains, Han comes to understand the cycles of change and fate. This is not to say that these different forms actually correspond to hexagrams; rather, like Yang Hsiung's *T'ai-hsüan*, Han Yü is creating his own complete range of possibilities.

The closing passage is a beautiful tribute to the creation of the mountain range and of the ordered universe. The mountains lie "between Heaven and Earth," between Yin and Yang, the polarities from which all change is generated. Within the multitude of forms there is order: "In perfect order like the body's ducts and veins." Han Yü then honors the creator of the mountains, the greatness of his labor and the skillfulness of his craftsmanship. Like the order of the mountains themselves, Han Yü's poem is "finely wrought" and shows the "application of axe and hatchet" (a phrase which, in Chinese literary criticism, suggests careful craftsmanship that is evident rather than hidden).

"South Mountains" is Han Yü's most ambitious poem and certainly one of his greatest. It represents the culmination of a long trend in his poetry toward the symbolic landscape, understood in terms of the cosmic order. The narrative plays a purely secondary role in the poem: Han Yü's personal experiences are merely examples of the multitude of possible changes. One could interpret the poem personally, politically, in terms of literature, or in any number of ways, but these are only partial aspects of the central theme, the creative power and cyclical changes of the universe. The abstract and the concrete are perfectly fused in this tribute to the organic, holistic universe. Its enormity matches the ambitiousness of the subject described.

11

Worlds of Disorder: Han Yü's Mythopoeic Poetry

Lo-yang, the eastern capital of the empire, was traditionally considered the cultural center, the city of poets. It had been to the branch of the State Academy in Lo-yang that Han Yü had requested transfer to avoid the political pressures mounting against him in Ch'ang-an. A year earlier, late in 806, Meng Chiao had taken up residence there under the protection of the former minister Cheng Yü-ch'ing, who had been made Prefect of Honan. Presumably, Han Yü also counted on Cheng's protection, and by 810 Han had risen to the post of Vice-prefect of Honan, the local magistrate of Lo-yang.

In Lo-yang Han Yü found himself surrounded by old friends and new admirers. Despite his frequent complaints of poverty, the years in Lo-yang, from 807 to 811, seem to have been among his happiest. He was comparatively free from political pressures and could devote himself to enlarging the literary reputation he had already earned for himself.

A fascination with the supernatural had long been an undercurrent in Han Yü's poetry, but in poems such as "Poem of Hsieh Tzu-jan," it had been treated as an object of scorn by hard-headed Confucian humanism. In one delightful poem, "Shooting the Hoothoot," Han Yü is confronted with a fiendish owl-demon; by a utilitarian, Confucian analysis of the problem he devalues it into an ordinary owl and, with humorous dispatch, shoots it.[1] The supernatural, with its associations of heterodoxy, early takes on the function of a world of disorder, set against a Confucian world of order.

Gods may, however, also play a role in a world of order, such as the mountain gods in "Visiting a Temple on Mount Heng" and "South Mountains." In the former poem, the god of Mount Heng

1. *HCLS*, p. 116.

was valuable as a metaphor to make a landscape intelligible in human terms. Parallel to his development of the symbolic landscape in the preceding year, during his stay in Lo-yang Han Yü created a mythopoeic poetry, a poetry of fantasy, in which gods and supernatural beings were used to make abstract problems of order and disorder comprehensible. In most of the mythopoeic poems the gods are treated with a burlesque humor that plays counterpoint to their divinity: they are at the same time omnipotent and incompetent, mighty and foolish, august and silly. They are anthropomorphic, but every human quality in them is exaggerated.

Han Yü developed the symbolic landscape to find a universal pattern in his own experience of exile and return: in "South Mountains" he reached admiration and acceptance of nature's cycles of change, the natural order. Inventing humorous myths as his vehicle, in the poems of this chapter Han finds a new way to oppose disorder, the "rectification of nature," which we shall discuss shortly.

The style of the following poems is the comically hyperbolic, descriptive style of the later linked verses, such as "The Campaign Against Shu." In each case this style is used to describe a world of disorder, and in the first poem, the promise of the restoration of order brings a change to a more balanced style. Although this hyperbolic style had its origins in the later linked verses, Han Yü was inspired in these poems to greater and greater extravagance by the poets of the "cult hermetic." One of the poems translated in this chapter is dedicated to Huang-fu Shih, a disciple of Han Yü's well known for his advocacy of "strangeness," and is expressly written to outdo a similar poem by the younger poet. Han's "Lunar Eclipse," which we did not have the space to include here, is in imitation of Lu T'ung's "Lunar Eclipse," abridging and reworking Lu's original.

The myth Han Yü creates in most of these poems to oppose a world of disorder is the "rectification of nature." In the organic universe, not only do nature and the human world reflect the cosmic cycles, nature and the universe may be organized and understood ethically, according to the ideal Confucian social model. There is no accident, no empirical causality, no divine whim or retribution. Error and imbalance in the natural world can be rectified by the proper moral action or expostulation. This is the pattern we saw in Meng Chiao's "Cold Creek"; the unnatural cold spell was rectified by inner purity and ritual action. If the fixed, cyclical patterns of change are violated, it is the poet's duty to confront nature, expostulate on the error, and order nature to correct the imbalance.

Although Han Yü seems to have had a sincere feeling for the natural cycles, as we saw in "South Mountains," it is doubtful that he believed (as Meng Chiao perhaps did) that the remonstrance of a moral individual could actually restore order to nature. The theme is a fiction in Han Yü's poetry, a myth that held special meaning for him, rather than an actual way to confront the phenomenal world, as it was in Meng Chiao's "Cold Creek." As a Confucian intellectual, the ethical and political pattern of the rectification of nature provided Han Yü with an intelligible way to perceive and participate in the world of nature and the cosmic order.

In "Suffering From the Cold," Han Yü makes a tongue-in-cheek expostulation with Heaven in regard to an unnatural cold spell. Although the date of this poem is less than certain, it was probably written at about the same time as Meng Chiao's "Cold Creek." In "Fire in the Lu-hun Mountains," Han Yü turns a forest fire into a rollicking combat between the fire-gods and the water-gods. When the water-gods complain to Heaven, Heaven explains the apparent disorder by a Chinese version of *concordia discors*: water will be the cause of disorder in another season, canceling out the present disorder of the fire-gods, and there is profound order beneath apparent disorder. The last poems of this chapter are, strictly speaking, not mythopoeic. The first two of these are playfully hyperbolic treatments of a monk's snoring as a sign of cosmic disorder. The last poem is a *propempticon* for the poet Chia Tao, using the hyperbolic style and the theme of hubris to describe the younger poet's literary daring; at the same time the poem reveals Han Yü's reservations about the propriety of this style and the poetry of fantasy in general.

At times, the contradiction between the playful humor of such poems as the above and the poet's stern Confucian ethics bothered Han Yü. In "Fire in the Lu-hun Mountains" he shows uneasiness at his own delight and success in such pieces:

> Huang-fu Shih made such a poem to stop his drowsiness,
> Its diction extravagant, erring from truth, so he burned it.
> He demanded I write a similar poem, even odder and more
>   difficult,
> Though I regret this loose tongue, I cannot stop it.

The talk of burning playful poems is disturbing. There is a certain amount of circumstantial evidence that Chia Tao did destroy his youthful extravagant poetry, or at least excluded it from his collection. That two of Han Yü's funniest poems, "Mocking the Snorer," were excluded from his collection and found again only later suggests that he may well have done the same. The few pieces that do survive, however, give us a good picture of what the style was like.

Suffering from the Cold

The four seasons are equally apportioned,
The spirit of one cannot coexist with another.
Fierce cold has usurped spring's succession—
Winter's lord has been greedy indeed.[2]
The God of Spring retracts his norms,[3]   5
And flees in terror—but does preserve humility.
He sends orders down to the Yellow Springs,[4]
That the sprouts, which curl and poke up, will perish young.
Grass and trees come out no more,
Sweetness and bitterness is lost in all foods.   10
Dire whirlwinds beleaguer the universe,
All suffer the jabs of their points, the hacks of their blades.
Though it is said sun and moon are august,
They could not preserve sunraven and moontoad.[5]
When Hsi-ho goes out to send off the sun,[6]   15
He cringes, peers around time and again.
The Blazing Emperor clutches the Fire-god,
He huffs and puffs but can't set him ablaze.
And we mortals at such a time as this—
How can we be bathed in spring's gracious light?   20
My skin grows hard as a tortoise-shell,
My robes become like knives and sickles.
The air so cold I can smell nothing,
Blood freezes, fingers won't grasp.
Warm wine seems to boil in my throat,   25
Then the mouth's corners freeze solid, as though gagged.[7]

2. "Winter's lord" is Chuan-hsü.   3. The god of spring is T'ai-hao.
4. The Yellow Springs is the underworld.
5. A raven was believed to inhabit the sun, and a toad, the moon.
6. Hsi-ho is the charioteer of the sun.
7. At first the warm wine seems boiling hot as it comes into contact with Han Yü's

When I'm about to take spoon and chopsticks to eat,
My fingers touch them as though arranging divination stalks.[8]
The cold gets in the stove, I feel no warmth,
Though I add charcoal time and again.   30
It does no good to stick your hands into boiling water,
How much less can you expect from silks and satins!
Tigers and leopards lie stiff in their caves,
Great dragons die sunken deep in the water.
Mars, the fire star, is destroyed on its course,   35
Ice pulls the whiskers from the sun's six dragons.
Far and wide, in the Great Cosmos,
I fear all manner of living things will perish.
The sparrows chirping at the window
Know not their own insignificance—   40
Raising their heads they sing to Heaven,
"We had wished that time would last longer for us,
But it would be better to die, shot by a pellet—
Then at least we'd get ourselves boiled or broiled."
If even the phoenix doesn't survive,   45
You little birds certainly won't be counted.
The rest, the crawlers and the wrigglers,
Will all die together, no special favor for any.
Though we men are known as most divine,
You we cannot protect.   50
Sorrowful lament stirs doleful sighing,
All emotions are hard to calm and cheer.
At midnight I stand, leaning against a wall,
A flood of tears goes rolling down.
"Heaven! Pity the guiltless,   55
Be kind to us, gaze down upon us!
Lift the crown's tassels from your eyes,
        Take the wadding from your ears,
Have salt and plum brought in to get the right flavor.[9]
Each day raise and employ the virtuous and capable,

---

cold mouth and throat, but it quickly freezes his mouth open.

8. This is a difficult metaphor. My guess is that the poet's frozen fingers are so stiff that he can't grasp his eating utensils. This, he imagines, resembles the stiff-fingered manner of a diviner consulting the oracle slips.

9. Han Yü is suggesting that Heaven bring in good ministers to "season" his government.

Dismiss the haughty and flattering.   60
Let the wind of life blow away the air of death,
Wide open, like raising a curtain.
Let the hanging icicles fall and shatter
And dawn's light enter the front eaves.
Let snow and frost melt forthwith,   65
Let the soil be rich and pasty.
Not the orchids alone shall flourish—
Extend it even unto the weeds.
I'll walk past sunlit blossoms lustrous,
Sit under wind-blown branches flapping.   70
O Heaven, if this were possible,
Though I die, my heart would be satisfied."[10]

Han Yü's comic myth about the cold spell contrasts sharply with
Meng Chiao's seriousness in "Cold Creek." Beneath the joking,
however, there lies a fundamental assumption of order; indeed, the
poem is organized by a cosmic hierarchy of beings. Beginning with
abstract statements on the natural order, Han Yü descends the
hierarchy of sufferers from the cold— from gods to men to beasts.
Each lower order then complains in turn to the order above it.
The first four lines progress from abstraction to personification. The
general principle, "The spirit of one cannot coexist with another,"
is made specific—"Fierce cold has usurped spring's succession"—
then personified in the myth of the god of winter's invasion of springtime. Through the myth, Han Yü makes a breakdown in the natural
order a culpable offense by an agent; he reduces a natural event to
human and ethical terms. Thus, as we have said, mythopoeia makes
nature and abstraction (order disrupted) intelligible in human
terms.

Countering Han Yü's treatment of natural phenomena in moral
terms as individual guilt, there is the openly comic handling of the
myth. For example, the god of spring's flight in terror is considered
to be "preserving his humility." Hsi-ho "cringes" in fear of the cold
as he "sends the sun off" in the morning, perhaps suggesting that he
didn't dare go along with it. Still more ludicrous is the scene in which
the blazing emperor is trying to blow flames onto the freezing fire-
god.

10. *HCLS,* p. 74.

From the world of the suffering gods, the poem moves to the world of mortals, specifically Han Yü. His suffering, though no less hyperbolic than that of the gods, involves everyday situations. Flesh hardens, clothes freeze, his mouth is frozen open, his fingers stiffen— even the stove and boiling water can't warm him. Following this, we move into the animal world, beginning with noble animals, tigers and dragons, and descending to sparrows and insects.

The sparrows, belonging to one of the lowest orders of creatures, raise their heads in hyperbolic imprecation: they long to be killed so that they will be cooked and thus kept warm. Though they address Heaven, it is Han Yü, the man and mediator, who responds and intercedes to Heaven for them and all things. Man may be at the top of the earthly hierarchy, the "most divine," but he is unable to protect them himself. Han, then, carries the expostulation up to Heaven, begging it to get rid of the baleful influences in the celestial government and restore harmony to the world. Han Yü treats the cosmic order as though it were the imperial Chinese court. He makes it clear that his request is for all things and not for himself alone; this is the purity of purpose and personal integrity ("Though I die, my heart would be satisfied") which is necessary to make such expostulation effective.

As suggested earlier, comic and serious elements balance each other throughout the poem. It would be a mistake to read the poem either as totally comic or totally serious. Han Yü mitigates each serious statement with playful hyperbole. Begging Heaven to pity those who suffer, he uses the comically hyperbolic metaphor of Heaven getting the crown's tassels out of its eyes and the wadding out of its ears. But beneath the comic treatment lies the serious theme of the concerned subject's expostulation with his ruler to get rid of evil and restore harmony to the world.

The outrageously hyperbolic language and imagery serve to actualize an extreme condition of disorder. In contrast, Han Yü's invocation of springtime has a more mellow tone:

> Let the wind of life blow away the air of death,
> Wide open, like raising a curtain.
> Let the hanging icicles fall and shatter
> And dawn's light enter the front eaves.

Hyperbole disappears, and the language is mollified in accordance with the situation for which Han Yü prays. The invocation similarly demythicizes the poem: the offending gods in the celestial court become simply the "haughty and flattering"—flattering courtiers being a literary convention that further humanizes the situation. Finally, the poem returns to the objective world in a description of how nature should be in springtime. Although it is only a prayer, the orderly and beautiful description of spring should, through word-magic, effect the same state in reality.

It is significant that in these mythopoeic poems, the supreme power of Heaven is curiously impotent to act. In this poem Heaven doesn't actually respond to Han Yü's expostulation, and in the following poem it responds with sophistry and evasion. Never does almighty Heaven interfere with earthly matters. Since Han Yü is using a political model, the Marxist critic might, with some justification, see a certain disillusionment with the imperial system and cynicism about its effectiveness.

The following poem leads us into an utterly different world, one in which Han Yü's fertile imagination could have free rein.

FIRE IN THE LU-HUN MOUNTAINS: FOLLOWING THE RHYMES OF A POEM ON THE SAME SUBJECT BY HUANG-FU SHIH

Huang-fu Shih was filling an office in ancient Lu-hun
The season was right in black winter
    When the marshes dry their streams.
Mountains went insane, valleys rampaged,
    As they spat forth and swallowed each other,
And the winds raged without ceasing, wranglingly.
Rubbing, chafing, they brought forth fire   5
    To incinerate themselves,
There was a sound in the middle of the night
    Startling all awake—none knew its cause.
Heaven leaped, Earth strode forward,
    The universe was toppled,
Scarlet, it shone upward to the furthest shores of the world.
Shredding all around to pieces, four horizons burning,
Gods broiled and demons blazed—no gate of escape.   10
Sun, moon, and stars were unstrung and shattered,
    They would come out to shine no more,
Tigers, bears, deer, boarlings, even the apes and gibbons,

Waterdragons, lizards, turtles, fish, and tortoises,
Ravens, owls, vultures, hawks, pheasants, snowgeese, and quail—
All boiled, broiled, roasted, ash-baked—   15
      Which of them could fly or flee?
The Fire-god was taking a day off to feast
      His godlings, the great and the small,
He set in order his firepearls, opened his splendid gardens.
Wild flights of lotus stuffed it with profuse freshness,
A thousand bells, ten thousand drums screeched,
      Droning in the ear,
There he amassed the jumbled toots and peeps   20
      Of fife and ocarina.
Rufous pennons, carmine streamers,
      Purple feathers and bandaroles,
Blazing civil servants from the Bureau of Heat
      In vermilion cap and uniform,
Lacquer their flesh red, down to thighs and butts;
With sunken chests and tumescent bellies,
      They heaved up the carriage axles,
Ochre faces and orange legs with paired leopard-skin quivers,   25
Rose-cloud carriages, rainbow pulling-straps,
      sun-hubbed surreys,
Cinnabar tassels on cerise canopies with ruddy pennants,
Red curtains and crimson tents
      Where they set sacrificial meats,
Wind and wave on pools of gore,
      Hills and mounds of flesh,
Immense chasms, gaping wide, are their plates of crystal;   30
The Five Mountains, their meat platters;
      The oceans, their four flagons,
As they merrily drink toasts and, laughing, chat.
The Lord of Thunder cleaves the mountains,
      Seawaters spread through,
Incisors bite and molars chew,
      Then the tongue goes back to the palate,
Lightning beams flash criss-cross   35
      From incarnadine goggle eyes.
Winter's Emperor and the God of the North retract their sway,
      Flee to the Roots of Darkness,

Leaving in panic their horses and palaquins,
    Turning their backs on their offspring.
Their bodies doubled over by secret panting,
    Roll up in a ball, shoulders to ankles,
Then in mutual pity subject and lord
    Grow still more tender and loving.
They sent out their black behemoth to spy,   40
    Fire burned its head,
Heaven's Gate so far, far away, it couldn't climb to it.
In dream it would reach the High God, to explain with
    bloody face,
Its body leaned forward, wanting to advance,
    It was shooed away by Heaven's gatekeeper.
The God bestowed the Nine Rivers to bathe its tear-streaks,
And summoned Shaman Yang to call back its spirit,   45
Slowly ordered it to approach,
    Asked what wrongs it had suffered.
    [The High God's reply to the behemoth's complaint]
"Since antiquity the Fire Element has been found in winter—
Besides, if I forbid them, it will break up their meal.
Lady Fire's a wife to Water, a marriage lasting for ages,
If you turn enemies in one morning, alas for your posterity! 50
Your season-element is due to return, take care now to hide,
And when the peach tree blossoms, you can take wing a little.
By August and September—advantage to showing your spite
    again.
Aiding you shall be five dragons following nine leviathans,
You shall inundate their towns, jail them in K'un-lun."   55
Huang-fu Shih made such a poem to stop his drowsiness,
Its diction extravagant, erring from the truth, so he burned it.
He demanded I write a similar poem, even odder and more
    difficult,
Though I regret this loose tongue, I cannot stop it.[11]

It is unfortunate that the original poem by Huang-fu Shih has not survived; in any case Han Yü's version probably succeeded in being "odder and more difficult." We find here the familiar pattern of natural imbalance, complaint to Heaven, and Heaven's response.

11. *HCLS*, 297.

The High God explains natural imbalance as two antithetical worlds of disorder that will balance each other out in different seasons. Fire's untimely and obstreperous behavior in winter will be matched by equally untimely and obstreperous flooding in late summer.

The water element is associated with north and winter in "five elements" theory, while fire is associated with south and summer. Instead of the hierarchical world of "Suffering From the Cold," here balance is achieved through two opposing and complementary elements, two extremes. Yet although this is Han Yü's most fantastic poem, the characteristic sense of balance and order still underlies it all.

The description of the feast of the fire-gods is one of the most outlandishly comic passages in Chinese literature. Han Yü has mustered a dazzling array of exotic vocabulary for the occasion. As he did in "South Mountains," Han Yü borrows fu devices for his own purposes. Lists, for example, the primary device of the epideictic fu, are put to comic uses, as in lines 12–15. This is the point in the poem where the hyperbole is first clearly comic. The list grows more absurd until the poet delivers a string of monosyllabic bird-names, then the string of cooking terms that are metaphors for the animals' dying in the forest-fire. When these cooked animals become the feast of the fire-gods, the situation becomes even more comic. Like the scene of the capture of the escaping rebels in the "Campaign Against Shu," humor sits uneasily beside violence and cruelty. However, beneath the extremes of destruction and comic hyperbole is the basic sense of order: each line represents the animals of land, water, and air, respectively.

The rectification of nature myth is subordinated to Han Yü's sheer delight in inventing metaphors and displaying his considerable command of exotic vocabulary. As a result the narrative suffers, leaving gaps which the reader and translator must fill in to make the events of the poem coherent. For example, line 40 is literally "Ordered black behemoth spy, burn its head." This must be amplified to "the two gods of winter sent their black behemoth back up to the world from the Roots of Darkness to spy out what the fires were doing, but the fires burned its head." Line 47 begins the High God's reply to the black behemoth, but this is neither indicated in the text nor is the complaint of the behemoth stated. Such ellipses

may suggest that Han Yü, usually very careful about the logical and
narrative structure of his poems, either composed this one carelessly
or did not take the trouble to revise it. This is a further indication
that playful poems such as this were not taken very seriously, even
though the brilliant style and fertile imagination displayed in this
poem make it one of Han Yü's most noteworthy. It may be that, as
with *tz'u* (art songs) later in the T'ang and in the Sung, conservative
taste brought authors to disregard some of their finest work.

The following two poems make use of the hyperbolic descriptive
style and the theme of a world of disorder for ends even less serious
than "Fire in the Lu-hun Mountains." Poems of "mockery" are a
common subgenre in T'ang poetry, though the mockery   usually
so gentle as to be undiscernable; Han Yü's mockery is more imaginative, using his early Yüan-ho style, and thus more obviously
mockery. These two poems were probably written in 811 when Han
Yü was in Lo-yang.

MOCKING THE SNORER

I

When Reverend Tan sleeps in the daytime,
What a cacophony are the sounds he makes!
A gale blows obstinately over rolls of fat,
Piling the boulder peaks into deep valleys.
With a manly oink he suddenly gags and stops,   5
Then each time begins anew, the robustness more than
    doubled.
It's somewhat like a corpse deep in hell,
Who, emitting long howls, suffers for his host of crimes.
He startles the horses and cattle so they won't eat,
All the demons gather, waiting for him.   10
His wooden pillow splits into an X-shape,
The face of the mirror grows blisters.
An iron Buddha frowns, hearing him,
Stone statues shudder, their legs quake.
Who says Heaven and Earth are kind?—   15
I intend to scold the Lord of Creation.
Seeking seclusion, lice explore his ears,
But the sounds' fierceness spreads waves over the seas.

The sun can't bear to shine any more,
So the flying wind-riders all grow drowsy.[12]   20
Suddenly it seems as though P'eng Yüeh and Ch'ing Pu
Were crying out the injustice, as they were ground to
        pulp.[13]
It's also like a tiger in a cage,
Screaming from its wounds and roaring in hunger.
Though you order a Ling Lun to play his flutes,   25
He could hardly change these bitter tunes.[14]
Though you order Wu-hsien to summon it back,
His soul will never again come into his body.[15]
On what mountain is there some magic herb
To cure this—I'd like to pick it for him.   30

II

The very instant Reverend Tan lies down,
There's not the least discomfort—he takes a long snooze.
Having had occasion to hear the sound he makes,
I was gravely worried least his inner organs were being
        destroyed.
Like the Yellow River it would spurt playfully downward—   5
But he dammed it up into a flood, just like stupid Kun.[16]
Then the Emperor of the South first wielded his bludgeon,
Bored holes, and Chaos leaked out.[17]

12. The "flying wind-riders" are birds. This line suggests that there will no longer be any pleasant bird songs left to counteract the noise of snoring.

13. P'eng Yüeh and Ch'ing Pu both served Liu Pang, later to be the first emperor of the Han Dynasty, in his struggle against Hsiang Yü. After Hsiang Yü was defeated, both were unjustly accused of plotting rebellion and were executed. As his punishment P'eng Yüeh was hacked to pieces.

14. Ling Lun was a legendary musician in the court of the Yellow Emperor.

15. Wu-hsien is probably the shaman of that name mentioned in the Li Sao. There was an ancient shamanistic practice of summoning the soul of the sick or dying to persuade it to return to the body. Han Yü imagines that Tan's soul is undergoing all the torments of hell, and if it can be summoned back to the body, all the noise will cease. It may also mean that Tan's departed soul couldn't bear to return to such pandemonium.

16. Kun was delegated by the emperor Yao to channel the floods of the Yellow River, but after nine years he proved unequal to the task. The point of Han Yü's comparison here is that instead of letting his breath flow freely, Tan seems to be damming it up inside him (as Kun did with the Yellow River), portending a flood of air even more horrible than usual.

17. Han Yü is playfully and improperly alluding to the last story of the "Ying Ti-wang"

Suddenly he expels his breath out to infinity,
From unfathomable depths, thousands of feet down,   10
You'd imagine it would stop there, but no!—
It keeps coming out with a resounding roar.
In the dark recesses of his tiny throat
A forest of trees and bushes luxuriates.
Though a robber be cunning and crafty,   15
His spirit would sink, wouldn't dare even peek around the
     door.
Like Chaos before Creation, a universal jumble,
Where weird phantoms discharge their violent dispositions.
All at once it seems a babbling competition,
Then instantly like a grumbling resentment.   20
The forms it takes are terribly dissimilar,
And there is no road to find the roots of the trouble.
How can I close off its source?—
The only answer is a full basket of dirt![18]

These poems, not in Han Yü's regular collection, were found after his death, and there remain some doubts as to their authenticity. However, there are two factors that make me inclined to accept them as genuine: first, the inimitable style is Han Yü's—no other T'ang poet writes like that—as well as the characteristic hyperbole, cosmic imagery, and hints of universal disorder; and second, these are just the sort of works Han Yü or his editor might have excluded from his collection.

As suggested above, there are hints of a rectification of nature myth in the first poem. Tan's snoring has clearly disrupted the natural order of things (see l. 10), to which Han Yü responds:

Who says Heaven and Earth are kind?—
I intend to scold the Lord of Creation.

But Han Yü does not carry out his intended reprimand; rather he elaborates further on the outlandish effects of the snoring. If the first poem describes the catastrophic effects of Tan's snoring, the

---

chapter of the *Chuang-tzu*, in which the emperors of the Northern and Southern Oceans, wishing to show their gratitude to Chaos, bored holes in it, with the result that Chaos died (holes differentiated the undifferentiated). Han Yü is suggesting, on the contrary, that through the bored holes Chaos leaked out, a metaphor for Tan's exhalation.

18. I.e. to stuff up his mouth. *HCLS*, p. 289.

second one minutely describes the snoring process in outlandish hyperbole. In the second poem we can see the blend of realism and fantasy which are characteristic of much of Han Yü's poetry of the early Yüan-ho period: every movement, inhalation, exhalation, each noise and hesitation, is present—this is not just snoring, but a careful observation of the *process* of snoring. Each particular sound or movement in that process, however, is blown up out of all proportion by hyperbolic metaphor.

Although poems such as the two above are hardly the heights of Han Yü's poetry, they do provide a fresh breeze of good humor amid the general seriousness of the age. In the following poem we find Han Yü beginning to show reservations about the extravagance of the early Yüan-ho style.

SENDING OFF WU-PEN [CHIA TAO]
    ON HIS WAY BACK TO FAN-YANG [EXCERPT]

In regard to Wu-pen's writing,
His body is large, but not as large as his gall.
I have indicated difficulties to him,
But advancing boldly, there's nothing he doesn't dare.
Dragons sport with horn and fang,   5
Yet in his confusion he wants to grab them.
Demon hordes, imprisoned in Hell's Great Gloom—
He peeks downward and descends the Dark Pit.
When the sun in the sky illuminates all the world,
He fixes his gaze on it without lowering his head.   10
Whales pop out of their lairs, rocs scrape the sky,
He lifts both and cheerfully gobbles them up.
Now how can his capabilities necessarily be so?—
Because he is utterly free of all ignorance and confusion.[19]
He makes his mad diction as lush as he pleases,   15
Fluctuates, showing expansiveness, then grief's constriction.
When his recklessness is gone, I marvel at the change,
How everywhere he creates lucid ease.
Wind-blown cicadas—shattered knots of brocade,
On green pools, spreading lotus.   20

19. This is a difficult couplet. I think Han Yü is simply saying that Chia Tao is able to perform such audacious literary feats because his heart is pure. There may also a be note of chiding Chia's naïvété in that purity of heart.

> Blossoms of magic plants lifting above wild medlars,
> Lone pinions rising out of joined reeds.[20]

Chia Tao (779–843), as a youth a Buddhist monk with the religious name Wu-pen, was to become the best poet of the first generation of the Late T'ang. At the time when this poem was written (about 811), Chia Tao was turning from the cult hermetic style toward the new Late T'ang style. At the same time, Han's own style was changing too, and this is one of the last poems using highly imaginative metaphors and extravagant hyperbole that can be dated in his works. Han Yü has become aware of the "difficulties" (l. 2) of Chia's Lo-yang style, that its gall is larger than its body—it pretends to be more than it is. Han is playing on the words *body* and *gall*, using them in their physical senses as well as "gall" as reckless courage and "body" as the size or capacity of a literary work. Chia's "recklessness" (l. 17), his youthfully exaggerated literary daring, no longer lures Han Yü to write a piece such as "Fire in the Lu-hun Mountains"; rather he uses that style to describe Chia Tao's daring and to suggest his own dissatisfaction with it.

Han Yü shows much more interest in the "lucid ease" of which Chia Tao is equally capable. The following four lines, in which Han Yü imitates that new style, show the dense beauty and delicacy of the Late T'ang:

> Wind-blown cicadas—shattered knots of brocade,
> On green pools, spreading lotus.
> Blossoms of magic plants lifting above wild medlars,
> Lone pinions rising out of joined reeds.

Though there are differences to be sure, still we can see a basic similarity between the Late T'ang style and that of the High T'ang. This dense, graceful, antithetical style had never really died out during the Mid-T'ang; it had simply lingered on in conventional poetry while the two primary Mid-T'ang poetic movements, those of Han Yü and Po Chü-yi, ran their course. This is the mainstream of the tradition emerging again, slightly altered but victorious. As the poetic fashion of the times changes, Han Yü's own personal taste and style change, and in his last years the old poet finally comes to terms with the tradition.

20. *HCLS*, p. 257.

12

The Cult Hermetic: 806-814

. . . If what one says is novel, then it's different from the ordinary [ch'ang]; what's different from the ordinary is "strange" [kuai]. If one's diction is lofty, it stands out from the average; if it stands out from the average, then it's unusual [ch'i]. The stripes [wen, also "literature"] of a tiger or leopard cannot help being brighter than those of a dog or a sheep. The sounds of a phoenix cannot help but be more melodious than those of magpies. The luster of jade and gold cannot help being more splendid than that of tiles or stones. [from Huang-fu Shih's "First Letter in Answer to Mr. Li"][1]

However obvious the above statement of critical theory may be, it is symptomatic of the prevailing poetic fashion among the young poets who gathered around Han Yü and Meng Chiao in the early Yüan-ho period. Ch'i, the "unusual," always carried a positive force in Chinese critical terminology, generally meaning the "unusually good." Here it is equated with kuai, the "strange." The argument of this passage is that whatever is better than average is unusual, but the implication is that whatever is strange is therefore better than average.

By 806 Han Yü and Meng Chiao had already made a name for themselves as poets. As we saw in the linked verses and in the preceding chapters, wit and hyperbole constituted one aspect of their new styles, and this aspect was easily seized upon and imitated. As young admiring poets began to seek the help and encouragement of the two older ones, it was natural that they turned to this "strange" style to impress Han Yü and Meng Chiao with their talent. Among these poets were Chia Tao, Li Ho, Lu T'ung, Liu Ch'a, Ma Yi, Huang-fu

1. *CTW*, c. 685, p. 8897.

Shih, and Fan Tsung-shih. Of the last three poets mentioned few works survive today. Chia Tao and Li Ho were both to exert a strong influence on the development of the Late T'ang poetic style, while Lu T'ung and Liu Ch'a are known exclusively for the bizarre imagination they displayed in this "strange" style of the early Yüan-ho. This is the "cult hermetic," the pose of exceptional talent which carried poetry beyond the comprehension of ordinary men.

Han Yü and Meng Chiao had long believed in their own moral superiority, and the change of emphasis to superior artistic talent was not a difficult one to make. As early as 806 Han Yü seems to have had something of this sort in mind, as we saw in "Drunk: To Chang Shu." However, while Meng Chiao and Han Yü certainly were the motive forces behind the cult hermetic, and while their own poetry between 806 and 814 was influenced by it, only a few of their poems can actually be called cult hermetic. These poems are, not suprisingly, usually those addressed to their younger admirers. As we have discussed in the preceding chapters, Han Yü's and Meng Chiao's concerns during these years went beyond a simple display of their own imagination and cleverness. With the notable exception of Li Ho, these younger poets were primarily concerned with impressing their mentors and each other.

An excellent example of cryptic bombast are the following excerpts from a poem by Lu T'ung (who, incidentally, was a contemporary of Han and Meng, not a younger poet, though his poetic activity began in this period).

POEM ON MAKING FRIENDS WITH MA YI

Between Heaven and Earth suns and moons pass without
    a care,
Lu T'ung, at forty, has had no chance to get together
    with you.
There is only a single heart, spleen, and bones,
Peak-craggy, jag-jutting, sheer abyss-creviced
Knives and swords as the peaks and cliffs,   5
While flatlands are let loose into heights like K'un-lun
    Mountain.
No place for it in Heaven,
Earth cannot receive it,

Nor do sun and moon dare steal from its splendor.[2]
Shen-nung drew the eight trigrams   10
Thereby piercing the heart of Heaven.[3]
Nü Kua was originally Fu Hsi's wife,
Who, fearing Heaven's rage,
Pounded and smelted five-colored stones,
Drawing the needle of the sun and moon.   15
And threads of the five stars, mended Heaven,

. . . .

Yesterday T'ung wasn't T'ung/the same,
Yi was of course Yi/different.[4]   35
This is to say for the most part the same/T'ung, and a
    little different/Yi.
Today T'ung is T'ung/the same
But Yi isn't Yi/different,
This is to say T'ung didn't go and Yi didn't arrive.
Right in the middle it moved Heaven and Earth,   40
Out of a jade-white badge hacked a heart of longing,
Out of golden ore forged tears of longing,
When suddenly in the sky I heard sounds of avalanches
    and valleys overturned.
Infinitely better than a billion bushels of perfect pearls,
Is buying a pair of concubines, real Hsi Shih's from the   45
    South.[5]
These concubines were sexy enough to drive a man mad,
Their arms of congealed unguents, their skirts of kingfisher,
They knew only of painting their eyebrows and daubing
    their lips crimson.
But ever since I got you,
I rap gold and whack jade passing up and over floating   50
    clouds,

2. "It" refers to Lu T'ung's "single heart, spleen, and bones."
3. Shen-nung was one of the mythical emperors of antiquity. He first taught people how
to farm, hence his name means "God-farmer." He, however, was not traditionally cre-
dited with the development of the eight trigrams. Lu T'ung may either be inventing this
theory, or he may be drawing on some esoteric tradition of which I am unaware.
4. Lu T'ung is punning on the two men's names: T'ung means "same," and Yi means
"different."
5. Hsi Shih was a legendary beauty and is used as a conventional metaphor for beautiful
women.

And looking back,
That pair of concubines isn't even worth mentioning.
All my life I've made friends like a petty man,
But I remember you right before my eyes as though
    actually seeing you.[6]

Not being one of the initiate, I cannot explain all the implications of this poem. The myth in the poem is perhaps a political allegory, a type of poetry for which Lu showed great aptitude. The witty punning on the two men's names does not mean a great deal. In line 36 the names are used cleverly in a common phrase, "for the most part the same, but a little different." Lu T'ung proceeds to express his longing for Ma Yi hyperbolically: Ma is more valuable to him than a pair of the loveliest concubines, who are in turn more valuable than "a billion bushels of perfect pearls." In the last part of the poem, untranslated, Ma becomes a composite of shimmering bones and knotty pine, an image reminiscent of the virtuous "cragginess" in Meng Chiao's late poetry.

This is, of course, more outlandish than anything Meng Chiao or Han Yü ever wrote, but compared to their poetry it is hollow bombast. Even as bombast, however, it is still far superior to Ma Yi's answer.[7] His poem is as hollow as the above piece but not as imaginative, even though he tried hard. Lu T'ung is primarily known for his "Lunar Eclipse," which was imitated by Han Yü. Though only a few of Lu T'ung's other poems can equal "Lunar Eclipse" and "Poem on Making Friends with Ma Yi" in bizarre imagery, his work is still the clearest example of the cult hermetic.

Only two of Huang-fu Shih's poems survive, one a prosaic encomium of Yüan Chieh's writing, and the other, "The Valley of the Stone Buddha," a characteristically obscure poem in the cult hermetic style.[8] However, we do know that he wrote a version of "Fire in the Lu-hun Mountains," Han Yü's most extravagant poem. As a disciple of Han Yü, Huang-fu Shih is better known as a prose writer and advocate of obscurity in prose style.

In the poetry of Li Ho we are dealing with the work of a major poet every bit the equal of Meng Chiao and Han Yü. Within the context of this chapter we cannot even begin to account for the full range and depth of Li Ho's poetry; rather, we must concern ourselves only

6. *CTS,* c. 388, p. 4383.   7. *CTS.* c. 369, p. 4155.   8. *CTS,* c. 369, pp. 4150–51.

with how his poetry relates to the cult hermetic style of the early Yüan-ho period. In his life Li Ho was most closely associated with Huang-fu Shih, but he also seems to have been well acquainted with Han Yü. It is unfortunate that more of the poetry of Huang-fu Shih does not survive, for in it we might have been able to establish an even closer link between Li Ho's poetry and that of the Han Yü group.

The traditional influences on Li Ho's poetry are diverse. Most important are: (1) the *Ch'u Tz'u*; (2) palace poetry; (3) *yüeh-fu* and Li Po; and (4) Chinese myth and the shamanistic tradition. Contemporary influences are equally varied: (1) the mythic poetry of Han Yü and Lu T'ung; (2) the self-image of the talented, suffering poet rejected by society, from Meng Chiao; (3) the satirical "new ballads" of Po Chü-yi and Yüan Chen; (4) *ch'uan-ch'i*, T'ang tales of strange phenomena; and (5) the contemporary currents in literary theory which equate the "strange" and the "exceptional." These contemporary influences exhibit the full range of literary fashion of the Yüan-ho period, and yet Li Ho's poetry is completely his own.

Although Li Ho never mentions Meng Chiao in his poems (any more than he does Po Chü-yi or Yüan Chen), he must have been familiar with Meng's poetry. Indeed, at times in Li Ho's poetry we can hear the voice of Meng Chiao far more clearly than that of any other of the contemporary poets who influenced Li. When Li Ho turns away from the eerie symbolism of his mythic poetry and from the lush eroticism of his "palace poetry" to his own sufferings and emotions, we read:

> My sick bones alone can survive—
> Have I missed any trouble that afflicts mankind?[9]

> Wind in wu-t'ung startles the heart, a bold man is bitter,
> Fading lamp, the crickets cry over cold, white silk.[10]

> A youth who embraces the bitterness of wandering,
> Weeping in dream turns his hair white.
> An emaciated horse pastures on ruined grasses,
> A frothy rain blows in gusts over cold gutters.[11]

> How chill is the stoney air!
> Old sedge like short arrowheads.[12]

9. *LCC*, p. 10.   10. *LCC*, p. 65.   11. *LCC*, p. 205.   12. *LCC*, p. 260.

and entire poems:

BALLAD OF A BROKEN HEART

Droning I imitate the songs of Ch'u,
Sick bones wounded by hidden poverty.
On an autumn form white hair grows,
Tree leaves cry in the wind and rain.
The lamp flame blue, its orchid oil gone,   5
In the fading brilliance flying moths dance.
Dust hardens on ancient walls,
As the soul of an exile speaks in dream.[13]

Knowing Meng Chiao's vision of the pure, suffering poet, would we
know that the following lines are by Li Ho?

Nowadays the Way is blocked up,
Why should I wait till my hair turns white?
In dismal suffering, Ch'en Shu-sheng,
Wearing coarse robes he cultivates the rites.
He imitates the style of Yao and Shun,
Thus rebuking the decadent antitheses of contemporaries.
The carriage rut freezes by your thatched gate—
As the sun goes down, gaunt shadows of elms.[14]

Ch'en Shu-sheng refers to Ch'en Shang, a minor disciple of Han Yü.
Poems such as those from which I have quoted the passages above
are often used to show the hardships and personal sufferings of Li
Ho—and rightly so, I believe. However, one should not ignore the
fact that this is the "party line": the "Way is blocked up," the man
of integrity "wears coarse robes" and suffers in poverty while holding
to the ideals of antiquity. Besides the general equation of virtue with
suffering in poverty, Li Ho seems to be familiar with Meng Chiao's
personal association of the suffering poet: "sick bones," screeching
crickets, "hidden poverty," "emaciated horses," freezing, etc. This
is meant in no way to detract from Li Ho's originality—he does not
"imitate" Meng Chiao, Han Yü, or any poet—it simply means that
he was strongly affected by the prevailing poetic fashion of his age.
Although these current poetic styles of the early Yüan-ho period did
not *determine* the kind of poetry Li Ho wrote, only then was such
poetry possible.

13. *LCC*, p. 124. The "exile" is probably Ch'ü Yüan.   14. *LCC*, p. 207.

There are an equal number of ways in which Li Ho was indebted to the work of Han Yü; however, in the following comparisons we will consider the great differences as well as the similarities between the two poets. I believe we can see that Li Ho is neither a "disciple" of Han Yü, as some traditional critics assume, nor is he totally separate from him, as some modern critics such as Chou Ch'eng-chen would have us believe.[15]

Both of the following poems are written to compliment a precious object belonging to a friend. This is a common subgenre in T'ang poetry, one of the requirements of polite society, but Li Ho and Han Yü infuse their poems with a hyperbolic gusto rare in more conventional treatments. Both poems apply supernatural terms to the object they describe to heighten its specialness. It is difficult to know which of these poems was written first, and although it would be absurd to say that Han Yü was influenced here by Li Ho, we do know from poems such as "Fire in the Lu-hun Mountains" and his "Lunar Eclipse" that Han Yü was spurred on to greater and greater literary extravagance by the daring of his young poet friends.

USING THE SAME RHYMES AS LU TING'S "SONG OF THE RED
    VINE STAFF: TO REPAY CH'IEN HUI"

Han Yü

A staff of red vine has never before been seen in the world,
Ch'ien of the Secretariat first brought one from Tien-ch'ih.[16]
Tien's king had his palace swept and left it for the envoy,
Kneeling offered it, bowing time and again, his speech,
    gibberish.[17]
You leaned on it, crossing rope bridges, and avoided falling,   5
When your life was in great danger, you received its support.
A hundred states your road passed, but none had ever seen
    such,
Lords and courtiers crowded to behold it, following your
    banners.
Traditions agree that Tien's god left the water to offer it,
A whisker pulled from the Red Dragon on which gushed his
    blood;   10

15. Chou Ch'eng-chen, *Li Ho Lun* (Hong Kong: Wen-yi, 1971), pp. 134–35.
16. Tien-ch'ih was a kingdom, nominally a client state of China, in the southwestern part of modern China.
17. The king's "gibberish" is doubtless his inability to speak Chinese.

They also say it's the fiery whip grasped by Hsi-ho,[18]
Who in darkness reached the remote west, and lost it sleeping.
In several layers you wrapped it, wrote your office title on it,
So as not to exalt yourself to barbarians by such treasured
    marvels.
Returning home you presented it to a colleague,   15
Its light floated over his hands—about to grasp it, he doubted.
As he slept one day in his empty hall, it leaned by a window,
Like flying lightning against the wall, it sought dragon form.
The South Palace, remote and pure—the Forbidden
    Chambers, intimate,
Their poems together are like two instruments played in
    tune.[19]   20
I cannot continue their charming phrases and lovely lines,
So this is sent only to comfort a while this minor official.[20]

Song of the Sword of the Collator
in the Spring Office

Li Ho

Sir, in your sword-case there are three feet of water,
Into a Wu pool it has gone and beheaded a dragon.[21]
The slanting brightness of moonlight through wall chinks,
    the chill of polished dew,
A white-silken sash rolled out flat, windblown but unrising.
Its sharkskin sheath old, the barb of a briar,   5
Grebe fat tempered its flash, a white pheasant's tail.
Really it is the whole of Ching K'o's heart,[22]
But don't let its shine light up words in the Spring Office.[23]

18. Hsi-ho is the charioteer of the sun.

19. The "South Palace" and the "Forbidden Chambers" are conventional kennings for the offices of the two men. The former refers to Lu Ting, the latter, to Ch'ien Hui. The second line of the couplet is literally, "Their singing in harmony is the kind as when playing ocarina and flute," which traditionally suggests brotherly friendship. See *Book of Songs,* ♯199.

20. *HCLS*, p. 309.

21. Chou Ch'u of the Chin Dynasty once beheaded a dragon in a lake.

22. Ching K'o unsuccessfully attempted to assassinate the first emperor of the Ch'in Dynasty; though a would-be regicide, he was greatly admired for his courage.

23. The "Spring Office" was a bureau attached to the crown prince. I believe that here Li Ho is saying that in his capacity as collator, his cousin has no need for arms; i.e. the sword is fine, but it has no place in the crown prince's library—especially since it is the

Twisted threads, beads of gold dangle from it,
Its divine light seeks to slice Lan-t'ien jade.   10
Drawn out, the White Emperor of the West was frightened—
Moaning, a demon mother weeps on autumn's moors.[24]

In comparing these two poems, the first element we note is Han
Yü's use of narrative: the concise and complex story of the red vine
staff is like a miniature *ch'uan-ch'i*, a T'ang "tale of the strange." Han
tells of the miraculous origins of the staff, how Ch'ien Hui came by
it, and the wonders that occurred after it was given to Lu Ting. In
Li Ho's poem there is no narrative, but the miraculous events associated with the sword are encapsulated in allusions. There is a
pseudoverisimilitude in Han Yü's poem: he is pretending these
miraculous events really happened. Li Ho uses his allusions purely as
metaphors for the preciousness of the sword.

It is characteristic that in Han Yü's poem there is a connection between the supernatural world and the human world: indeed, the
main points of interest in the poem are those when human beings
confront the supernatural. Everywhere we find the hierarchical patterns of human relationships: the deference of the king of Tien-ch'ih
to the envoy, the god "offering" the staff to the king of Tien-ch'ih,
the friendship of Ch'ien and Lu, and Han Yü's own deference to
them. The supernatural is interesting, but it must not be given precedence over what is really important, the political and social structure of the human world:

In several layers he wrapped it, wrote his office title on it,
So as not to exalt himself to barbarians by such treasured
     marvels.

It is more important that Ch'ien Hui be recognized by the barbarians as the Chinese envoy rather than as the possessor of some
magic staff. The sword Li Ho describes is, on the contrary, completely outside the human world, except for the curious line: "But don't
let its shine light up words in the Spring Office!" This line was perhaps added lest anyone in the court, reading the poem, grow under-
standably uneasy about the comparison of the collator's sword to the
regicidal heart of Ching K'o.

---

heart of Ching K'o, a would-be regicide.
    24. LCC, p. 28. After the founder of the Han Dynasty had killed a large snake, he had a
dream in which an old lady appeared and told him that he had killed the son of the White
Emperor, the legendary god of the West.

The sword belongs to a dazzling world of metaphor and myth; though men carry it, they do so only in the remote past and against supernatural creatures—it has very little to do with its owner. The red vine staff may be magic, but it is still a good staff and very practical—it helps Ch'ien over the dangerous mountains. Han's poem is mythopoeic: he creates his own story. Li Ho, by relying on traditional myths and stories, makes the object less human and genuinely supernatural; the closing couplet is truly eerie, and one believes that the sword is actually haunted.

Now let us look at four poems by Meng Chiao, Han Yü, and Li Ho, showing different treatments of the same theme.

LISTENING TO A LUTE

Meng Chiao

Moaning in the wind, a faint rain subsides,
Blown fluttering, leaves of the chestnut-oak sing.
The moon sinks west of wild peaks,
Faint and melancholy, three or four stars.
Across the creek before me, suddenly a lute is strummed,   5
On the other side of the forest, a chill tinkling.
When I hear the sound of a major piece being played
I can't bear to listen just lying on my pillow—
I bring back my candle, straighten my hairpins,
Wash in a stream, then stand in the middle of the yard.   10
With firm stance, the teeth of my clogs set deep,
My manner, trancelike, my eyes in darkness.
As a faint wind blows over my robe,
I even recognize the faint sounds of the *kung* note.
I have studied the Way for thirty years,   15
But have not escaped worries over life and death;
Listening to the playing through the entire night,
I knew every emotion in the universe.[25]

LISTENING TO THE REVEREND YING PLAY THE LUTE

Han Yü

Intimately, a boy and girl talking together,
Whether tender or bitter, each calls the other "darling."
Then cutting off abruptly, he changes to the haughty,

25. *MTYSC*, p. 162.

Valiant warriors going off to the field of combat.
Then floating clouds and willow floss without roots,   5
Through the vastness of Heaven and Earth, continue soaring
   upward.
Or as amid chattering flocks of all kinds of birds,
Suddenly one perceives the solitary phoenix.
Or climbing up—can't go even an inch, even a mite higher,
Then, strength failing, one long fall, over a thousand feet
   down.   10
But unfortunately these two ears I have
Have never listened to such music.
Since I've heard Reverend Ying play,
I'm transfixed in this single corner.
I push his hand away and abruptly stop him—   15
Streaming tears have sopped my clothes.
Ying—you're really a master at this,
But don't go setting ice and charcoal together in my heart![26]

Song on Listening to Reverend Ying Play the Lute

Li Ho

Clouds from Parting's Shores return to the isle of cassia flowers,[27]
In the strings of a Szechwan lute, two phoneixes speak.[28]
Leaves of the lotus fall, rocs part in autumn,
Or a king of Yüeh rising at night to wander T'ien-mu
   Mountain.
Pendants of a virtuous courtier in darkness, crystals clinking,   5
Moth-eyed maidens crossing the oceans, leading white deer.
Who can see one, clasping his sword, going to the long bridge?[29]
Who can see one, dipping hair in ink, writing poems on
   spring bamboo?[30]

26. *HCLS*, p. 441. "Ice and charcoal," opposite and incompatible extremes of emotion.

27. "Parting's Shores" refers to the spot in the Milky Way ("River of Heaven") where the Spinning Girl Star and the Herd Boy Star are permitted to meet once a year. The "isle of cassia flowers" is the moon.

28. The two phoenixes supposedly refer to the lutanist's hands, although the allusion to the Spinning Girl and Herd Boy above, as well as Han Yü's intimate chat, suggest a musical impression of lovers.

29. This refers to the story of Chou Ch'u beheading the dragon in the lake.

30. The High T'ang eccentric Chang Hsü was famous for practicing calligraphy in this unorthodox manner when drunk.

An Indian monk stands before me at my gate,
A sculpted arhat of a Buddha Hall, august the arch of his
    eyebrows.   10
His ancient lute with huge pegs, eight feet long,
An old tree of Mount Yi-yang, no mere wu-t'ung branch.
Hearing its strings in the chill hall startles this sick wanderer,
Medicine-bag that I am, I leave my mat of dragon-whisker rush
    for a while.
For a song about your playing, best ask a great minister—   15
The office of Supervisor of Ceremonies is low—what can it gain
    you?[31]

BALLAD OF LI P'ING'S HARP

Li Ho

Wu silk, Shu wu-t'ung stretch to high autumn skies,[32]
Clouds harden over empty mountains, crumble and don't move
    on.
River goddesses weep on bamboo, the Pale Girl grieves,[33]
Li P'ing in the heart of the nation is playing his harp.
K'un Mountain jade shatters, phoenixes cry out,   5
Lotus weeping dew, fragrant orchids laugh.
It melts cold light before the twelve city gates,
Twenty-three strings move the Purple Emperor.[34]
Nü Kua melts stones to patch the heavens,[35]
Stones break, heavens tremble, letting through autumn rains.   10
In dream he enters the gods' mountain to teach the Witch
    Goddess,[36]
Old fish leap from the waves, lean dragons dance.

31. *LCC*, p. 372.

32. Silk and wu-t'ung wood are metonymies for the harp and its music. The best silk for lute strings came from the province of Wu; the best wood for the body of the lute came from Szechwan (Shu).

33. The "River Goddesses" are the wives of Shun who, on hearing of their husband's death, wept on the bamboo of the Hsiang River region, leaving it speckled forever. Later they committed suicide and became the goddesses of the river. The Pale Girl, a consort of the Yellow Emperor, once played such unbearably sad music that the Yellow Emperor broke her fifty-stringed lute into two lutes of twenty-five strings each.

34. The Purple Emperor is a high figure in the Taoist pantheon.

35. Nü Kua mended the sky when a demon broke it; see "Poem on Making Friends with Ma Yi."

36. The Witch Goddess was known as an accomplished harpist.

> Wu K'ang doesn't sleep, but leans on the cassia tree,[37]
> As dewdrops fly slanting to soak the cold Hare.[38]

Though they are on similar subjects, there are great differences between each of the four poems quoted here; furthermore, these differences are indicative of a progression into the "strange" style of the early Yüan-ho period. Meng Chiao's poem is intense, personal, and straightforward; the example by Han Yü shows a greater concentration on metaphor and is about human relationships rather than inner experience. In the first poem by Li Ho the metaphorical element dominates, but there is still a trace of the human world. Finally, in the last poem, one of Li Ho's finest, the supernatural world ceases to be hyperbolic metaphor and becomes another level of reality in itself.

Meng Chiao does not need the lutanist and scarcely needs even the music. His poem is characteristically inward, centering on the listener. The conventional theme, appearing in all the poems, of the endless variety of moods stirred up by the music, is stated with power, simplicity, and absoluteness: "I knew every emotion of the universe." In his solopsistic world, Meng cares only for his experience of the music and not for the music itself.

Han Yü's poem is in two parts—one consisting of metaphors for Ying's music, and the other, of Han Yü's reaction to the music. The metaphors are drawn mostly from the human and natural worlds: lovers, warriors, clouds, floss, chattering birds. Ying's runs up and down the scales are described with a violent energy characteristic of Han Yü:

> Or climbing up—can't go even an inch, even a mite higher,
> Then, strength failing, one long fall, over a thousand feet down.

Han Yü's reaction to the music is playfully hyperbolic: the emotional excesses the music has stirred in him have caused his clothes to become soaked in tears, thus parodying a poetic convention. Unable to endure such moving music, he must stop Ying. Of the four poems, Han Yü's emphasizes most strongly the relationship between the listener and the musician.

In Li Ho's first poem the lutanist is not simply a human "master,"

37. Wu K'ang is a mythological figure who lives in the moon, forever trying in vain to chop down the immortal cassia tree.
38. *LCC,* p. 1. The Hare is another mythical immortal inhabitant of the moon.

as he was in Han Yü's poem; rather, he is a figure of supernatural power: "A sculpted arhat of a Buddha Hall, august the arch of his eyebrows." The human metaphors for the music in Han Yü's poem become bizarre visions in the hands of Li Ho. The structure of the two poems is similar: first there are a series of metaphors for the music, followed by a statement about the lutanist. But how different are Han Yü's clouds

> Then floating clouds and willow floss without any roots,
> Through the vastness of Heaven and Earth, continue soaring
>   upward

from Li Ho's clouds: "Clouds from Parting's Shores return to the isle of cassia flowers." Han Yü is trying to stay close to what the music might actually suggest, while Li Ho is using the music as a starting point from which to enter a private fantasy. One wonders if any music by itself could suggest "moth-eyed maidens crossing the oceans, leading white deer." To Han Yü the music, though impressionistic, is genuinely mimetic; to Li Ho it is a gateway to the supernatural.

The last poem by Li Ho is a tribute to the harp music of Li P'ing and to the power of music in general. It is an extremely complex poem and I do not have the space here to even begin an adequate explanation of it.[39] Music dissolves the clouds, inspires dragons to dance, and makes the eternal chopper, Wu K'ang, rest from his labors. The human listener is altogether gone from the poem and the harpist himself is scarcely present. Li P'ing is playing his harp in *chung-kuo*, "the heart of the nation," "the central states," China. His music emanates from the capital (also suggested by *chung-kuo*), the center of the world, and spreads through the cosmos. The real world disappears and a bizarre, supernatural world remains—a supernatural world not metaphorical for Li P'ing's music but a different level of reality, one stirred by the power of music.

The bizarre, imaginative poetry of Li Ho should be seen in the context of the cult hermetic poetry of the early Yüan-ho, though it clearly transcends it. The literary values and poetic directions set earlier by Meng Chiao, Han Yü, and Lu T'ung made Li Ho's private, hermetic world possible. By themselves, however, they cannot account for his genius.

39. For a good discussion of this poem see Chou, pp. 28–38.

Chia Tao was a poet of great talent, but unfortunately none of that talent lay in the direction of the cult hermetic. Nevertheless, Chia seems to have tried very hard. We have already seen the strong impression Chia Tao's early poetry made on Meng Chiao and Han Yü, though it seems that impression was not altogether favorable. They considered Chia's poems to be audacious and radical. Since only a few such poems survive today in Chia Tao's collected poetry, we can only assume that Chia excluded the majority of them as youthful indiscretions.

Like Han Yü, between 812 and 814 Chia Tao began to turn away from the "strange" style, while Meng Chiao (until his death in 814) and Li Ho (until his death in 817) continued in the early Yüan-ho style. As the poetic tradition reasserted itself, Chia Tao found his true voice as the representative poet of the first generation of the Late T'ang. Some of what he had learned during his apprenticeship in the cult hermetic style had an influence on his subsequent development:

1. The desire to shock. This is the most salient feature of the cult hermetic style; in his early poetry, this urge appears in the form of fantastic metaphors and images, but in his later regulated verse, it becomes the unusual use of one or two words in a line.

2. The concentration of language. Here Chia Tao follows the poetry of Meng Chiao, rather than the looser, more discursive style of Han Yü and Lu T'ung. This combines with a natural tendency of regulated verse toward linguistic density.

3. Ethical concerns. These appear more strongly in Chia Tao's early poetry, but Meng Chiao's ideal of the "lean," suffering poet remains with Chia Tao throughout his career.

The changes that begin to occur between 812 and 814 are symptomatic of the new Late T'ang poetic style. These include:

1. An increasing preference for regulated verse rather than "old style" verse.

2. Stylistic smoothness, avoiding the grating harshness of Meng Chiao, the prosaic sturdiness and stylistic tours de force of Han Yü, and the simplicity of poets like Po Chü-yi.

3. A tendency toward objective description, especially of scenes from nature.

4. A strong emphasis on the couplet as a unit. This is very important in the development of the Late T'ang style and goes along with the preference for regulated verse. In contrast to the poetry of Han Yü and Meng Chiao, in which a couplet usually cannot stand apart from the entire poem, Chia Tao focused much of his craftsmanship in turning out perfect, jewel-like couplets.

5. Last and most important, there is a trend toward a poetry of intimation, a poetry of mood, rather than the symbolism, didacticism, and narrative concerns of Meng Chiao's and Han Yü's poetry. Instead of the logical (or more often illogical) "argument" we find in Meng's and Han's poetry, Late T'ang poetry tends to parataxis. The new poetry tries to appeal directly to the emotions rather than making demands upon the intellect, as Han Yü's and Meng Chiao's poetry did.

Beyond this general indication of the directions Chia Tao's poetry took, we cannot make a full study of it here. Instead, let us look at some of Chia's poems written before 815 to see what survives of his apprenticeship in the cult hermetic style.

The following poem is from 810 and is the earliest datable poem by Chia Tao. In that year he left his home in Fan-yang to go to Ch'ang-an and Lo-yang to meet Han Yü, Meng Chiao, and Chang Chi.

WRITTEN ON THE ROAD WHILE TAKING RECENT
COMPOSITIONS TO CHANG CHI AND HAN YÜ

In my sleeves I have poems, recently composed,
Wishing to show them to the venerable Han and Chang.
No wings grow on the green bamboo mailing tubes,
So I took one step on that thousand mile road.
Looking up, I gazed on the dark blue sky,   5
Clouds and snow press down on my brain.
I've lost Mount Chung-nan,
And sorrow fills my heart.
How can I get a northwest wind?—
My body wants to change to a tumbleweed.   10
The earth gods hearing these words,
Will burst forth, startling me upside down.[40]

40. *CTSC*, p. 15.

The last couplet of this poem shows a youthful arrogance and bravado characteristic of the cult hermetic style: Chia, wishing to become a tumbleweed blown northwest (homeward) by the wind, finds his wish granted as the earth gods pop forth and startle him, causing him to fall over backwards, thus beginning the revolutions of the wind-blown tumbleweed. Then there is the line: "Clouds and snow press down on my brain," yet another awkward attempt at cult hermetic wit: the snow both presses down on his head physically and is likewise an emotional weight of depression. From the title and the first lines of the poem it is evident that Chia Tao is trying to show off his talent to the two older poets, and it is significant that he chooses such witty lines to do so. Aside from these flashes of wit, however, the poem is dreadfully dull and its sentiments highly conventional, though the terms in which those sentiments are expressed are not.

Almost all Chia Tao's surviving poems in the Yüan-ho style are dedicated to one or another of the poets of Han Yü's circle. This could suggest that Chia preserved mainly those poems which confirmed his association with famous poets like Meng Chiao, Han Yü, Chang Chi, etc. The following poem is a blatant imitation of Meng Chiao's style, but is utterly devoid of the passion and strength that inform his work. The clever last couplet is somewhat reminiscent of Meng Chiao's wit but is more contrived.

JOY OF A WANDERER

A wanderer's joy is no real joy,
A wanderer's sorrow is no real sorrow.
Letters reaching home a hundred times
Are worth less than going home myself just once.
Not yet gone home, I always sigh from sorrow,   5
Sighing from sorrow increases the feelings within.
Opening my mouth, I spit forth sorrowful sounds,
Which come back into my ears.
Always I fear that my dripping tears be so many
That they will harm the radiance of my eyes.   10
Though there be strands of white silk by my locks,
I cannot weave of them clothes against the cold.[41]

White hair is often called "strands of silk" and Chia Tao is suggesting that he weave winter clothes out of it. His white hair reinforces

41. *CTSC*, p. 9.

rather than protects him against the cold of the "winter" of his life. It is tempting to think of this poem as an excellent parody of Meng Chiao's style; but, alas, I fear Chia Tao was quite serious.

Through Chia's early years, try as he might to imitate the bizarre wit of the cult hermetic and the rugged ethical style of Meng Chiao, the real directions of his own talent occasionally break through. In another poem to Meng Chiao, Chia begins.:

> I have tears that lament the past,
> Nor do I weep facing a crossroads.
> I wipe away my tears which sprinkle in the evening sky,
> Dripping and sticking on the branches of the cassia.[42]

The second line refers to the epicurean philosopher Yang Chu, who wept at a crossroads because he did now know which "Way" to go. By not weeping, Chia Tao shows that he knows the proper Way. The tone of these lines shows just how bad fu-ku poetry can be. Later in the same poem, however, Chia Tao speaks with his own voice:

> One alone, seated, evening, a snowy gate,
> A stream sinks under when it reaches the stone bridge.

or literally:

> sit   solitary   snow   gate   evening
> stream   fall   stone   bridge   time

Unlike the ambiguity of referents we find so often in Meng Chiao's poetry, the ambiguity of this couplet lies in the grammar and in the definition of the scene's significance to man. The compact scene sets an undefined *mood;* it is not symbolic, as we might expect in Meng Chiao's poetry. The poet speaks by intimation; the message is carried in the mood itself. The style is paratactic and nominal: words are used as building blocks to create a static picture.

By the time Meng Chiao died in 814, Chia Tao was well on his way toward a Late T'ang style. One of his laments for Meng Chiao is inappropriately a regulated verse, a genre Meng usually scorned. In the following poem from 815 we can see the full extent of Chia Tao's talent.

42. *CTSC*, p. 13.

WEEPING FOR THE ZEN MONK "CYPRESS CRAGS"

The moss covers his stone bed fresh,
How many springs did the monk occupy it?
Sketched and detained his form as it practiced the Way,
But burned away his body which sat in meditation.
The pagoda garden closes in snow on the pines,   5
While the sutra room locks in dust in the chinks.
I myself hate that this pair of tears comes down,
But I am not a man who understands the Void.[43]

The "freshness" of the moss contrasts with the long time for which
the monk has occupied the bed. The sketch of his "form" survives, as
opposed to his real body, which has been cremated. Thus the pagoda,
the charnel-house in which the ashes of the burned body are kept, is
seen in images of purity and integrity—snow on pines. On the other
hand, what remains of the monk as he was, the sketch, is in the dusty
library—dust being symbolic of the foulness of the phenomenal
world. Cremation is purification, abandonment of the worldly body,
and thus still beautiful; the attempt to hold on to the "form" implies
the foulness of this world. Though he is aware of the contrast between the purity of the spirit and the foulness of the body, Chia Tao
still weeps over the monk's death. The reason he gives is that he
doesn't "understand the Void"; he feels only the tragedy of death,
not the Buddhist sense of the futility and painfulness of life.

The genius of this poem lies in the careful craftsmanship, perfect
balance, and restrained dignity of Chia Tao's style. Indeed, it is as a
stylist that Chia was known and appreciated in later ages. For example, the third line:

hsieh   liu   hsing   tao   ying
sketch   detain   practice-Way   image

The use of "detain," *liu,* gives the line much of its force. *Liu* is commonly used to mean "to detain a guest," to keep him from returning
home. The monk has departed, his soul has *returned* to the void, and
only the "form" or "image"—an ephemeral thing—has been
successfully "detained." But it is a form which has been detained in
the act of "practicing the Way," which also means "walking the
road." Thus there is a subtle irony in detaining this image from leav-

43. *CTSC,* p. 25.

ing—an image that is in the act of learning the futility of life, learning to "walk its road" homeward to the void. The use of "sketch," *hsieh* (or more properly "copy"), and "form" give the picture a sense of falseness, of illusion, the very nature of life in the phenomenal world. It is the interplay of associations in such carefully chosen words which give the line its beauty in Chinese. But equally, this poem signifies the end of the Mid-T'ang style: it is a poetry of subtlety rather than of extremes.

13

Affirmation of the Tradition: Han Yü

Toward a Poetry of Balance, 811–812

In 811 Han Yü returned to Ch'ang-an to take a post as auxiliary secretary in the Bureau for the Organization of Military Regions (*chih-fang yüan-wai-lang*). It did not take long for Han to find himself in trouble once again. In 812, having defended a certain Liu Chien who was later convicted of malfeasance, he was demoted to his third term as professor in the State Academy. In 813 he took a post as a compiler and redactor in the College of Annalists, where he wrote the "Veritable Records of Shun-tsung" (*Shun-tsung Shih-lu*), presented to the throne in 815.

The four years between 811 and 814 saw not only the death of Meng Chiao and the demise of the flamboyant Lo-yang style of Han Yü, it also marked the end of the Mid-T'ang poetry of extremes and the reemergence of the mainstream of the T'ang poetic tradition, a poetry of sentiment rather than of thought or imagination, of concise and balanced form rather than of freedom and unrestraint. Some imitators of the Lo-yang style lingered on; Li Ho continued to develop that style in his own personal way until his death in 817. But in general a new poetic fashion emerged, a process we can see in Han Yü's poetry of 811 and 812 on his return to Ch'ang-an.

One may find in this new poetry Han Yü's finest work, a mature control over and balance of his widely varying talents. On the other hand, one may also see this later poetry as a flagging of Han Yü's lively intellect and imagination, and as a surrender to the mainstream of the poetic tradition. It is futile to speculate on the causes of a new literary fashion; in Han Yü's case it would be tempting to see these changes as the result of new friendships with more orthodox poets, the death of Meng Chiao in 814, and his return to the central government. It may be that the self-consciously "strange" style of the Lo-yang had simply worn itself out or gone too far: both Meng Chiao and Han Yü had expressed dissatisfaction with Chia Tao's excesses in this direction. In any case, the last twelve years of Han Yü's life show a poet at peace with himself and finally coming to terms with the poetic tradition.

This new conventionality in Han Yü's poetry did not occur all at once, nor was his compromise with the tradition a characteristically Late T'ang one, as was Chia Tao's. In this chapter we have one long poem and a series of eleven poems exemplifying the important changes that took place in the years 811 and 812. The two primary aspects of Han Yü's later poetry may at first seem contradictory, but they are closely associated in T'ang poetry. These are an expressionistic poetry of emotion and a sense of balance and control—especially in style. The Romantic association of intense emotion and freedom of expression make it difficult for us to associate intense emotion with a highly controlled style, but this is the balance characteristic of High and Late T'ang poetry. Unlike the worlds of disorder in Han Yü's Lo-yang poetry, his new style represents a world of order.

Han Yü's compromise with the poetic tradition is a poetry characterized by balance and decorum: it is a poetry of the "mean." Intense emotion may be present, but it must be expressed within certain accepted modes without ingenious metaphor or the overwhelming intensity of Meng Chiao's poetry. The new style is never rough, never jarring, and shows control rather than experimentation. It may use narrative, didactic, or descriptive modes, but never exclusively or in the extreme. The manner is humanistic and personal, avoiding private symbolism, imaginative flights, and overt didacticism. Except where emotion is concerned, it is a poetry of understatement.

Considering Han Yü's earlier propensities to impose order on his experiences and to restore order to a disordered world, it would seem that the style of the "mean" would be the natural place for his poetry to come to rest. But, as has been evident throughout Han's artistic career up to this point, he is a poet of many contradictory tendencies, and his new balanced style develops at the expense of his fertile imagination and aggressive energy. In the "Song of the Stone Drums" (811), one of Han Yü's finest works, the concision, balance, and restraint of the new style exists side by side with the characteristic vigor and imagination of the Lo-yang style.

The "stone drums" were a group of ten dolmens from the Chou Dynasty on which had been carved a number of poems similar in form and style to those of the *Book of Songs*. They attracted a certain amount of interest during the T'ang: Tu Fu mentions them, and Wei Ying-wu had written his own "Songs of the Stone Drums." Han Yü believed them to have been composed during the reign of King Hsüan of Chou (828–782 B.C.), a period of the restoration of Chou power, although modern research has shown them to have been written somewhat later. Since the Yüan-ho period (806–20), during which this poem was written, was considered to be a "restoration" (*chung-hsing*) of T'ang power, the stone drums had a special meaning for Han.

SONG OF THE STONE DRUMS

Master Chang holds the stone drum poems in his hand,[1]
Urging me to write a stone drum song.
At Shao-ling there is no one, the "banished immortal" is
　　dead,[2]
My talents are meager, so what can I do about the stone
　　drums?

The order of Chou rule was on the decline,　　　　　　　　　5
　　　all within the four seas seethed in turmoil,
When King Hsüan rose zealously,
　　　wielding a Heaven-granted spear.
He opened wide the Hall of Light,
　　　received nobles paying their respects,[3]
Swords and girdle-pendants of the feudal lords
　　　rang as they rubbed one another.
He held spring hunts at Ch'i-yang,
　　　where galloped bold men and fine steeds
For thousands of miles, birds and beasts　　　　　　　　　10
　　　all caught and netted.

1. There is some debate as to whether this refers to Chang Chi or Chang Ch'e. What he is holding is a rubbing or copy of the poems.

2. Shao-ling refers to Tu Fu; the "banished immortal," to Li Po.

3. The Hall of Light, *ming-t'ang*, was a royal temple of cosmic significance, associated with the Chou mandate to rule.

He had their merit engraved, their accomplishments carved,
    to tell myriad ages,
They bored out stone to make the drums,
    tearing up lofty mountains.
Attendant courtiers of talent and ability,
    each one, first rate,
Were chosen and selected to compose and carve them,
    Then left on the mountain slope.
Rains drenched them, the sun baked them,   15
    wild-fires burned them,
But ghostly beings stood guard on them,
    taking the trouble to chide offenders and shoo them away.

Whence, sir, did you get this copy on paper,
Complete to the smallest detail, without variant or error?
The diction, stern, the meaning, dense—hard it is to
    understand,
The forms of the words are unlike ordinary script.   20
It is deep in years—how could it avoid having missing strokes?
But a keen blade chopped them, making dragons and
    crocodiles:
Rocs soar, phoenixes mount, while a band of immortals
    descends,
Trees of emerald and coral, crisscrossing branches and boughs,
Golden ropes and iron cables, bound and locked fast,   25
Ancient tripods leap from the water, dragons fly from shuttles.[4]
Some foolish scholar compiling the *Songs* did not include them,
Now the two books of formal odes are cramped in scope,
    not expansive.
When Confucius went west, he didn't reach Ch'in,
Thus gathered the constellations, but overlooked sun and
    moon.[5]   30

4. The first of the allusions refers to a Yin Dynasty tripod possessed by the Warring States kingdom of Sung. This tripod sunk into the waves of a lake when the temple in which it was lodged was destroyed. Because it was a symbol of unified empire, the first emperor of the Ch'in Dynasty tried unsuccessfully to salvage it. A certain T'ao K'an of the Chin Dynasty caught a shuttle while fishing and hung it on his wall. During the night it changed into a dragon. Had Yü is engaging here in a pictographic fantasy about the ancient inscriptions, probably because he cannot read them.

5. This implies that the poems chosen for the *Book of Songs* were lesser luminaries, while the really important poems of the Chou, the stone drum poems, were omitted.

Alas that I, though I love antiquity, was born terribly late,
In face of this, my tears stream down both eyes.

I remember when I had first been summoned to be a
    professor,
The reign title had just been changed to Yüan-ho.
An old friend of mine was in the army at Yu-fu,   35
For my sake he considered excavating them from their
    depressions.
I cleaned my cap and bathed, went to inform the Dean—
Certainly not many treasures as perfect as this survive.
"Wrapped in carpets, rolled in mats, they can be brought
    at once,
Only a few camels will be needed to carry ten drums.   40
We shall offer them to the Imperial Temple—equal to Kao's
    tripod,[6]
Then their splendid value will certainly increase over a
    hundredfold;
Or, if Imperial Grace permits, they can stay in the Academy,
Here students can compete discussing and explaining them.
We'll be inundated with tourists as when they put the
    classics on display at Hung-tu school,[7]   45
From all the states they'll come rushing in waves to stare fixedly.
Pare off the moss, scrape away the lichens, reveal the edges,
Set them firm and secure, level and not tilting.
A great hall with deep-set eaves will give them shelter,
They will endure far into the future, I hope, with no change." 50
But this great official of the central government, experienced
    in his work,
Why would he not sympathize with me, instead of being
    uselessly indecisive?
Herd boys will strike fires from them, oxen grind their horns—
Who will apply his hand to wipe over them any more?
Each day they wear away, each month they erode, finally
    they'll be buried,   55
For six years I have gazed westward, singing of them in vain.

6. Kao's tripod was a famous ceremonial vessel of antiquity.

7. The Eastern Han emperor Ling founded the Hung-tu School and had a text established for the five classics. He then had a famous scholar, Ts'ai Yung, engrave them on stone. They became a major attraction and the school was filled with sightseers. Han Yü is suggesting that the stone drums would attract similar crowds to the Academy.

Wang Hsi-chih sought lovely form in his ordinary calligraphy,
Still he could barter several sheets of it for a white goose.[8]
Eight dynasties of war and strife following Chou are ended,
What can be the reason that no one will gather them up?   60
Right now we have an age of peace, daily our troubles
    disappear,
Those in power rely on tradition, honoring Confucius and
    Mencius.
How can I explain this to the emperor?—
I would avail myself of a debater's mouth, flowing like a
    waterfall.
My song of the stone drums will stop here—   65
Alas! How my will stumbles and falters.[9]

In this poem we see many faces of Han Yü: there is the persuasive rhetorician arguing for the preservation of the stone drums, the antiquarian emotionally stirred by these artifacts he does not understand, and Han Yü the political "philosopher," seeking patterns and parallels in history, finding in the reign of King Hsüan a parallel to the Yüan-ho period to which the drums will serve as a symbolic link.

In the exordium Han Yü maintains a humility appropriate to the persuasive aspect of the poem. Though he claims that Tu Fu (of Shao-ling) would have been more qualified to compose such a poem in praise of the drums, he cleverly uses a passage from Tu Fu claiming similar lack of ability in a similar situation: the last four lines of Tu Fu's "Song of Li Ch'ao's *Pa-fen* Small Seal Script" are:

East of Pa I met Li Ch'ao,
For more than a month he asked a song of me.
I'm now old and decrepit, the force of my talent, meager,
Ch'ao, O Ch'ao—what can I do about you?[10]

The structure of Tu Fu's epilogue and Han Yü's exordium are quite similar: a meeting, being urged to compose a song on calligraphy, disavowal of one's talent, and an exclamation that the poet doesn't know what he can do. In contrast to Han Yü's

---

8. Wang Hsi-chih of the Chin Dynasty was the most famous Chinese calligrapher. He had an inordinate fondness for white geese, and an old Taoist once exchanged an entire flock of them for a copy of the *Tao-te-ching* in Wang Hsi-chih's hand.

9. *HCLS*, p. 346.   10. *CTS*, c. 222, pp. 2360–61.

earlier imitation of Tu Fu, in which he used Tu Fu's line in an entirely different context and tone (see chapter 7), here Han Yü uses Tu Fu's experience as a parallel—Han is affirming the poetic tradition; he is organizing his experience through a similar experience of another poet rather than through some extraliterary pattern, as he did in his exile poems and his symbolic landscapes. Although he uses Tu Fu's experience with Li Ch'ao as a comparison, Han Yü's exordium has a self-conscious dignity and gravity entirely distinct from the straightforward and emotional statement of Tu Fu. For example, Han Yü says, "holds *in his hand,*" instead of simply "holds," in order to focus on the objective scene rather than on the situation. When Tu Fu says that Li Ch'ao "urged" him to write a poem, he simply recounts what happened; given the objective scene of Chang Chi (?) holding the copy of the poem in his hand, the "urging" has a present-tense immediacy that further dramatizes the situation. Instead of saying, "Tu Fu is dead," Han Yü uses the periphrasis, "At Shao-ling there is no one" ("Tu Fu was from Shao-ling and since he is now dead, there is no one capable of writing the song you ask"). Furthermore, there is the calculated irony of "the 'banished *immortal'* is *dead.*"

Next, Han Yü proceeds to give a concise history of the stone drums, as he imagines it to have been. In contrast to the epideictic treatment such a subject would probably have received in the preceding period, Han Yü allots only one couplet to each essential event in their history. The Chou Dynasty declines in one line, and King Hsüan counteracts that decline in one line; the erring nobility are brought to submission in one couplet, and a hunt is given and completed in one couplet, etc. The style is still verbal—twenty-six verbs in twelve lines—but rather than suggesting nervous activity as the verbal style in Han Yü's earlier poems did, here it is used simply to complete the narrative quickly. Except for an archaic "at" in line nine, archaisms and characteristically prose usages are absent.

We can see an interesting conflict in this passage between the stylistic formality which lends solemnity and dignity to the story of the drums, and Han Yü's natural tendency toward exuberance and hyperbole. This conflict is central to the transition from the Lo-yang style to his new balanced style: does one lend a topic importance by exaggerating it or by treating it with dignity and restraint? On the one hand, the king's attendants are hyperbolically: "tearing up lofty mountains," to make the drums. On the other hand, there are the *tautologia* which lend solemnity:

> He had their merit engraved, their accomplishments carved,
> . . . .
> Were chosen and selected to compose and carve them.

The epideictic, ennumerative mode survives, but it is stripped of descriptive ornament, rendered concise, and shortened in length:

> Rains drenched them, the sun baked them, wild-fires
>   burned them.

Indeed, the great beauty of this passage lies in the combination of Han Yü's earlier exuberance and his new sense of stylistic control.

The next section concerns the rubbing of the stone drum poems Chang shows him. Though unintentional, there is a certain humor in the first five lines. At first, Han Yü makes a point of complimenting the perfection of the rubbing, but then finds that he cannot understand it. Reconsidering, he then decides that maybe the rubbing isn't so perfect after all: "It is deep in years—how could it avoid having missing strokes?" Han Yü simply cannot read the script. Unable to decipher the rubbing, he indulges in a more satisfying fantasy about the exotic shapes of the characters. At this point, he slips into the Lo-yang style: the illegible characters become dragons, crocodiles, rocs, phoenixes, immortals, coral trees, golden ropes, etc. Caught up in his own hyperbole, Han exceeds all bounds, saying that the man who compiled the *Book of Songs* was a "foolish scholar" who gathered only lesser luminaries and omitted the stone drum poems, the sun and moon of Chou poetry. This is excessive praise (especially since he cannot understand the poems)and in later dynasties would have been tantamount to blasphemy.

When Han Yü turns to recount his previous experiences with the drums, he immediately falls into the leisurely and chatty narrative style which took shape in the late 790s and remained with him throughout his life.

> I remember when I had first been summoned to be a professor,
> The reign title had just been changed to Yüan-ho.
> An old friend of mine was in the army at Yu-fu.

For a different tone, Han Yü could easily have condensed this into one line. In the course of the narrative, he recapitulates his arguments for the preservation of the stone drums in his version of his speech to the Dean of the State Academy. As we have seen Han do before, the master rhetorician skillfully blends compliment and censure:

> But this great official of the central government, experienced
>   in his work,
> Why would he not sympathize with me, instead of being
>   uselessly indecisive?

Han Yü then heightens his censure by the tragedy of the ruin of the stone drums: "Herd boys will strike fires from them, oxen grind their horns—." The last section concludes his plea for the preservation of the drums with a concise argument: if Wang Hsi-chih's "ordinary" (in comparison to that of the drums) calligraphy was worth something, how much more are these relics of antiquity worth; we have an age of peace which shall last forever and in which Confucianism is honored, therefore why will no one spare a few camels to preserve these invaluable writings?

"Song of the Stone Drums" is an amalgam of Han Yü's different attitudes and styles: he is alternately the visionary antiquarian, the poet of fantasy, the chatty storyteller, and the persuasive rhetorician. But in this very balance of styles and attitudes we can see one characteristic of his later poetry, nothing in the extreme—his experience with the stone drums has been made up of many different aspects, and all those aspects must be present for a *balanced* treatment of the subject.

The "autumn meditation" is a meditation on transitoriness in face of an autumn scene. Going under a wide variety of titles other than "autumn meditation," the conventions of this subgenre were firmly established during the Wei and Chin Dynasties.[11] Though autumnal melancholy is absent in the *Book of Songs,* the theme is usually traced back to "Sung Yü's" *Chiu-pien.* Commentators emphasize the affinity between Juan Chi's "Singing My Emotions," *Yung-huai,* and Han Yü's "Autumn Meditations"—"Singing My Emotions" being, as we may remember, one of the principle models of High T'ang *fu-ku*

11. An excellent treatment of this theme in Late Han, Wei, and Chan poetry can be found in Obi Koichi, *Chugoku Bungaku ni Arawareta Shizen to Shizenkan* (Tokyo: Iwanami, 1962), pp. 52–120.

poetry. To the T'ang poet the title "Autumn Meditation" would bring to mind Hsieh Hui-lien's "Autumn Meditation" in chapter 25 of the *Wen-hsüan,* the standard anthology of pre-T'ang literature and requisite reading for the examination.

Thus, the tradition of such meditations on transience is old and strong. However, in the hands of T'ang poets the theme took on a new complexity. Tu Fu's two major sequences, "Autumn Thoughts" and "Autumn Wastes," transform the simple lament into a complex sequence of poems brooding on the relation of past and present. Meng Chiao's "Autumn Meditations," a nightmarish, interior contemplation of the meaning of the past and the individual's relation to time, carries the theme even further away from its melancholy origins.

Characteristic of Han Yü's new-found acceptance and affirmation of the poetic tradition, his "Autumn Meditations" seek to restore the theme to its original simplicity. In contrast to Tu Fu's and Meng Chiao's use of the poetic sequence, Han Yü uses the series form, variations on the theme, an older form than the poem sequence. He tries consciously to work within the traditional style and conventions of the subgenre, avoiding the stylistic tours de force and clever arguments which have so often characterized his poetry. The restrained tone achieved by working within the tradition is proved by the contrast with the one exception, the ninth poem of the series, which is a contrived fantasy in the Lo-yang style.

Han Yü's "Autumn Meditations" have been considered by many critics to be his masterpiece. The great Ch'ing scholar Ch'ien Chien-yi made the following curious statement about them: "If you look for autumn meditations in Han Yü, you will find Han Yü's Autumn Meditations in *him,* and if you look for Han Yü in his Autumn Meditations, you will find Han Yü in them."[12] This seems to be saying that these poems exemplify the melancholy autumnal feeling in Han Yü, and that the poems are characteristically Han Yü's own. It is true that, for all his affirmation of the tradition in this series, here we see clearly the attempt of a sophisticated poet to recapture a simple style but separated from genuine simplicity by his own sophistication. But still, we should consider the difference between this series of poems and "South Mountains," also called Han Yü's masterpiece. The earlier poem applies self-conscious artistry to dazzle the reader,

12. Quoted in *HCLS*, p. 245.

to show off, while the later series applies the same energy in a self-conscious effort toward dignified simplicity. The poems resemble earlier fu-ku poetry in this respect.

AUTUMN MEDITATIONS

I

On the two fine trees before my window,
The crowds of leaves are bright and verdant.
Once the autumn wind puffs over them,
Rustling, they sing without end.
A faint lamp shines on an empty bed,   5
As they enter my ears, especially at midnight.
Sorrow and melancholy come for no reason,
Stirred to sighs I end up rising and sitting.
When the sky grows bright, I gaze on the faces of the leaves,
They don't resemble what they used to be.   10
Hsi-ho drives the sun and moon,
So swiftly we can't depend on them.
Though there are many roads in this floating life,
There is only one track, racing toward death.
Why recklessly make oneself bitter?—
We should get wine and enjoy ourselves a while.

In this poem I shall point out some of the echoes of Han and Wei treatments of the autumnal theme. Unable to do so for every poem because of the limitations of space, I hope this analysis will give the reader some idea of the complex relation the series bears to the tradition.

The first couplet is a free variation on the first couplet of the ninth of the Nineteen Old Poems:

In my yard there are wondrous trees,
Their green leaves emit a glossy splendor.[13]

The first line is a location formula, common at the beginning of a poem: "at *x* [there is/are] *y*." Han Yü's first line is literally: "Before [my] window, two good trees," using this formula without the "there is/are," *yu*. In Han Yü's earliest poem, "The Far North," he used the formula with the "there were," *yu*: "There were vagabond

13. Ting ed., *Ch'üan Han Shih,* p. 71.

wings in the far north." But whereas in his early poem Han Yü had turned to the Han and Wei style as a model of ruggedness and strength, here he turns to it as a model for classic simplicity. Consider, for example, the convention that grief seems to come from nowhere: in Han Yü's poem: "Sorrow and melancholy come for no reason," echoing the simplicity of the Emperor Wen of the Wei Dynasty's

> Melancholy comes from nowhere,
> No one knows where.[14]

In contrast, there is Meng Chiao's almost paranoid echo of the convention in the second of his "Autumn Meditations":

> These feelings of doubt are based on nothing,
> Listen in vain to things—mostly without cause.

("without cause" and "for no reason" are both the same phrase, *wu-tuan*). Meng Chiao uses the purposelessness of autumnal melancholy to reject his own wild fantasies—he *hopes* it comes "for no reason." Meng uses the convention not because it is part of the tradition, but because it fits into the larger context of his sequence.

Although Han Yü is trying to stay with the tradition, his own innate sense of order betrays him as a T'ang poet. The Han or Wei poet would construct his autumn lament by the association of themes and images; Han Yü's poem is constructed in a strict chain of causality. The trees in the first couplet are static; upon these static objects the wind acts, making the leaves rustle, making the poet unable to sleep, making him restless until dawn; dawn leads him to think of the movement of the sun and moon, in turn bringing him to contemplate transience, leading him to resolve his melancholy by the carpe diem theme. This is not association; this is the careful delineation of a chronological chain of causality. Another revealing point is an echo of the first poem of Juan Chi's "Singing My Emotions":

> In the night I could not sleep,
> Rising and sitting, I strum my singing lute.[15]

Han Yü, the sophisticated poet, finds it difficult to be that direct; instead we have: "A faint lamp shines on an empty bed." Thus we know it is night and the poet cannot sleep.

14. Ting Fu-pao, ed., *Ch'üan San-kuo Shih,* in Ting, ed., *Ch'üan Han San-kuo Chin Nan-pei-ch'ao Shih,* p. 188.

15. Ibid., p. 300.

The logical order of the chronological chain of causality is characteristic of Han Yü's poetry, but there are other structural aspects of
the poem which are characteristic of T'ang poetry in general, in
contrast to the Han and Wei models. The poem builds in intensity
from static objects to faint movement, the rustling of the leaves, then
to more intense movement, the "singing without end." The natural
world affects the human world, and the intensity keeps increasing to
the nervous "rising and sitting." This builds to a frenzy of movement:

> Hsi-ho drives the sun and moon
> So swiftly we can't depend on them.

Then the goal of this race is revealed: "There is only one track,
rushing toward death." In face of this frenzied speed and intensity,
the carpe diem theme is more than just a convention—it is real
resolution.

Such intensity could easily have found expression in the bizarre
hyperbole of the Lo-yang style (as indeed it does in the ninth poem
of this series); however, here that intensity is kept under control by
the self-conscious conventionality of statement. The poem's artistic
value lies in the very simplicity and clarity of Han Yü's understanding of autumn and his meditative process. Since it is a conscious
effort, this poem is more direct than most of the Han and Wei poems
on the theme Han Yü is imitating. Meng Chiao had to struggle to
find personal meaning in autumn; Han Yü finds comfort in the
straightforward and time-honored responses of the tradition, though
he organizes those responses in his own characteristic way.

II

> White dew descends on all the plants,[16]
> Together orchid and thatch wither and waste away.[17]
> Green, green, beneath my walls,
> They have grown again, filling the earth.
> The cold cicadas have just grown silent,   5
> While crickets sing as much as they please.[18]
> The cyclical movements of nature never end,

16. Sung Yu, *Chiu-pien* III: "The white dew has descended on all the plants." Han
Yü has merely adapted the *Ch'u Tz'u* line to the five-character *shih* line.

17. Orchid is the representative of superior plants; thatch, of common plants.

18. Again from the *Chiu-pien:* "The cicada is silent and makes no sound"; "The cricket
sings here in the north hall."

But the spirit, endowed by Heaven, is terribly altered.
At the appointed time, each thing gets its proper place,
Even the evergreen need not be honored.[19]   10

The traditional symbolism and philosophical meditation of this poem give it an emblematic and intellectual tone, unlike the preceding poem. Very untraditional, however, is the compression of time in the first four lines: no sooner have the plants died in autumn than they are growing again in spring. The simplicity with which this is said mitigates its strangeness.

The nature and attributes of the cycle of the seasons are fixed in tradition. Thus in the "Yüeh-ling" chapter of the *Li Chi* we read: "A chill wind comes; the white dew descends; cold cicadas sing"— these are characteristic of the seventh month, from mid-August to mid-September. In the poem "Seventh Month" from the *Book of Songs*:

In the tenth month the cricket
Gets under my bed.

Thus the traditional insects set the parameters of autumn, and Han Yü is describing the eighth or ninth month.

From this observation of the fixed order of nature's cycles, Han Yü begins his philosophical meditation. The cycles never cease their movement, and all must accord with the pattern of change. Both the good and the bad perish when their time comes (l. 2). The traditional response invoked here, unlike the traditional carpe diem response in the first poem, is unconditional acceptance of nature's changes.

III

How rapidly passes this thing, time—
But how much further my will extends!
A Kung-sun Yen, who in vain loves drink,
A Lien Po, who can still eat.[20]

19. I.e. although they last through the winter, this endurance is part of their nature, and they too have a time to wither.

20. When Kung-sun Yen, an official of the Warring States kingdom of Wei, was asked why he liked to drink so much, he replied, "Because I have nothing else to do." The Prince of Chao once sent a deputy to see if his aging general Lien Po was still of any use to the state. At this Lien Po ate a tremendous meal, put on his armor, and jumped on his horse

In the study hall, nothing to do each day,   5
I ride my horse off, going where I please.
Far and wide the roads that lead from my gate,
I want to leave, then urge myself to stay a while.
Returning home, I look over my books—
Words everywhere, millions and millions.   10
Who now can really match their great deeds?
My base desires are not their noble gifts to man.
As a grown man, there are those of my thoughts that endure—
It's for a woman to be full of resentment.

Han Yü's sentiment in the first couplet lies between the famous passage in the "Yang-sheng" chapter of the *Chuang-tzu*, "My life has limits, but what I can know has no limits," and the Horatian, "et spatio brevi/spem longam reseces." Han Yü's "will," which extends beyond the limits of his life, is to accomplish great deeds. Against these noble desires is set his real situation in the second couplet—frustrated, idle, unemployed to the full extent of his capabilities.

The next three couplets vividly portray Han's dissatisfaction with his idle life. Unable to study, he rides off into the countryside; then wanting to go back, he forces himself to stay a while, because he knows that there will be nothing for him to do on his return. When he does come back, he looks over his books, which seem only a jumble of words; or, Han Yü may be saying that the great deeds of men of the past recorded in those "millions and millions" of words are not possible for him. At this point Han Yü checks his despair and opposes it: his ambition for public renown is only a "base desire" and not a desire to make a "noble gift to man." He resolves to hold stoically to his principles and not to give himself over to resentment: this is in sharp contrast to the carpe diem resolution of the first poem and the passive acceptance of fate in the second poem.

The emphasis on the analysis of his personal emotions we see in this poem is something new in Han Yü. His earlier poetry had been consistently directed outward. Here we have an interior monologue in which Han analyses his emotions and actions and tries to resolve them. Although he closes the poem with stoic resolution, it is to oppose a sense of despair rather than to affirm ethical principles.

---

to show that he was still vigorous. These two allusions mean, "I have nothing to do, but can still be of use to the state."

IV

Autumn's spirit gets daily more forlorn,
Autumn's sky gets daily chillier and more remote.
Above there are no cicadas on the branches,
Below, no flies on the plate.
Can I help being stirred by the season?— 5
I have gotten rid of what was hateful to ear and eye.
When I roll up my books and sit on a clear morning,
South Mountain reveals its high ridge.
Beneath it there's a tarn of clear water,
With a dragon I could net as it gets colder. 10
But alas, I can't get to go there,
Though no one can say I lack the ability.

Here Han considers the positive aspects of autumn, the destruction of insects hateful to man and the lethargy of the dragon, rendering it vulnerable to netting. The dragon usually suggests great power, though its exact use here is uncertain; probably it simply means the ability to do great deeds.

V

My heart shattered, in it hangs aimless grief,
Melancholy, I embrace meaningless warnings to the heart.
Dew drips as tears from autumn trees,
Insects mourn through the long cold nights.
Withdrawing, I reach a new timidity, 5
And am grieved by my former frenzy, the busy rushing.
Returning to simplicity, I recognize the level road,
To draw from the well of antiquity, I have gotten a long rope.
Still there is shame at my insubstantial fame,
Though truly I feel blessed at how little I enjoy the world. 10
I wish I could leave behind regret and blame from others,
And be hidden, be screened away right here.

Here we have another interior monologue analyzing the poet's state of mind. In face of personal crises, the Chinese intellectual always had the option of withdrawal, severing emotional and social ties with the external world and retreating into the self. The responses of these five poems are traditional, but they are all different, even mutually exclusive. The tendency toward exclusive positions seen

in Han Yü's earlier poetry has here given way to the characteristically
T'ang approach to such traditional responses: from the variety of
different—and often contradictory—responses offered by the
tradition, the poet chooses whichever response seems satisfying or
appropriate to the situation.

In broader terms, the withdrawal Han Yü speaks of in the above
poem can be seen as a rejection of his former energy and flamboyance
("my former frenzy, the busy rushing") and an affirmation of "simplicity" and the "level road." The first four lines of this poem bear a
striking resemblance to lines in Meng Chiao's "Autumn Meditations," but the intellectual analysis of Han Yü's emotions in the
second part of the poem is alien to Meng Chiao.

VI

This morning I didn't finish getting up,
But sat straight until the sunlight was gone.
Insects sang, the room grew darker and darker,
Then the moon came forth and my window shone brightly.
Emotions lost, and it seemed I'd strayed from my course,   5
Floating thoughts, as intense as though a thorn were in them.
I am weary of paying my respects to this foul world,
Haphazardly I dash off my words.
Still I must strive hard against this stubbornness—
There are audiences and attendances in royal affairs.   10

Again Han Yü combats depression with resolution. He knows that
his broodings are insubstantial ("floating," l. 6), but he still feels
the pain of them, "as though a thorn were in them." In the last
couplet he opposes the "stubbornness" of his depression with the
practical requirements of participation in society, the "audiences
and attendances." But the delineation of his depression is concise and
grim: it renders him immobile for the entire day, which passes
even more quickly and meaninglessly than usual.

VII

Autumn nights never seem to dawn,
Autumn days darken with terrible ease.
Since I lack restless, bustling ambition,
Why do I have such sorrow as this?[21]

21. This directly contradicts III.1–2. Here Han is saying that, since he lacks any ambi-

Cold chickens wait in their roosts in vain, 5
I'm annoyed so often to see the waning moon.[22]
Having my lute here, I tune the stops and strings,
Strum again and again, it gets ever fainter to my ears.
The ancient sounds sank into oblivion long ago,
And we have no way to tell the true from the false. 10
Then lower your heart and rush after present fashion—
I try terribly hard, but can do so for only a while.
It's somewhat like riding a boat in the wind,
Once let loose, it cannot be moored.
Better to scrutinize literature, 15
To work at punctuating and collating.
Why need one seek more than this?—
What is essential is to have a keg or two of rice.[23]

Here we have a third alternative to the poet's ennui: he should neither strive with great ambition nor should he withdraw altogether, but rather he should be content with little, with doing insignificant jobs like "punctuating and collating" and with just enough food to live. In the first part of the poem there is an overpowering sense of encroaching darkness, both real and metaphorical. The nights are getting longer with the approach of winter, civilization is also declining. True music was lost long ago, and even the music Han Yü is playing is gradually overcome by silence.

VIII

Coiling round and round, leaves falling to earth,
They rush in the wind past the porch before me.
The sound of their singing seems to have meaning,
Whirling over and over, they hurry after one another.
In my empty hall on a dusky evening. 5
I sit silently, not speaking;
My boy comes in from outside,
Lights the lamp right in front of me.
He asks how I am—I don't answer,
He offers me food—I won't eat. 10
He goes back and sits by the west wall,

---

tion, why should he care that time passes swiftly.
22. I.e. he is impatient that the night lasts so long.
23. I.e. to have just enough to satisfy one's needs and nothing more.

And reads through a few poems.
The man who wrote them is no man of today,
He's already a thousand years in the past from me.
But there's something in the words that touches my heart,   15
Once again making me feel the pain.
I look at him and say, "You, boy—
Put away the books and go to bed.
A grown man has things he must think about
And work to do that never ends."   20

This may be Han Yü's finest short poem; it shows a depth of
humanity peculiar to him. Still primarily an external poet, Han
finds great meaning in acts and gestures; through them the internal
world is revealed. Internal poets such as Tu Fu or Meng Chiao are
at their best when describing emotions or casting the external world
in terms of their emotions (this is only partially true of Tu Fu). Tu
Fu and Meng Chiao view the world from the inside outward, whereas
in this poem Han Yü's eyes are somewhere else in the room, watching
himself and his son.[24]

The first four lines are an objective description of the autumn
leaves falling. But they "seem to have meaning," seem to have
purpose in their confusion of movement and noise. Falling leaves
are traditionally associated with impermanence, but here there is
another level of meaning in the leaves' helplessness as they are
carried by the will of the autumn wind. Watching this scene, the
poet falls into *silent* brooding on his aging and impending death,
the "autumn meditation." But maintaining the external point of
view which sees only actions, the poet's thoughts are never explicitly
revealed.

As in the preceding poem, the oncoming dark, "a dusky evening,"
is part of this general autumnal movement toward death. Against
the growing darkness Han Yü's son comes in and lights the lamp
for his father. The boy asks the father how he is, offers him food, and
reads him poems, but the father, deep in brooding, does not respond.
The older man is involved in the world of death, while the young

24. A lot in this poem depends upon the interpretation of *t'ung-tzu,* a general term for
young boys. I follow Shimizu Shigeru, *Kan Yu* (Tokyo: Iwanami, 1958), p. 65 and my
own inclination in taking it to refer to the poet's son. *T'ung-tzu,* however, sometimes refers
specifically to a servant-boy and is so understood here by a number of commentators and
translators. Such an interpretation presents a number of anomalies in the poem which are
difficult to explain.

boy belongs to the world of life. Thus the things the boy offers his father are the things of life—light, concern for how he feels, food, and companionship. Becuase they belong to different worlds, there is a gulf between them; here the boy tries to bridge that gulf with his gestures of life, and later the father tries to bridge it.

In reading poems to his father, the boy is offering the old man company; but these poems, probably concerning death and impermanence, have a special meaning for the father and he cannot bear to listen to them. From his experience of life, the father can understand the boy's intentions; but the boy cannot possibly understand the meaning such poems have for the father, nor can he understand why the father rejects all his gestures of kindness. Therefore, as a gesture of love for his son, the father comes out of his trance and speaks to the boy. As the son showed filial concern through his words and deeds, the father shows an equal, paternal concern by telling the boy to go to bed, literally to "sleep peacefully." Since he realizes that the boy has no way of understanding his world of dying, the father doesn't explain it, but says: "A grown man has things he must think about," as if to apologize for his failure to respond to his son's gestures of love. The last line seems to contrast how much Han Yü feels he should do with the little life left remaining to him. This is the only hint he gives his son (and the reader) of his broodings, and it is significant that he tells his son only what he feels his son will understand; in other words, that he has much to do—great ambition —which is the life aspect of his internal struggle between the desire to accomplish much and his awareness of impending death.

The almost neoclassical control of language and emotion are clear in this poem. The falling leaves are not a symbol in the poem; rather, they are a symbol *to the old man* in the poem and a real part of events. Deep emotion is present, but it is kept hidden within the old man and his son. The close relation between them is never stated explicitly or analyzed, but it is revealed in words and gestures. The language is neither awkwardly archaic and prosaic, nor is it exotic and flamboyant; it is plain, smooth, and straightforward. Most of all, the poem is magnificently human, without a note of falseness, the intensity all the more real because of the controls placed upon it.

IX

A frosty wind intrudes upon the wu-t'ung,
All its leaves are dry, stick to the tree.

On the empty stairs a single leaf falls,
And tinkles like shattering jade.
I imagine that night's spirit has vanished,   5
And Wang Shu has meteored his globe:[25]
Having nothing to rest on in the dark blue sky,
His flying course is precarious and insecure.
Startled I get up, go out the door, look,
Then leaning on the railing, I weep a long time.   10
In sorrow and melancholy I wasted fleeting time,
Sun and moon are like bouncing balls.
Gone astray while returning, I thought not of the distance,
But now I stop my dusty saddle because of you, O Moon.

For all its exaggeration, this poem ends in resolution like several
other poems in this series. In tone and style it stands in sharp relief
to the preceding poem, as Han Yü gives free rein to his fantasy.
Possibly because of the context of the other poems of the series, this
ninth poem has disturbed many critics; for example, there is the late
Ch'ing scholar Tseng Kuo-fan's amusing understatement: "In this
poem, because a leaf has fallen, he imagines that the moon has
fallen; our bold scholar certainly has unusual emotional associations."[26] It is not, however, as unusual as a forest-fire becoming a
feast of the fire-gods.

The reader is told the real situation in the first two couplets: he
knows what the "fallen moon" really is. Unlike the other "Autumn
Meditations," this poem is symbolic. The faint movement of a
single leaf blown down *is* a titanic calamity, like the fall of the moon,
for it is a symbol of the awesome power of autumn and the destruction it brings. Han Yü captures a sense of autumn's violence by
describing the wind as "intruding upon" or "invading," *ch'in,* the
wu-t'ung tree. The faint effect of the wind's movement is the fall of
a single leaf, but that single leaf has in its fall the destructive power
of a heavenly cataclysm. This symbolic value of the falling leaf
becomes the poet's private fantasy: Han Yü imagines that the moon's
course through the sky is unstable and that, having lost its energy,
it is fallen on his steps. At this point in the poem there is a flurry of
movement as the poet "startles," "gets up," "goes out," and "looks"
—four verbs in a five-character line.

25. Wang Shu was the charioteer of the moon.
26. Quoted in *HCLS*, p. 244.

The moon's fall would suggest that time has stopped, since the passage of the moon is closely associated with the passage of time. Han Yü sees that the moon is still on its course, time is still going on, and that the real situation, the fall of the leaf, indicates even more forcefully the passage of time. The meditation that follows this strange incident is concise: first, Han Yü grieves at the passage of time, then says he is wasting what little time he has by such grief and resolves to correct his error. Han has "gone astray" in imagining that the moon might fall and time stop. To correct his error and to give pattern to the experience he has just had, he draws a phrase from the discussion of the "return," *fu*, hexagram from the *Book of Changes*; he has "gone astray while returning," *mi-fu*. Han Yü therefore resolves to "stop his dusty saddle" ("dusty" suggests the foulness of the world) on this road of error and, no matter how far astray he has gone, return to the right Way. The fantasy world of the first part of this poem (and of the early Yüan-ho style) is a world of error, and it is rectified at the end of the poem.

X

As the evening grows darker, the guests that came leave,
Each of all the bustling noises gathers in its sound.
Calmly I recline in night's silence,
As it advances, I embrace autumn's brightness.[27]
Worldly entanglements suddenly come to my cares,   5
Then external griefs encroach on my sincerity.
Strong emotions, taut but not stretched full,
Weak broodings, the gaps have been filled.
Though I shun the pitfalls of words, warped and twisted,
In the vagueness I touch on weapons in their hearts.[28]   10
Defeated, I consider casting away a thousand in gold,[29]
Though what I gain is like the blossom of a tiny flower.
Understanding shame is enough to make one brave,
Self-possessed, who could command you?

27. I.e. the moon.
28. This seems to suggest that, although he has avoided making open enemies, he feels the hostility of others.
29. In the "Mountain Tree" chapter of the *Chuang-tzu* there is a story of a man who, fleeing a calamity, cast away jade pieces worth a thousand in gold in order to save his baby son. This is representative of a choice between the natural and the artificial.

This is the most cryptic, most abstract, and most interior of Han Yü's meditations. For example, the couplet

Strong emotions, taut but not stretched full,
Weak broodings, the gaps have been filled

is virtually unintelligible. Extrapolating from the preceding couplet, Tseng Kuo-fan identifies "strong emotions" with his "basic will," *pen-chih*, seeking peace of mind, and "weak broodings" with the "proclivities of the age," *shih-ch'ü*.[30] Because he is simply extrapolating from the preceding couplet, Tseng's interpretation makes the most sense of several possible ones, but referents of these phrases remain basically unclear.

The poem begins with the transition from companionship to solitude; however, in his solitude he finds little tranquillity because external worries intrude upon him. Whatever the couplet discussed above does mean, it is an image of tension, of extension, and then concentration ("the gaps have been filled"). Because of hostility from the external world, the poet has found isolation rather than tranquil solitude. His response is to choose the natural, his fundamental nature, "casting away a thousand in gold," worldly glory. Retreating into himself, the poet finds "the blossom of a tiny flower," his nature and heart ("tiny," *ts'un*, is literally "inch," which is a cliché for the heart). Only after being sure of what is within can he face the external world: he is "brave" because he understands shame, and "self-possessed," at no one else's command.

Not at all unlike western meditative poetry, Chinese meditative poetry tends to dwell on certain problems and to abstract them far beyond the point where we can see their relevance to a specific situation. Han Yü deals with a genuine sense of despair in the only intellectual terms available to him, those of inner and outer selves. Feeling failure in the external world, Han Yü retreats into himself to try to find what part of him is constant and unaffected by that external world. Once he finds that identity which is not defined in relation to externals, he can emerge again and face the outside world with courage and a sense of autonomy. "Courage" is to do what is right because one has a personal sense of shame, the knowledge that one cannot be lured or forced into doing wrong.

30. Quoted in *HCLS*, p. 245

XI

Fresh, chrysanthemums amid the frost,
It is late—what good is their beauty?
Fluttering upward, butterflies that sport in their scent,
It is even less early in your lives.
Now that the cycle ends you both meet,   5
Lovely and close, preserve one another as you die.
The west wind brings snake and dragon to hibernation,
All the trees wither and decay.
For always Fate's portion has been thus—
Why even mention the destruction, the obliteration?[31]   10

Han Yü closes his series with this lovely poem bringing together the chrysanthemum, symbol of goodness ("fragrance"), and the butterflies, things of beauty, surviving alone amid the general destruction wrought by autumn. The message is simple: to endure, to preserve what is good and beautiful, and to accept what is fated.

Despite the wide stylistic range represented in "Autumn Meditations," these poems are generally closer to the poetic tradition than Han Yü's earlier poetry, and certainly more personal. They show a stylistic precision, purity, and sense of control rare in his earlier poetry, as well as a conscious toning-down of any elements that might be obtrusive. Though Han Yü does counter his emotions with a sense of moral resolution in many poems, the morality is inward and personal, not a restatement of fu-ku ethical conventions.

31. *HCLS,* pp. 237–45.

14

Han Yü's Later Poetry: 813-825

The last thirteen years of Han Yü's life were occupied with moving from one post to another in the upper echelons of the central government. This succession of relatively high posts was punctuated midway by his famous memorial criticizing the official worship of the Buddha's bone, and his subsequent exile to Kwangtung. Closely associated with the minister P'ei Tu, Han accompanied the latter on the Huai-hsi expedition to put down a rebellious satrapy (*chieh-tu-shih*). On his return he was made vice president of the Board of Punishments (*hsing-pu shih-lang*). A year later in 819 came the affair of the Buddha's bone and his brief exile. Thereafter he held a succession of good posts until 824 when, at the age of fifty-six, he took sick leave and died at his villa south of Ch'ang-an.

The range of Han Yü's later poetry is extensive. The bulk is made up of witty, gracious vers de société in regulated verse. Han Yü had hitherto disdained such poetry, and when called upon for the usual parting poem or praise of a social gathering, he had tried to give such occasions some universal significance. Finally at home within the poetic tradition during these last thirteen years of his life, Han Yü no longer tried to avoid the firmly established conventions and set poses of occasional poetry.

For more serious poetry, Han Yü also turns to the tradition for themes and responses. His style in such poetry is one of mature balance and understatement, the style of the "mean" that we saw developing in the preceding chapter. His vision of himself as an old man is entirely traditional: slightly eccentric, loving tranquillity, and longing to retire from office. In this later poetry we first find genuine nature poetry—nature no longer actualizes the cosmic order but is valuable in itself. Nature may be described with the objectivity of a Wang Wei or may form an emotionally tinted scene that stirs traditional responses in the poet.

Although the flamboyant Lo-yang style had all but disappeared, a few excellent poems were written in other earlier styles. Because his new sense of stylistic and structural control smooths over the energetic awkwardness of his earlier work, many critics feel that these poems are the best of their kinds: indeed, from the point of view of polish and incisiveness, "To Be Shown My Son" may be Han's best didactic poem, 'To Ts'ui Li-chih" his finest character sketch, "Clerk at the Rapids" his finest personal narrative, and "The Girl of Mount Hua" his finest straight narrative. However, apart from the application of structural and stylistic control to earlier styles and manners, these poems contain nothing new in Han Yü's poetry and are too long to be studied within the scope of this chapter. We will consider one of Han's later didactic poems, "Fu Studies South of the City," both as an example of his new handling of older styles and as representative of his humanistic values.

In all of Han Yü's later poetry we can easily recognize the taming of his talent; he no longer seeks to startle the reader with his moral rectitude or stylistic ingenuity. The main faults of Han's early poetry were garrulousness and awkwardness; that of his Lo-yang poetry was overingenuity, trying too hard to dazzle the reader. Yet these are all faults of an excess of energy, trying to be "ancient" or brilliant, or simply talking too much. The flaw we often see in Han Yü's later poetry is exactly the opposite, a lack of energy. Often we find him mechanically churning out conventions, platitudes, and pointless periphrases. Many of Han Yü's finest poems were written during these years, but the quantity of bad poetry greatly exceeds that of the good. The reader will mercifully be spared such bad poetry, but it is important to remember that Han's affirmation of the tradition was not without its costs.

"Fu Studies South of the City" is a versified didactic essay extolling the merits of study, but it closes with a note of genuine emotion and paternal concern characteristic of Han Yü's later poetry. It is perhaps the kind of poetry he would have liked to have written in the early 790s.

FU STUDIES SOUTH OF THE CITY

That wood reaches the pattern of square or circle
Resides in the craft of carpenter or wheelwright.
A man's capability to be human

Comes from having the *Songs* and *Shu* by heart.
Persevere and you shall have the *Songs* and *Shu*,   5
Not persevere and your heart shall be empty.
I'll tell you of the power of study—
Sage and fool have the same beginnings,
But from one's inability to study
He thereby goes in a different gate.   10
Two families each give birth to a son,
As babes in arms they're just the same.
Somewhat older they join playing games,
No different than two fish in a school.
But on reaching twelve or thirteen   15
Their youthful physiognomies are slightly different.
By twenty they gradually develop apart,
As a pure canal shines against a stagnant gutter.
By thirty their frames are complete,
Then one's a dragon, one's a pig.   20
The magic steed Flying Yellow bounds away,
Unable to gaze on such a toad.
One becomes a runner before the horses,
Worms grow in the whipwelts on his back;
One becomes a Lord or Minister,   25
Who lives remote in his office.
If you ask why this is so—
It's a case of study and failure to study!
Though gold and jade be valuable treasures,
If you waste them you'll accumulate nothing;   30
Learning is stored in the body,
And if the body survives, there's always plenty.
The Good Man and the Lesser Man
Are not bound to their parentage—
Have you not seen how Lord and Minister   35
Raised their persons from the plow and hoe?
Have you not seen the posterity of a great Lord
Cold and starving, go without even a donkey?
Why do you think literature is honored?—
It's a field sown with the learning of the classics.   40
There is no source for muddy trickles in the street;
At dawn they're full, by evening already gone.

If a man cannot span past and present,
He's just a horse or ox wearing clothes.
In their actions they shall fall into unrighteousness,   45
Even less can they hope for much praise.
The season is autumn, the long rains are clearing up,
A fresh chill enters the hills and moors.
One can feel a certain kinship with the fires in the lamps,
And one can roll and unroll scrolls of books.   50
Of course I think about you day and night,
And worry that the days and months pass for you.
Indulgent love and righteousness take me over by turns,
So I compose this poem to encourage you in your hesitation.[1]

Despite the unfortunate parallels with the speech of Polonius, this, one of the latest of Han Yü's didactic poems, is the best of its kind, both in the dignity of its style and in the paternal feeling that transforms the drier aspects of the lesson. If one had read only Han Yü's prose, this is the kind of poetry one would expect him to write. In contrast to his early didactic poetry, here he avoids awkward turns of phrase and is generous in his use of metaphor. Also, one may note that this is the ethics of success, in sharp contrast to his youthful ethics of failure or of as yet unachieved success: now to Han Yü the one who is "cold and starving, . . . without even a donkey" is the frivolous child of an important family who failed to study and thus to achieve worldly success. In his early poetry the same line would have characterized the poor but upright scholar. For the first time, Han has come to identify worldly success with morality.

In the first two couplets, Han Yü follows the pre-Ch'in philosophers in arguing by analogy, and as is so often the case among them, the analogy is inaccurate. The correct analogy for Han Yü's statement of human perfectability would have been: "Wood's reaching the fullest of its potential resides in the carpenter or wheelwright having a square or compass." However, the point of the analogy is clear: like wood, man is initially only potential material whose perfection depends on his being made to conform to a given pattern.

The style is prosaic but flowing. Caesura is violated in two of the first four lines. In addition to Han Yü's feeling that a prosaic style is appropriate to the didactic mode, there are other aspects of its use in

1. *HCLS,* p. 445.

this case. Occasionally, as here, when Han is being didactic, he speaks with an aggressive, ex cathedra tone, to which the authority of *ku-wen* prose style, the style of the classics, lends credence. Han Yü and many of his friends rose from the ranks of lower official families to secure relatively good positions in the central government; hence he finds justification in the meritocratic ideal, as did the bourgeoisie in the West. This ideal in itself would not be offensive, but Han Yü is stating at with particular forcefulness here. Greatness is "not bound to . . . parentage." This line ends with an archaic, emphatic particle, as if to emphasize the "ancient" truth of what he says. The style of the classics is to validate the context in which he says this. No doubt there were a number of high officials of the age who felt differently.

In the poem learning is a great deal more than simply a gateway to office, it means one's "capability to be human."

> If a man cannot span past and present
> He's just a horse or ox wearing clothes.

Knowledge is of the past, of precedent. In contrast to human life without learning, which is like

> . . . muddy trickles on the street
> At dawn they're full, by evening already gone,

the tradition gives man a sense of and a place in eternity. And what is *knowable* about eternity is the past, not the future. The tradition makes human life more than a short space of awareness, a theme Meng Chiao treated in the fourteenth of his "Autumn Meditations."

In the last section Han Yü lyrically suggests his own love of study as well as his love for his son (thus raising the poem from simple didacticism and separating it from his earlier work). It is not difficult to sense the scholar and bibliophile in:

> The season is autumn, the long rains are clearing up,
> A fresh chill enters the hills and moors.
> One can feel a certain kinship with fires in the lamps,
> And one can roll and unroll scrolls of books.

Throughout the poem, Han Yü's sense of humanity comes through, severe though it may be, but in the last couplet the moralist falls away and Han becomes fully human. He speaks of an "indulgent love," a love that makes the father want to let the son follow his own inclinations. It is precisely such "softness" on Han Yü's part which prompts the severity of the poem. Han finds himself caught between a desire to be indulgent and the knowledge that his son needs to study, not simply to gain official position but to become human. Thus, whatever its didactic content, this poem is written to *explain* to his son why he should study. Instead of ordering his son to study or berating him for his failure to do so, Han Yü, because of his paternal love, tries to reason with his son.

The following two poems are not new treatments of an older style like "Fu Studies South of the City"; they are, like "Autumn Meditations," a personal re-creation of a traditional theme and style. The poems are, however, less intellectual than "Autumn Meditations."

STIRRED BY SPRING [TWO OF THREE]

I

By chance I sat beneath a vine-covered tree,
At the end of spring, during its last week.
The shade of the vines could shelter me,
But still there were falling petals far and wide.
Slowly but surely the new leaves grow larger,   5
Parched white as jade, late blossoms dry.
But the blue sky is high and empty,
Save for a pair of butterflies that fly fluttering.
It is proper and fitting that the season be thus,
But melancholy emotions still come for no reason.

From the poet who transformed nature into an intelligible symbol of the cosmic condition, Han Yü has become the traditional passive nature poet, responding emotionally to what nature is in itself. His final emotional response, which we have seen before in "Autumn Meditations," is appropriate to the death of flowers in late spring. In poems such as this it seems that Han Yü is virtually seeking anonymity within the tradition. In the last couplet we see clearly the victory of traditional response over Han's independent intellect:

It is proper and fitting that the season be thus,
But melancholy emotions still come for no reason.

First, we have the intellectual assertion that the state of spring is *proper*; however, the traditional response of melancholy at the passage of spring comes anyway. In early poems Han Yü often specifically rejected the emotional responses, as in "The Far North":

> . . . that babyish attitude,
> That broken-hearted grieves over poverty.

Han consistently rejected emotional truth for intellectual truth. Still there are occasions when an intellectual truth cannot account for a problem, as in the intellectual pseudotruth Han Yü offers Meng Chiao in "Meng Chiao Loses His Son," where Han uses a hollow fatalism to account for the death of the old poet's baby son. In many of the "Autumn Meditations" intense personal emotion was present, and the intellectual truths of resolution, ambition, and fate were successful antidotes to Han's despair. Here, finally, emotion is more powerful than intellectual understanding: the wise fatalism of the eleventh "Autumn Meditation" is not proof against the melancholy of spring's end. This melancholy is the most conventional of responses despite the neoclassical control of style in the poem.

II

> Yellow, yellow, the flower of the turnip,
> The work of peach and plum is past.
> A whirlwind winnows the bare elms,
> Their pods lie helter-skelter on the great thoroughfare.
> Spring's seasonal position is entirely thus, 5
> How can you rely on the youth of your features?
> Who can harness the birds and fly his carriage?—
> I'd follow him to look beyond the seas.[2]

Again, the style of this poem is consciously traditional, as is the response of escape to the world of the immortals. Transcendental longings have been quite rare in Han Yü's poetry, but they are to be expected following his yielding to the melancholy of transience that we saw in the preceding poem. The first line is one of the most traditional openings in Chinese poetry: a reduplicated adjective followed by some natural object. The second line, however, betrays Han Yü's personal manner, literally: "Peach and plum, their work has

2. *HCLS,* p. 430. I.e. travel to the land of the immortals.

withdrawn." This interesting anthropomorphic description of flowers implies that they, like man, perform their duties (of blossoming) and then retire from the scene. Such an understanding of natural phenomena in human terms is characteristic of Han Yü's earlier poetry.

From the formal order of the second line, the poem moves into harsh words of destruction and disorder—"whirlwind," "winnows," "bare," and "helter-skelter." The destruction of natural beauty in late spring is reminiscent of an autumn scene. In the pods, however, lies the potential for rebirth. Characteristically, such observations of the pattern of growth and destruction in nature lead to abstraction, "spring's seasonal position." But the abstraction is no longer sufficient consolation. Instead, the impact of transience is primarily emotional, stirring the traditional response of longing for the timeless world of the immortals. He longs to escape the disorder on "the great thoroughfares" by a "flying carriage."

The following set of four poems shows Han Yü in a mood of restrained playfulness. As poems on fishing, they may be well contrasted with "To Hou Hsi" (p. 83) and "Fish-spearing" (p. 112). Here we find no effort to make the fishing experience metaphorical or to increase its importance by sheer descriptive ingenuity: the fishing trip is a personal experience, valuable in itself, with its own simple beauty.

FISHING ALONE: FOUR POEMS

I

The forest lodge of this princely house is superb,
It happened that I came here for a chance to dangle my fishing pole.
Twisted trees lead the vine pods,
The level pond scatters dishes of lily pads.
When the wings of the fly sink, I know the bait's been taken,   5
As the line grows taut, I realize how hard it is to pull in.
I'd like to catch enough to brag to my children,
I'll tie them with an elm-twig stringer to my servant's saddle.

II

The entire path slants toward the pool,
Around the banks of the pond, wild plants and flowers.

There's been a lot of rain—the mushrooms by the willows have
    increased,
The waters have risen, cutting down the number of reed sprouts.
Just now I'm sick and tired of involvement in the power to
    punish,[3]   5
So I steal a chance to come, my fishing reel at my side.
In this age of peace there is little official business—
I'm not at all far from resembling the "hermit clerk."[4]

III

Alone I went to beside the southern pond,
An autumn morning, the scene was stimulating.
Dew bent down the plants on all the banks,
The wind bound together duckweed over half of the pool.
Birds came down, seeing the stillness of the man,   5
Fish came smelling the fragrance of the bait.
It bothers me that there was no one to invite along—
So I can't empty my jug of wine.

IV

Autumn's mid-point, most things are changing,
The fish of the creek go off and don't come back.
The wind can split the beaks of the lily pads,
Dew also dyes the cheeks of the pears.
Distant summits merge in layers,   5
Chrysanthemums, flowers of the cold, blossom scattered.
The one I made a date with never came,
So with whom shall I turn back at sunset?[5]

In contrast to the careful control of the hints of playfulness and
melancholy in the preceding poems, the following five quatrains are
playfully witty and self-mocking. Yet in this wit there is gentleness
rather than the aggressive exaggeration of the linked verses. And
there is a sense of the human delight in little things.

3. At that time Han Yü was attached to the Board of Punishments.
4. The "hermit clerk" is Lao-tzu. The point is that, by not becoming embroiled in
political struggles, one can be a hermit even when in government service.
5. *HCLS*, p. 478.

BASIN POOL

I

This old fellow's acting just like a kid—
He draws some water, buries a basin, and makes a little pool.
All night long green frogs sing until dawn,
And it's just like when I'm fishing at Fang-k'ou.

The playful, colloquial tone of this little poem is reminiscent of
the self-conscious carelessness and spontaneity practiced by Po
Chü-yi and his group. We can see such carelessness in the pointless
redundancy of the third line: "all night long . . . until dawn."
Analogous to his earlier microcosms, this miniature version of a pond
is gently humorous, both in its approximation of the real thing and,
as we shall see in the fifth poem, in its discrepancies.

II

Don't say my basin pool isn't completely finished,
First I planted lotus stalks and they're already growing evenly.
From now on, when it rains, you must remember
To come listen to the melancholy sound beating on the leaves.

III

The water of this pond is naturally clear in the morning,
Countless little insects whose names I don't know.
Suddenly they scatter—no trace or lingering echo,
And there are only the fishies, moving in a school.

IV

How can a muddy basin, shallow and small, become a pool?
But at midnight the green frogs showed sagely wisdom.
Once permitted, they came in darkness bringing companions,
Nor was I bothered by their singing and croaking as they fought
    over mates.

V

Light on the pool, reflections of the sky—both blue,
To make it strike the bank, one need add only a few pitchers of water,

Just wait until deep in the night when the bright moon is gone,
And take a look at how many stars are submerged in the water.[6]

Here Han Yü is playing with the Taoist theme of the relativity of things. The pool may be tiny, so tiny that a few pitchers of water can make it overflow, but it can reflect the entire sky and submerge all the stars.

The light cleverness of the above series is also found in the vers de société which form the bulk of Han Yü's later poetry. The following poems will serve as examples of this kind of verse; they were written in 817 when Han went along with the entourage of the Minister P'ei Tu to Huai-hsi to punish the rebellious satrapy.

STAYING IN THE FIELD ON THE WESTERN BOUNDARY IN THE
    SERVICE OF MINISTER P'EI TU: A POEM WITH LI CHENG-FENG

On all sides, stars and planets, bright upon the earth,
Smoky fires, burning scattered, put Imperial troops to bed.
We don't care that, having broken the rebels, we must return and
    report on the campaign,
But rather to take advantage ourselves of the New Year to
    congratulate His Majesty on the Great Peace.[7]

The necessary economy of the *chüeh-chü*, the regulated quatrain, makes severe structural demands on a poem. As a result, the poem is often mechanically divided into two couplets, one being a well-wrought descriptive couplet and the other containing the "message" of the poem. The campfires of the imperial army here become an array of stars and planets, extending the traditional metaphor of the emperor as the sun and his chief minister, the moon. Thus, the military finds its proper place in the orderly universe, in conjunction with, but clearly subordinate to, the emperor and his minister. The last couplet is an interesting version of the traditional view that civil matters have primacy over military ones: the officers are less concerned with reporting victory than with congratulating the emperor on the New Year and the new peace.

STAYING THE NIGHT AT SHEN-KUEI:
    I INVITE LI CHENG-FENG AND FENG SU

Wild mountains and rivers through the moors shine in the evening
    sunlight,

6. *HCLS*, p. 415.   7. *HCLS*, p. 470.

Only then do winter crows, pecking in the snow, fly off, availing
    themselves of the last light.
I spend the night in the pavilion of the post station, so sad I can't
    sleep,[8]
I hope you'll come here to me, covering yourselves with your
    uniforms.

This is a poem of invitation, one of those social situations that
evolved into virtually independent subgenres during the T'ang. Han
Yü uses one of the standard conventions of the subgenre, inviting
friends to dispel loneliness. This regulated quatrain well illustrates
the disintegration of a poem's unity in regulated vers de société. The
first couplet, describing the sunset, is masterful, but it bears little or
no relation to the invitation extended in the second. Were there a
relation, it would be the mood of melancholy loneliness. As mentioned earlier, one central characteristic of the developing Late T'ang
style is a focus on the couplet at the expense of the unity of the poem;
another characteristic is a vague unity of mood. Han Yü, though not
fully in the Late T'ang style in his later work, nevertheless shows the
influence of the new poetic fashion.

IN PEACH GROVE AT NIGHT: CONGRATULATING P'EI TU, NAMED
    DUKE OF CHIN

Torch riders coming from the west shine the mountains red,
At night we stay in Peach Grove, the last month of winter.
In your hand you hold the Badge of Enfeoffment and the
    Minister's Seal,
At one time a double appreciation of your prime merit.[9]

The first line is a beautiful description of the emperor's emissaries
coming with the news of P'ei Tu's enfeoffment; however, the rest of
the poem is nothing more than gracious compliment, as Han wittily
plays on the number of two major titles at one time.

The three preceding poems are sufficient to illustrate his vers de
société during this period. Han Yü ends up writing precisely the kind
of poetry he had reacted against during the early 790s.

In 819 Han Yü was banished to Ch'ao-chou in the far south for
his famous "Memorial on the Buddha's Bone." In 820 he was recalled
to the capital, where he lived until his death in 824. Some critics feel

8. *HCLS,* p. 471.   9. *HCLS,* p. 472.

that it was during these years that he wrote his best work. There is no noticeable stylistic change from the years immediately preceding 819, but one feels that the poet's hand is surer, the vision of himself and the world even deeper, and his tone even mellower.

BANISHED AND DEMOTED, I COME TO THE LAN-T'IEN BARRIER: FOR MY NEPHEW HSIANG

In the morning a sealed memorial was presented through the nine layers of Heaven,[10]
By evening, dismissed to Ch'ao-chou, an eight-thousand mile road.
I wanted to remove certain vile matters for the sake of sagely perspicacity,
Little did I realize that as a decrepit old man I would pity my remaining years.
Clouds stretch across the Ch'in Range—where is my home?   5
Snow stuffs Lan Barrier, my horse won't go ahead.
I know that when you come from afar, it must be for this reason—
Showing the kindness to gather my bones from beside those pestilential rivers.[11]

This poem is built around a series of calculated and subtle ironies. The emperor is as *remote* as Heaven; he is also the symbolic center of the world and the empire. Han Yü's memorial penetrates this remoteness at the center of the world but results in his being sent to equally remote regions at the edge of the world. The irony of the second couplet is more obvious: Han Yü's intention to do good was requited by personal ruin. In the third couplet the poet is immobilized, clouds and mountains blocking a return home northward and snow blocking his movement southward. Clouds, we remember, are the conventional metaphor for slanderers who hide the emperor's "brilliance/perspicacity" from a loyal subject. Thus Han Yü's wish to clear up "sagely perspicacity," so that the emperor could clearly see the state of things, brought about the hiding of that very "brilliance/perspicacity" from Han, in the form of the clouds blocking the view back to the capital.

In the last couplet, Han Yü addresses his nephew Hsiang, project-

10. The memorial is the "Memorial on the Buddha's Bone." The "nine levels of Heaven" is a cliché for the palace and the emperor who dwells remote from ordinary mortals.
11. *HCLS,* p. 484.

ing himself forward to his imagined death in the south. There is a further irony in Han's use of "bones" in this context: while his own bones, those of a loyal official, will be found in the remotest corner of the empire in exile and disgrace, the bone of the Buddha will be honored and allowed to continue to disrupt and pollute the state.

Despite the great bitterness of this poem, Han Yü keeps that bitterness well veiled in irony. Likewise, he avoids discussing the ethical problems involved in his banishment, hinting at them only in the "clouds" and the "bones." The subtle indirectness of this poem provides an interesting counterpoint to the straightforwardness of the "Memorial on the Buddha's Bone" itself. As in his earlier exile, Han has again "become chastened to subdue himself."

The following regulated quatrain has been considered by many traditional critics to be Han Yü's finest.

On the Temple of King Chao of Ch'u

Tombs and mounds fill my eyes, the robes and caps are gone,
Walls and towers stretch to the sky, trees and grass grow over
   them.
Yet still there are men of his state who feel his former virtue,
And in this single-roomed thatched hut, they pray to King
   Chao.[12]

The central theme here is the endurance of virtue and the memory of virtuous men amid the ruin and transience of the material world. The whole world seems full of tombs and ruins that "fill the eyes" and "stretch to the sky." Though this evidence of their former grandeur remains, the men themselves, the "robes and caps," have perished. In the second line Han Yü begins by summoning up that former grandeur: "Walls and towers stretch to the sky," then destroys it with "trees and grass grow over them." In this first couplet, the Late T'ang tendency toward parataxis appears in the juxtaposition of complete predicates, setting one condition against another.

The kings of the Warring States kingdom of Ch'u were not particularly known for their moral qualities; King Chao, however, was among the better ones. All that survives of Ch'u is the memory of King Chao's virtue. The use of the phrase "men of his state," *kuo-jen*, refers to the local inhabitants, even though the state of Ch'u had

12. *HCLS,* p. 489.

long since disappeared. The use of this phrase suggests that the people's cohesion as a nation and their sense of continuity exist only through the memory of King Chao. Even though the sacrificial temple is only a "single-roomed thatched hut," appropriate to the deterioration of the state's grandeur, virtue and respect for virtue survive and are as strong as ever: King Chao is still prayed to. The conventional contrast between former grandeur and present ruin is counteracted by the unchanging respect for virtue. We see a trace of Han Yü's former affirmation of ethical principle over emotion (here, lament over the passing of former glories) without the rugged style that once went with such assertions. The result is that the melancholy remains side by side with the affirmation of virtue, forming a more mature and complex whole. Certainly the endurance of King Chao's virtue, no matter how impressive the fact may be, does not entirely mitigate the ruin of his great palaces and the melancholy irony of his temple becoming a tiny thatched hut.

The following poem is another of Han Yü's finest regulated verses. Intense and genuine emotion is consciously restrained up to the last line, where it bursts forth with violence.

> Last year I was dismissed because of wrongdoing from a position as secretary in the Board of Punishments, to become Governor of Ch'ao-chou. I went on the post road to my new position. Later, when my family was also banished and followed me, my youngest daughter died on the road, and they buried her at the foot of the mountain beside Tseng-feng Station. Receiving Imperial forgiveness, I return to court and stop by her grave. I left this poem on the portal of the post station.

> Several strips of vine bind your coffin of bark,
> Buried in the grass on a wild mountain, your white bones cold.
> Fear and trembling entered your heart, your body already sick,
> All knew the hardships of taking your body along on the road.
> Nor was there any time to circle your grave three times to call back the soul,
> And I heard that there was only a single bowl of rice set as an offering.
> It happened to you who were guiltless through my wrongdoing,
> A hundred years of pain and shame and tears streaming down.[13]

13. *HCLS*, p. 529.

As we read this poem, it is important to remember that in traditional China, especially for a staunch traditionalist like Han Yü, ritual and ceremony were the most valid expressions of deep feeling. The omission of ceremony can be a humiliating failure of a father to show love for his dead daughter. This is, of course, bound up with his personal sense of responsibility for her death. The image of the bark coffin bound with vines shows the haste and primitive conditions under which she was buried. Her burial in such a lonely, desolate place, "her white bones cold," far from her family, stirs Han Yü to the heart. The poem becomes Han's personal apology to her, imagining her fear of death and pathetically explaining to her the practical considerations that prevented the family from taking her body along.

The third couplet again concerns the neglect of the funeral ritual—no offering but a single bowl of rice and no time for the ritual calling back of the soul. In the last couplet, the personal sense of guilt which transcends ritual comes forth; his daughter died because of his own wrongdoing and through no fault of her own. The hyperbole of the last line is nevertheless restrained—a hundred years, a lifetime—rather than a thousand or ten thousand. Yet it is only through hyperbole that Han Yü can express the extent of his remorse in emotional terms rather than through gestures. The genuine depth of feeling in this poem is unlike anything in Han Yü's earlier poetry. To suggest the changes he has undergone as a poet as well as a man, we need only compare this poem to the emotional frigidity of "Poem of Hsieh Tsu-jan" (p. 43).

The three following poems are thought to be Han Yü's last. The Confucian poet, the humorist and the wit, the rhetorician and the myth-maker have all disappeared, and what remains is the most traditional of self-images of a poet—that of the old man traveling through the landscape, appreciating and reflecting on nature and on himself.

FLOATING ON SOUTH CREEK FOR THE FIRST TIME:
THREE POEMS

I

I paddle my boat onward beneath South Mountain,
Upward and upward, never getting the desire to return.
Feelings of seclusion grow many, following my goings,

Who cares whether it's near or far?
I pass under joined trees, thick and shady,   5
High and then low, I come to a slope across my path.
Stones harsh, wantonly rubbing and grinding me,
Waves evil, stubbornly dragging at me.
Sometimes I'm a fisherman on an inclined bank,
Then finally reaching a sandflat I'll eat my meal.   10
Spot after spot, the evening rain spreads out,
A faint sliver, the new moon lies flat.
Apprehensive that the years remaining to me are not many,
And grieved that my day to quit service is already late.
It's only because sickness makes it so,   15
And not from any desire to transcend the world.

II

South Creek is also clear and rushing,
But there are no boats or oars on it.
Mountain farmers are startled to see this one,
And following me, they won't stop staring.
Not just a group of young boys—   5
Sometimes there are white-haired men leaning on staffs.
They offer me melons in a basket,
And urge me to linger here.
I say that I've come home on account of sickness,
And feel particularly on my own here.   10
I hope I'll have a chance to use my remaining salary
To set up a dwelling here on the western fields.
Rice and grains shall fill the granaries,
And I'll have no worries from dawn to dusk.
I never got any satisfaction from rising to a high position,   15
Coming down from it, I'm also perfectly at ease.
I only fear that I'd be a nuisance to the village,
At times troubling them when there is urgent business.
But I would like to be one who shares their cult,14
And with pigs and chickens, feast the springs and autumns.   20

III

My feet are weak—I cannot walk,

14. "Shares their cult," i.e. becomes a worshiper of the tutelary village god. This is
equivalent to saying that he would like to be accepted as their neighbor.

Naturally it's fitting I cease my visits to court;
My frail form could be taken by palaquin,
But how could I give up seeing these lovely sights?
It's right here beneath the slope of South Mountain,   5
Where so long I've heard there are stones and waters—
I've brought my boat into their midst,
Right where the current of the stream is strongest and
    clearest.
I'm not able just to follow the waves,
Far better to thrust my pole into the jutting rapids.   10
An egret rises as if to lead me on,
Flying ahead of me twenty or thirty feet.
High and splendid, the willows belt the sand,
Round, pines crown the cliffs.
When I return home it's already the end of the night—   15
Who could say this isn't as hard as court service?[15]

In contrast to "South Mountains," the human being is very much
in the landscape here; in contrast to the narratives of his first exile,
the landscape is no mere appendage of human experience. The landscape has a stability and identity all its own, as the poet himself has.
Description, narrative, cliché role, and introspection are combined
to form a mature appreciation of an experience and its relation to
one's life. There are lines which are prosaic, colloquial, and densely
poetic; the feeling is that the poet is writing completely at his ease,
using whatever style comes most naturally to his perception of the
moment. It is this sense of stylistic ease which reflects Han Yü's experience with the boating trip.

In the course of these three poems, Han Yü moves through a wide
variety of roles. There is a trace of the cantankerous old humanist
refusing to admit that he wants to become a hermit and "transcend
the world"

> . . . grieved that my day to quit service is already late.
> It's only because sickness makes it so,
> And not from any desire to transcend the world

as well as a mature suspicion about his own motives, as when, at the
beginning of the third poem, he says he is too lame to go to court,
then reflects that he could go by palaquin, and finally admits his real

15. *HCLS*, p. 566.

motive, laughing at himself: "But how could I give up seeing these lovely sights?" In the second poem Han plays the pastoral poet, and throughout we see traces of the objective landscape poet; but mostly there is an active relation between the poet and the landscape, a sense of two wills, two separate identities—sometimes working together, sometimes at cross-purposes:

> I'm not able just to follow the waves,
> Far better to thrust my pole into the jutting rapids.
> An egret rises as if to lead me on,
> Flying ahead of me twenty or thirty feet.

This poet who, most of all T'ang poets, sought a sense of separate identity, of exclusiveness, ends up like other poets, culling whatever role strikes his fancy, moving at ease within the tradition. And ease is the key word here: these poems have none of the forced assertiveness of Han Yü's earlier poetry—this is the work of a man at peace with himself, a man in an ordered and intelligible world, a man who is happy to have escaped his role as literary reformer and bold innovator.

Index-Glossary

289